MW00634890

ROAD&TRACK

HENRY MANNEY
AT LARGE & ABROAD

Reprinted From
Road & Track Magazine

ISBN 1 870642 473

Published By
Brooklands Books with permission of Road & Track
Printed in Hong Kong

Titles in this series:

Road & Track on Alfa Romeo 1949-1963
Road & Track on Alfa Romeo 1964-1970
Road & Track on Alfa Romeo 1971-1976
Road & Track on Alfa Romeo 1977-1984
Road & Track on Aston Marton 1962-1984
Road & Track on Audi & Auto Union
   1952-1980
Road & Track on Audi & Auto Union
   1980-1986
Road & Track on Austin Healey 1953-1970
Road & Track on BMW Cars 1966-1974
Road & Track on BMW Cars 1975-1978
Road & Track on BMW Cars 1979-1983
Road & Track on Cobra, Shelby & Ford
   GT40 1962-1983
Road & Track on Corvette 1953-1967
Road & Track on Corvette 1968-1982
Road & Track on Corvette 1982-1986
Road & Track on Datsun Z 1970-1983
Road & Track on Ferrari 1950-1968
Road & Track on Ferrari 1968-1974
Road & Track on Ferrari 1975-1981
Road & Track on Ferrari 1981-1984
Road & Track on Fiat Sports Cars
   1968-1987
Road & Track on Jaguar 1950-1960
Road & Track on Jaguar 1961-1968
Road & Track on Jaguar 1968-1974
Road & Track on Jaguar 1974-1982
Road & Track on Lamborghini 1964-1984
Road & Track on Lotus 1972-1983
Road & Track on Maserati 1952-1974
Road & Track on Maserati 1975-1983
Road & Track on Mazda RX-7 1978-1986
Road & Track on Mercedes 1952-1962

Road & Track on Mercedes 1963-1970
Road & Track on Mercedes 1971-1979
Road & Track on Mercedes 1980-1987
Road & Track on MG Sports Cars
   1949-1961
Road & Track on MG Sports Cars
   1962-1980
Road & Track on Mustang 1964-1977
Road & Track on Peugeot 1955-1986
Road & Track on Pontiac 1960-1983
Road & Track on Porsche 1951-1967
Road & Track on Porsche 1968-1971
Road & Track on Porsche 1972-1975
Road & Track on Porsche 1975-1978
Road & Track on Porsche 1979-1982
Road & Track on Porsche 1982-1985
Road & Track on Rolls Royce & Bentley
   1950-1965
Road & Track on Rolls Royce & Bentley
   1966-1984
Road & Track on SAAB 1955-1985
Road & Track on Toyota Sports & GT Cars
   1966-1986
Road & Track on Triumph Sports Cars
   1953-1967
Road & Track on Triumph Sports Cars
   1967-1974
Road & Track on Triumph Sports Cars
   1974-1982
Road & Track on Volkswagen 1951-1968
Road & Track on Volkswagen 1968-1978
Road & Track on Volkswagen 1978-1985
Road & Track on Volvo 1957-1974
Road & Track on Volvo 1975-1985

Road & Track – Henry Manney At Large & Abroad

Distributed By

Road & Track
1499 Monrovia,
Newport Beach,
California 92663, U.S.A.

Brooklands Book Distribution Ltd.,
Holmerise, Seven Hills Road,
Cobham, Surrey KT11 1ES,
England

Contents

Like an enormous number of long-time *Road & Track* readers, I grew up savoring every word of Henry Manney's reports on things automotive and the condition of the world. Many years later, when I joined the staff of the magazine and Henry resumed residence in California (after his many years of living in Europe), I actually met and became friends with this delightful human being.

Henry Manney was one of those larger-than-life characters we encounter very rarely. An individualist, with very strong notions of right and wrong; a car enthusiast, with an addiction to automobiles, as long as they had panache. This compilation of Henry Manney stories is a never-ending treasure, always there for sampling when you need to escape from the trials of everyday living. Keep it close to hand at all times.

Those L. Bryant, Editor
Road & Track

Copyright 1989 © CBS Inc.

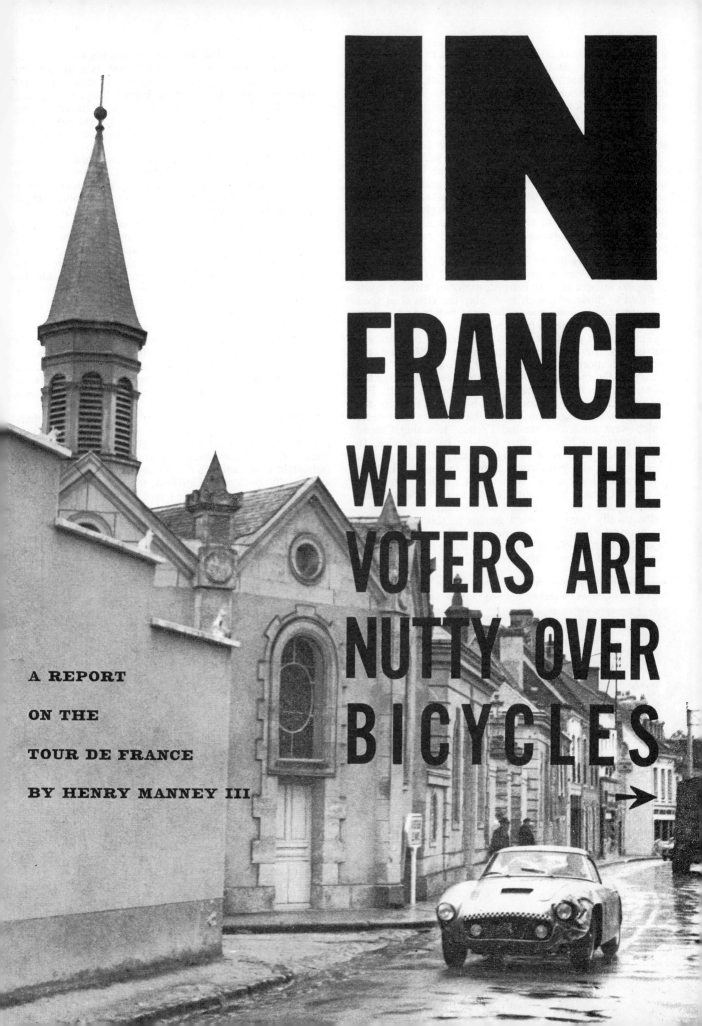

IN FRANCE

WHERE THE VOTERS ARE NUTTY OVER BICYCLES

A REPORT

ON THE

TOUR DE FRANCE

BY HENRY MANNEY III

IN FRANCE, WHERE THE VOTERS ARE NUTTY over bicycles because that is what they use for transportation (and none of that nonsense about why don't they drive cars . . . remember what happened to Marie Antoinette after her reflections on the baking situation), there is an event known as the Tour de France.

In this form of legalized sadism, producing only a smidgen less attrition than the Colosseum (Tipo Roma) of Nero's time, various muscular types pedal a bicycle clean around the country, up Alp and down dale, in sickness and in health, through snow, sleet and hail. Fame and fortune await the winner of this marathon; invitations to endorse athletic equipment and glucose drinks flow his way, beautiful women are found under his bed by other beautiful women, and some even start their own political party.

The organizers of the Tour also do well, it appears—otherwise the event would not continue. "Tour" editions of papers sell out all over Europe, many advertising rights are sold to those who wish to display the virtues of their product across some rider's *derriere,* hotels and restaurants along the route do big business.

This shower of publicity and its attendant benefits was not lost on the automotive department at *L'Equipe,* the big French sporting daily, and in 1951 journalist Maurice Henry, *L'Equipe* and the Auto Club of Nice got together to put on the first 4-wheeled version of the Tour. For obvious reasons, stages could be a bit longer than for the push-bikes and there were five of these *etapes* on a route which went clockwise around France, touching Ostend and Geneva en route, before it came back to Nice. In spite of being a sort of regularity run with hill climbs, speed events and gymkhanas thrown in, enough interest was aroused for some 97 starters (of which 77 finished) to embark onto the teeming roads in early September, when anyone who owns wheels is on vacation.

Practically from the word go (or in this case, *allez*) the team of Pagnibon/Barraquet took the lead on points in a 2.6 Touring-bodied Ferrari roadster and held it to the finish. If I remember correctly, it was this Ferrari

Annie Soisbault, top French rallyist, inspects the back of her Coupes de Dames winning Porsche Super 90.

which was sold to Phil Hill and started his long association with that Maranello concern. Peron/Betramnier and Checcacci/Schell followed in similar models. A 1300 Porsche was 4th in the hands of Picard/Farge and having it, an 1100 Fiat and a 4-CV Renault scattered among several Jaguars leads me to believe that regulations were not too stringent as far as modifications were concerned, although class prizes were awarded.

In 1952 we found displacement categories split up from the former four (from below 750 to unlimited) to six, with an extra classification for cars *strictment de serie* and, of course, a Ladies Cup as before. Pagnibon entered again, this time with a newer model Ferrari, but in the course of the three stages (with seven circuit tests), Nice-La Baule, La Baule-Reims, Reims-Nice, which comprised the Tour, mechanical failures allowed M. and Mme. Gignoux (DB Panhard) to take the lead from him and Peron (Osca) on the last stage and keep it. Of the 108 starters, 58 finished, and the little DB beat out a choice selection of competition machinery besides the usual Jaguars, Panhards and Porsche 1100's.

For the 1953 version the pot really began to boil, with a classified separate category for production cars, both modified and unobtrusively so. Bigger and better prizes and races attracted 114 starters, of which 59 finished, the top money being taken home by the persistent Peron (Osca Mt-4) who just edged out the late Jean Behra (3-liter Gordini).

The next year emphasis swung back to the high performance sports cars and 124 competitors set forth to cover a changed course of Nice-Brest, Brest-Nancy and Nancy-Nice. Fog and thunderstorms bedevilled the hardly rally-style entry and after a stirring battle between Pollet and Guelfi, both with Gordinis, the former escaped the clutches of Storez (Porsche) and Peron (Osca) to give the Paris firm a win. In this event the Index of Performance, beloved of French mathematicians, was introduced to confuse the foreigners and a new name, that of Olivier Gendebien, appeared on the scene with 7th overall in an Alfa TI.

Mid-season of 1955 saw Pierre Levegh's tragic accident at Le Mans and a panicked Government, weathercocking with the breeze as politicians will, straightway heeded the yammering of anti-sport elements and cancelled anything that even looked as if it might involve putting numbers on cars. By the next year, when the Tour crept back, it was a shadow of its former self and had taken the form in which we see it today, with a 38-mph obligatory road average, secret controls, shorter stages with more rest time, and was restricted to GT and touring cars.

Shell of France got into the act and boosted the prize money, but even then the number of starters (103) was down from earlier years. Furthermore, many people found that with the new schedules there was no possibility of forging ahead and then stopping to fix something; the 37 finishers did not include Pollet (winner of the previous Tour), whose Ferrari had broken a rocker arm, but propelled de Portago into the big time, followed by Moss (Mercedes) and Gendebien (Ferrari).

Having the baby left on their doorstep, as it were, the AC Nice stuck with that formula and as if in sympathy for the *status quo,* Gendebien collected the next three events in a row, battling every inch of the way with such stalwarts as Trintignant, Mairesse, De Silva Ramos and Schild. That brings us up to the 1960 event.

The Tour is still a regularity run, with maximum and minimum road averages to please the always worried French authorities, but studded around the route are seven hill climbs and seven circuit races. Because the road sections are mostly duck soup for an experienced rallyist, their only sting lies in the nocturnal mountain sections where one can get lost and in the odd case, not check in

Three Tour cars sweep through Bellême in the rain.

Dusk at Le Mans and the race goes on for a few.

on time because of some mechanical derangement.

This year a system was adopted by which everyone's standing was rated in kilometers covered. If an entrant was late at a control, these minutes were treated as a function of the average speed for that section and he was docked in distance. Hill climbs were arranged as if the competitor had continued for a much longer period . . . say 15 minutes . . . at the same speed when it actually took him only five, his kilometrage being then worked off what he would have covered at his average speed. The circuit "races" were handled in a similar manner. At Le Mans, for example, all cars circulated for two hours. The winner covered the optimum distance while those behind had their seconds behind expressed in terms of kilometers and then subtracted from the optimum, thus giving the true distance covered. If one didn't finish an event, he was docked the amount he didn't do. Work carried out in the *parc fermé,* where cars were stored before speed events and during the rest stops, cost 50 kilometers, but if this seemed like an open invitation to rebuild the complete automobile between races, the cylinder head, block, differential casing, starter (pushing was penalized) and generator were marked against substitution. In addition, the gearbox, sump and rear end were sealed with wire so any fiddling about or swapping of bits lost 15 kilometers. And in case someone found a way to counterfeit the whole car, there was a secret mark put on somewhere!

As the first of 115 starters, Ancelin/Romel (NSU) moved out of Nice on Sept. 15 en route to the Col de Braus, it was raining like California and continued doing so through that night's rest (at Nice) and the next day, which encompassed the hill climbs of Mont Ventoux and Col de Rousset. On all three, people came unstuck (like Simon-Ferrari) or dropped points because of the wrong tires (Gendebien-Ferrari) or went like gangbusters (Mairesse, Consten, or Walter's Porsche Abarth). By the time the Nurburg Ring was reached, the pattern had been set, with Mairesse streaming wildly ahead of his fellow countryman, Gendebien, and Consten who, having made up a large lead on the Ventoux, sitting back and slipstreaming Jopp in another 3.8 Jaguar to lose only .154 km.

It was plain that Gendebien, who is very experienced in such matters, was waiting for the importunate Mairesse to crash or break the car and what were a few kilometers here and there? However, there is such a thing as letting the opposition get too far ahead and Olivier had a bit of bad luck at Spa, the next morning, when he had the race in the bag, but ran out of gas at the last corner. In the touring category, Jopp's co-driver Baillie (one driver could only perform in a certain number of events) halved Consten's lead but both, plus 3rd man Jose Behra in another 3.8, had to step smartly to stay ahead of Rosinski, Oreiller, and Trautmann in Conrero Giulietta TI's.

After Spa, it was around in the bushes at night (during which Mairesse clobbered Spinedi's Ferrari while the lat-

ter was making a U turn) and off to Montlhery, where Gendebien and Mairesse pulled exactly the same routine as at Spa and Consten and Jopp ditto Nurburg Ring. All slept in Rouen, and on the Essarts circuit the next morning, Baillie whittled another 2 km off Consten while Gendebien picked up almost that amount from Mairesse, whose Ferrari was not handling its best in spite of the fact that the whole front suspension had been replaced at the Montlhery control before checking in.

It was off to Le Mans next and goodbye to the big money for Gendebien; his Ferrari coughed a piston, probably brought on by running lean twice, and although the works mechanics changed it in just over two hours, there was a 200-km penalty for missing the race, plus 150 for unsealing the sump. Canny Consten slipstreamed Jopp throughout and took the lead just at the end, when his competitor's tank momentarily ran dry. Pons' Alfa blew its head gasket, Behra's 3.8 slipped its clutch, and many tired engines got more tired.

On the long night's run to Clermont-Ferrand Gentilini took his Jag over a railway embankment and blocked the main Paris-Brest line for two hours. Consten split the Puy Mary and Puy de Dome (which his co-driver Renel did) with Jopp and Baillie, but after that, with the hill climbs of Le Tourmalet, L'Aubisque and the circuits of Auvergne and Pau, this clever driver was far in front.

Oreiller, who had moved up to third in the Touring class, was put out when he found sand in his engine at Clermont-Ferrand, thus climaxing the skulduggery found in this event when keys were swiped (Berney), car papers pinched (Soisbault) and so forth, but Oreiller's teammate Rosinski took over his place. All Mairesse had to do was keep it on the road and sure enough he did, cruising into Biarritz on the evening of September 23 with a broad smile to collect more francs than I like to think about.

It all sounds a little on the dull side, but the atmosphere at the controls is fantastic. Service wagons from the principal makes are lined up along the side of the road, together with the leading accessory and fuel people. Spectators are wandering all over, scattering as an Alfa, say, comes whooping in with hysterical blasts on its air horn, peak revs in third. It sweeps to a stop, a disheveled driver leaps out and waves his arms about, whereupon a regiment of mechanics dive under the hood.

The Marchal (or Cibie) men change a squashed foglight while the Cibie (or Marchal) fellows align another with their portable rig. The BP (or Shell) man pumps fuel in the back. Meanwhile, if there is enough time, the co-driver wanders off to the barber for a shave, or perhaps to the Shell buffet tent for a bite to eat.

These wonderful Shell people, incidentally, after putting up most of the prizes and feeding the multitude at every stop, suffered the indignity of finding that Consten and both Index winners were running on BP. Nevertheless, what's to keep an event like this from being run in the U.S.? Seems like a crackerjack idea to me. ◉

I WANT 3000 WORDS BY MONDAY, THE EDITOR SAID,

ON WHAT TO DO IN EUROPE

. . . you know, the lot. And it was already Wednesday. But his orders are orders and he has even been over here to see where the interesting cars come from, so I can't just come on with any old flannel. However, the subject is obviously impossible to cover completely in our pages and, in fact, one could write a book. People have, y' know, and these are known as travel books; I advise you to go buy one or two and bone up on the more mundane aspects of the problem, such as what to do about passports, how to travel, what kind of money is used, and what have you. There are several that I have found useful which you can buy in the U.S., notably the Hallwag "Europa," ————————— which is full of maps, a reasonable commentary on each country, and quantities of hotel and garage lists which you can largely disregard (except in times of stress), as I get the feeling that they are paid advertisements.

Many people swear by Fielding's Guide and it certainly makes good reading even if it is not strictly a guide in the classic sense, and I have a selection of Fodor guides which are as satisfactory as any other. In Europe, the "Guide Bleu" and/or Baedecker can be saved for those who wish a really close look at the country. If one plans to spend some time in the well known *endroits* of France, Benelux, Italy and Spain, the various Guides put out by the Michelin tire people are absolutely essential, as they give you town plans, eating places, hotels, prices thereof, and, in their numerous regional guides, a superior rundown of sights to be seen. I wouldn't stir without mine. Yes, the important ones can be gotten in English.

If Germany is your target, the Varta battery people publish much the same sort of thing as the Michelin "France" and I would recommend this as well when you get to Deutschland. For those who think mostly of the inner man (as I do), then I would also prescribe the purchase of Sam Chamberlain's "Bouquet de France" and "Italian Bouquet," with possibly the addition of a good boozing book like Lichine's "Wines of France" or Simon's "Noble Grapes" and the "Great Wines of France." More on these later, but all of them make fascinating reading for months beforehand and it is well to bone up

enough so you won't be absolutely lost on arrival here.

First things have been first, and I will now pass by the matter of transportation by saying that traveling by plane or ship is a highly individual matter. I took a steam packet once across the great grey heaving Atlantic and shan't do it again unless I have simply stacks of baggage. However, if you are a good sailor and don't mind plastic cuisine, millions of kids, running a gamut of open palms at the end, or only plan to drink your way across (the nurse on our Dutch liner prescribed gin for seasickness), do take a ship. But reserve early, or you may find yourself stuck in the same cabin with some unlikely and uncongenial companions.

Airlines are much the same, really, if you avoid the wheatfield efforts. Traveling tourist, one might as well be in a Greyhound bus but you get there at the same time as the first-class passengers up front, and for a lot less money. I think the economy classes also cut down on baggage, but the seasoned traveler doesn't bring much anyway . . . and that should be drip dry, as both laundries and dry cleaning cost the earth. Also, I am told by economizing friends of mine, that it is just as well, if one is not returning in a peak period, to purchase the return ticket in Europe and avoid some dollars of U.S. tax. This same friend also advised me to look into Icelandic Airlines, which flies to England from New York with propeller-driven planes and, taking more time than the jets, charges less money. There are also deals from time to time, in which one may get in on some "club" which has chartered an airliner. But just one word of advice: re-confirm the minute you get here. Slip-ups on return reservations are not at all uncommon.

Inasmuch as you are readers of *Road and Track,* we will assume for the moment that you are planning to do

PHOTO BY JOSEPH PARKHURST

BY HENRY MANNEY III

some touring in Europe. If you enjoy motoring, then Europe is the place for you. Roads are comparatively uncrowded, motorcycle cops do not lurk around every corner, and, except for towns and construction zones, etc., there are no speed limits. It is a waste of time to take the train if you wish to see the bare bones of the country and be your own boss. At present, I will not go into the subject of *which* car to buy, except to note that gasoline is much more expensive than in the U.S. and it behooves one to watch the pocketbook. There is no point in bringing a domestic automobile to Europe, as roads are generally narrower, among other things. So it is a good idea to trundle around to your nearest dealer's and have a good hard look at those imports you think would suit you. Peer around. Work a swap with other members of your car club or your workmates for a day. Stick your nose in the shop at a dealer's and see what is giving the most trouble. Ask people on the street. You can't have too much information or cockpit time in a car if you are going to be living in it . . . which is what it amounts to, really.

Right now I will go on record as saying that unless you are young and/or a sport, you should not get a convertible if you plan to spend longer than three or four months. Europe is farther north than you think and it rains a good deal of the time. Also, there is a bit of petty thievery and anything seen may get pinched sooner or later, to the accompaniment of a cut top. For the same reason, I wouldn't buy a station wagon, as it is tiresome taking all one's junk into the hotel every night. Of course, what you plan to do with the car at home is the overriding factor.

Having settled on the car of your choice (I will attempt to give a short buyer's guide later), you should visit a reliable dealer and place an order. How do you find a reliable dealer? Same method as picking the automobile. Now you have two paths open . . . to purchase the car and bring it back with you or to sell it here. Agents for some makes have a package arrangement to cover either eventuality, guaranteeing repurchase in Europe or shipping it home. If the latter may seem high (it cost me, for

instance, a little under $200, including insurance, to ship a VW from Le Havre in France to New York through American Express), you can probably ship it for less by one of the fine firms in Rotterdam, as a couple of friends of mine did.

As far as selling the car (in Europe) is concerned, it *can* be done, but what with local ground rules, customs regulations, and the knowledge of the canny buyer that he has you over a barrel, important money is liable to be lost, plus the pleasure of your trip. Nobody enjoys sitting in an expensive hotel room, feeling like a country cousin in the hands of the slickers, and watching his departure date grow near with the vehicle still unsold. Your used car buyer over here is generally a lot closer with his money than his stateside equivalent.

Conversely, buying used equipment is fraught with peril besides being expensive, as most countries have internal or purchase taxes which have been absorbed. The snips in the back of *Motor Sport* look very enticing, it is true, and if you have time to spare there might be some advantage in looking for something special, like a bumblebee Frazer-Nash or 30/98 Vauxhall. However, most of the stuff has been used very hard indeed, and the English dealers have had many more years' practice concealing the bad points of dubious machinery than even our bandits at home.

Your car can be delivered to you almost anywhere on the Continent, but common sense dictates that a French car be picked up in Paris where the plane lands, and so forth. Of course, your VW can be waiting in Agrigento, Sicily, as you are brought ashore by war surplus landing barge from the Conte di Fettucine, but it will cost extra. The whole business of delivery charges is an invitation to print money and should be better regulated by the factories concerned. You see, your automobile occupies a special category in most countries with its "Tourist" plates, which it rates by reason of having been paid for in dollars. Customs duties, where applicable, and some local taxes will not have been paid, neither do they have to be for periods from three months (in Germany for road tax) to a year. This basic dollar price for each car

is the same all around Europe, but the difference between picking a VW up at the factory and in Paris will be an added charge of roughly $100. It varies with different makes and should be looked into. Alfa charged a friend of mine $230 extra to pick up his Veloce in Paris . . . a bit steepish. This money . . . VW's hundred bucks and Alfa's two hundred plus . . . includes transportation from the factory, pre-sale preparation, customs documents and perhaps enough gasoline to fill your lighter. The documents include your owner's certificate, *carnet de passage,* and various other papers supplied by the automobile club . . . including a membership thereof . . . that has arranged the bookwork. However, there is no reason that the charge for them should exceed $15. What can cost you the earth, though, is insurance arranged by dealers, so just set it up with your own agent before leaving home. Tell him you need the International Green Card, which is third party cover and required by most countries, and have him send it to the pick-up dealer in Europe.

Also be sure that you have left enough time to order and collect the car of your choice. VW's and Mercedes, for example, are in very short supply in the season. However, it is known that in certain countries, such as France and Germany, where licensing formality is not the order of the day, one can walk into the showroom and get what one wants in most cases. Jerry Sloniger tells me that VW's are available within a day or so in Germany now. But don't count on it . . . just useful in case you come over here on a bicycle and hit the *Lotterie Nationale.* Which I, personally, have never seen anyone do.

That leaves only the problem of warranty service. It is plenty tough enough getting anything done on a new car in its own country, without expecting warranty service all over. The service manager in a big BMC garage in Paris bluntly refused to replace faulty parts on guarantee in my car, but then VW is about the only house I know of that doesn't worry much about frontiers. In my experience, the others don't even want to give you the 500-mile check and that stuff; you get stalled off for weeks or they just take the coupon and never touch the automobile. On the associated problem of where-can-I-get-parts-for-it, I am afraid that VW again scores with its network of well policed agents, although Renault now has agencies in Germany besides being assembled by Alfa in Italy. Fiat is represented most places, although it is weak in France. For the English cars, the Channel is still there to stop Bonaparte, and away from Benelux and Switzerland (both of which have agencies for most European makes), sometimes you feel mighty lonely. A parts pack of the more easily consumable items should be carried anyway, no matter what you are driving.

To finish up this installment, we will tidy up a couple of questions that have probably been bothering you. The biggest of these is Money. Europe can be very expensive if you follow the "play-safe" policy of staying in palace-type hotels and eating in big restaurants twice a day. Playing it cool with the Michelin Guide, picnicking at lunch, and bothering to add up the bill can cut expenses in half. Most of the couples we know have figured $20 a day all-up for two; whereas this can be excessive, what slops over is taken care of eventually by an oil change, that jazzy bottle of wine, or those darling copper pots . . . made in Newark. The smaller hotels and restaurants are quite often superior to their big brothers in aspects of *gemütlichkeit* and cleanliness and will save you money as well. The only places where it pays to be a little careful about the soap and water aspect are Italy, Spain, Portugal and England. Of course one finds the obvious fleabag which one would not enter even at home, but, unlike the U.S., a look at the room beforehand is not considered strange at all. Neither is a firm request for the price of the room including taxes and service, and it may save some addition in the morning.

You may divine from some of my comments the feeling that you are going to get cheated from time to time. Sure you are. Money comes hard over here, and prices being what they are for the native as well as tourist, the hotel keeper or restaurateur is often tempted into fiddling the clients a little to make ends meet. They even do it to each other, especially in Switzerland, where nobody is safe.

GENÈVE 17 Km

INTERNATIONAL ROAD SIGNS
△ DANGER SIGNS ○ SIGNS GIVING DEFINITE INSTRUCTIONS ■ INFORMATIVE SIGNS.

DANGEROUS CURVE	ROAD INTERSECTION	UNEVEN ROAD
LEVEL CROSSING WITH GATES	LEFT CURVE	DOUBLE CURVE
DANGER	RIGHT CURVE	LEVEL CROSSING WITHOUT GATES
OPENING BRIDGE	DANGEROUS HILL	ROAD NARROWS
MEN WORKING	SLIPPERY ROAD	PEDESTRIAN CROSSING
WATCH OUT FOR CHILDREN	NO ENTRY	ROAD CLOSED
BEWARE OF ANIMALS	INTERSECTION WITH SIDE ROAD	MAIN ROAD AHEAD
STOP AT INTERSECTION	NO LEFT (Right) TURN	DIRECTION TO FOLLOW
SPEED LIMIT	CLOSED TO MOTOR VEHICLES	END OF SPEED LIMIT
CLOSED EXCEPT TO MOTORCYCLES	TRAFFIC CIRCLE	PARKING

Approaching Salvan in the Valais.

SWISS NATIONAL TOURIST OFFICE PHOTO

You can obviate this to a certain extent by sitting down and figuring out what the money is worth, but mostly by taking out your pencil and adding up the bill again. Don't be diffident . . . every Frenchman does it. But don't let the thought spoil your trip; in tourist places you are going to get taken like a tourist and you might as well accept it. Nothing personal, or because you are an American.

Don't worry about the language problem, as chances are you can't learn enough between now and then to help. You may think what you learned in school sounds like French/German/Italian, but Ha!!! What a shock when you walk down the street for the first time. Speak English slowly and precisely . . . a great many people do understand a little and in certain places (Scandinavia and Holland) it is a second language. Above all be pleasant . . . don't necessarily grin like an idiot, as they will think something is wrong with your head, but a smile goes a long way. Honey catches more flies than vinegar. (Thank *you*, Mr. Khrushchev.) However, a familiarity with the international road signs and knowing what *Vorsicht! Baustelle!* and *Teggenliggers* mean (in your Hallwag) may possibly save a shunt. And when you roll smoothly up to a frontier in the Ferrari and the man asks if you have anything to declare, you can say No in English. It means the same all over Europe.

Well, kiddies, away with dull care and next month out comes the old ball bat on such matters on Touring. What to See, Weather If Any, Where to Eat, Where to Get a Factory Ride, How to Sneak Into The Races, Shopping, What Clothes to Bring, What Season to Come In (any time but July and August), Whether to Bring Smokes and Food (No), or Nescafé (NO!), or Your American Girl Friend (Definitely No!!!), The Rundown on Foreign Cars, Camping (See "Through Europe in 2nd Gear," April 1960), Whether You Should Buy a Modified Car (that depends), and anything else I may have forgotten or you can write me about (quickly!) in the meantime *Ciao!*

MOTORING IN EUROPE

PART II
BY
HENRY
MANNEY
III

DRANG NACH OSTEN means drive toward the East (colloquially translated), which is, of course, what you will be doing soon after setting foot on the Continent of Europe. Now, there are many reasons why you might want to come here, and talking to the average tourist unearths some pretty strange ones.

Some visitors have come to see antiquities of various sorts; here in Paris or in that vast granite drafty barn of a cathedral in Reims, rather chipped around the edges from the war years, one can celebrate Mass elbow to elbow with ghosts attending the consecration of Charles VII in the presence of Joan of Arc in 1429, which makes the California Missions seem like pretty small potatoes. Other tourists flock, Michelin Guide in hand, to calcify their livers prematurely at the establishments of Hotel Cote d'Or (Saulieu), Pére Bise (Talloires), Pyramide (Vienne), or Laperouse (Paris), researching just why the words "French Chef" should be an advertisement for a restaurant.

Still more, Wagner throbbing through their blood, will make tracks for the Rhine, to disappear without trace into a pool of cool Rhine wine, salmon mayonnaise, view mit castles and *gemütlichkeit*. Certain sober couples, or sometimes men alone, make serious pilgrimages to the battlefields of Mons, Chateau-Thierry, the Argonne or the Ardennes in memorial-studded France, where the smallest town has 30 or 40 names listed on the church. And one finds the same sort of thing on the other side of the Rhine; just fewer names. Strong young men, or some-

times older ones optimistic about their condition, make tracks for the fleshpots of Paris, Brussels, London or Hamburg, where those who are going to make out will do so without any advice from me. Certain outdoor types, supervising their wine from the grape as it were, haunt the teeming secretary-spread beaches of the Riviera where one will see more bare skin in five minutes, thanks to France's national costume, the Bikini, than in a whole evening at Joe's strip joint. Still more fundamental ones seek out the Ile de Levant near Toulon or North Germany's Island of Sylt, where everybody runs around starkers. They say you get used to it. . . .

As one can see, the possibilities are endless and one could go on in the above vein indefinitely, but we at R&T are primarily concerned with motoring. And a good thing it is, too; otherwise we would be working for a movie fan magazine or something else profitable. However, it takes only one trip over here to discover that, for the average downtrodden U.S. motorist, driving in Europe is heaven. If posted speeds (about 35 mph generally) are observed in towns and notice is taken of no-passing zones, you never need glance apprehensively into the driving mirror for the dreaded American cycle cop, found in certain "speed trappy" sections of the U.S.

Long straight roads are yours for the asking; gradual curves, sharp bends, hairpins, asphalt, *pavé*, mountain passes, all generally with quite a low traffic density so you can blow the cobwebs out of the engine and see just why handy sedans and full-blooded sports cars developed here. Follow Marcel Renault's tracks to Bordeaux in the ill-fated Paris-Madrid. Head bowed reverently, trace the classic Mille Miglia course in Italy . . . Brescia, Verona, Padua, Rovigo, Ferrara, Ravenna, Forli, Rimini, Pescara, L'Aquila, Roma, Siena, Firenze, Bologna, Modena (convenient), Piacenza, Cremona, Mantova and Brescia again. You will wonder how on earth people covered it at anything up to 98 mph in open cars, and light a candle for Portago, who probably would have given his life *not* to end the Mille Miglia's history.

But then, as you trace your apprehensive way through the proliferation of motorized plankton that infests every Italian road, you will probably agree with a cheerful competitor who used the race as his annual vacation; everybody was going the same way he was, traveling at the speed he usually did, and he could look around without inadvertently collecting a bicycle.

Some of you will undoubtedly say, "Zounds! An idea!" And so it is. While the pukka Mille Miglia is in the same boat as the dodo bird, there are plenty of events where you can frighten yourself almost as badly. As far as the smaller rallies are concerned, organizers are a little more hidebound over here about somebody just turning up at the start with a gas company map, ready to run, but you can set your face in a broad smile and try. If you are planning to spend some time in a district, scout out the local automobile club or read the sporting papers and fix yourself up. Most enthusiasts are glad to have you along. There is the odd stuffy b . . . . . . , but Europe has no monopoly.

Racing is a little more formal, naturally, but for those willing to slop over into both types of events, a good GT car is the answer. Lots of GI's run in races over here and you just have to nose around and ask questions of them or the locals. For the big big events, both rallies (such as Alpine, Monte Carlo, Liege-Rome-Liege, and the other International ones, none of which are anything to trifle with), and races (1000 km of Nurburg Ring, Le Mans, Targa Florio and the TT), you might be able to wangle an entry if you write well in advance and spin a big line about how good you are. And if they don't have to pay you starting money it helps. The classic way, of course, of fiddling a ride is to buy a car from some temporarily impecunious manufacturer and have him enter it. I myself have been offered a DB for Le Mans and from what one sees in the 24-hour race I have a feeling that this policy still operates. Mind, it would be pretty hard to find a safer or more reliable car to do Le Mans in, but don't expect to be faster than Laureau. Lots of other manufacturers have resorted to this sort of thing from time to time and still do, as can be obvious to any thoughtful student of Le Mans, even in 1960. I could mention names who arrange this sort of thing, but you would only curse me when you got fleeced.

The first step, though, if competition motoring is planned, is to acquire an FIA competition license, which you will need for both racing and rallies on the calendar . . . plus karts, in Germany. England is a hotbed of motor sport and if you like it there, take out a domestic

RAC license, as a good percentage of their events in which you have any chance of winning something will be national. But the competition is rough!

The same applies to any other country viewed with residence in mind, but for anyone who wants a few bashes here and there and then go home, arrange with the FIA on Place de la Concorde, Paris, to issue one of their International Licenses. It is just as well to furnish them with a copy of your racing/rallying history as well . . . excluding the times, of course, that you have been on your head. The way it works here is that as soon as the entry form is completed, you send it to the governing body (FIA, RAC or whatever you have) with the entry fee. They "visa" the application blank and forward it to the organizer; their approval is regarded as at least tacit proof that you are capable of tackling the course. Once there, you are on your own about such businesses as warding off crooked organizers, etc., as nobody takes you by the hand, although the English privateers are generally the salt of the earth if anyone is really in trouble.

If you are here in September and like racing *and* rallying, you might try the Tour de France, which meanders between seven hill climbs and seven race courses. Details from L'Equipe, Paris. Liege-Rome-Liege wears the car out, the Monte involves going 65 mph on sheet ice, and the Alpine . . . brr.

At this point we will sandwich in a few words about what to bring to Europe. First comes money. Some of this was covered in the last issue, but there can never be too much. What you have with you is best carried in traveler's checks, and the American Express type seem to be the best known. Change these (which should be in 10 or 20 dollar units to avoid getting stuck with too much of the same sort of foreign currency at one time) at a bank, Cooks or Amexco agency if possible. Change-

St. Gotthard pass at Schoellenen Gorge.

SWISS NATIONAL TOURIST OFFICE

offices at borders will take advantage of you, as will hotels, restaurants, and shops, some just because they have to take their percentage on top of the bank's which eventually has to do it anyway. *Never* transact business with plausible little men on street corners. It is well, incidentally, to provide yourself with $20 worth of the money of your first foreign stop before you leave the U.S.

But what about the credit card? At the risk of making some people angry, I will just pass on to you reports garnered from friends who made use of some of the better known cards, that establishments bearing these signs on their door often seemed to have the worst sort of tourist trap atmosphere, besides having prices sadly out of line. At best, they have to make enough money to support all the paperwork on top of their normal retail charges. Generally, you can get off much cheaper by not seeking out these places; for that matter, we are always wary of shops advertising that "We Speak English." Use your Michelin Guide and remember that the common people over here are patient and kind, just like home. You won't starve.

Clothes? Depends on the season (avoid July and August if possible, as everyone else is on the roads,

Automobile plates identify country of origin.

hotels are jammed, prices are up . . .) and what you plan to do. Just bring as much drip dry as is practicable for that sort of clothing and, above all, don't bring too much, as you will always be hauling it in and out of the car. A few plastic hangers and a portable clothesline (adjustable for length) is a very good idea, but unless you use something special like Woolite don't bother bringing soap flakes. I personally would recommend to men that they invest in a *good* drip dry suit (like Brooks Bros.) with two pairs of trousers and in a dark color. People are more formal here, class differences are greater, and generally you are taken for the type indicated by your dress.

It would be advisable to have some absorbent slacks, wool or cotton, for driving, as drip-dry may cause your *derriere* to itch and/or make you feel that you are sitting in a hot bath. Provision should also be made for enough warm clothes if you come in spring or fall, but it can be very cold in summer. Some good compromises for driving are made by Lacoste and others in the form of long sleeved sweater-shirts.

The above remarks about formality are not meant to say that a hotel doesn't expect you to arrive looking like anything but an unmade bed, but it is nice to dress for dinner. Get anything drip-dry or nylon before you leave home, as the Continental varieties are expensive, nasty, or both. Imported shirts and things, of course, will be cheaper here and save room in the luggage. Above all, do not come with a selection of gaudy garments, especially sports shirts to be worn outside the trousers. Good grief!

Bring good, comfortable shoes, preferably with ripple soles, for all the walking about. Some Continental cars

(like Dauphines) are difficult to drive with large-soled shoes, but Italy has some nice thin ones. European feet, however, are different from ours, sometimes shorter and higher in the instep, and unless you are so constructed you may not be comfortable. My wife reports that ladies are better off, but then, as far as I can see, women will put up with anything short of a boot full of molten lead if it's stylish.

Speaking of the ladies, I can't imagine why anyone would want to bring one over here, but there you are . . . some people are sentimental. As far as clothes are concerned, the same remarks apply as above, with the proviso that nice females are a bit more covered up; sleeveless dresses or blouses are fine, but you should always have a sweater handy for hiding your nakedness in churches. Capri pants are worn (usually in resort areas or when actually traveling), but for pity's sakes leave the Bermuda shorts home; they are the laughing stock of Europe. Also forget the finely boned, plastic, tailored bathing suit and buy a bikini for a dollar on the Riviera. Give the old man a thrill. He might even start looking at you again.

In case you don't bring your own, or plan to collect one here, suitable traveling companions can often be located with a little scratching around (England is easier, in view of the language problem, if nothing else), and most Continental hotels are not particularly interested in whether you are married or not. Paris is also good (all this is hearsay, be it noted), although French girls on the whole are very moral, but you might try Lausanne, Switzerland. This seethes with pretty creatures, especially in the summer when all the little Scandinavian lemmings thunder down from the North for a few brief hours of sunshine. For obvious reasons, I can't go into more detail.

We can finish up the What-to-Bring-Dept. with several Noes. If you are enamored of American cigarettes, do pack them, but you will get much more of the flavor of the country if you fumez the local stuff. Plus another type of lung cancer. I personally prefer Gauloise, a black French mix that gives off sparks and makes you talk like Piaf. But then my taste buds have been atrophied for years . . . but not so much that I still refuse to smoke plastic American cigarettes, whose only virtue is that they are cheaper when brought from home. Have your own pipe tobacco unless you plan to go to Holland or someplace like that, but I prefer Dutch, Belgian, German and Swiss cigars to the American variety. French and Italian cigars shouldn't happen to a dog, and English ones are taxed out of reason . . . but so are their cigs, unless you get them on a boat or plane.

Don't import your own booze. Besides the local beers and wines, there is a great variety of hard likkers named cognacs, calvados, armagnacs, or *eaux de vie,* which latter are clear popskulls made from fruit and very dry. Regardless of what the red-faced bloke in the advertisements tells you, most of the good stuff stays here. This especially goes for Italian wines, which I have never found very good outside Italy, but not for English spirits in England, which are about 70 proof and all right for ladies, I suppose. It is possible to get used to their body-temperature beer, but one can get iced lager now. Avoid French or Italian beer like the plague (there is something called Panther Pils), but the Dutch, Danish or German beer is the real thing—especially on its home ground where it hasn't been pasteurized or otherwise neutered.

I am a wine man and don't get me started on food as well. If we have any room at the end, I will come back to it.

Bring any medicines that you are especially hooked on. If you are a junkie I hear you can get a fix in England on the National Health scheme. Better ask some musician who's been there. All the normal things like aspirin, of course, are here and then some. However, Kleenex costs the earth most places. You will also hear horrible tales of what drinking the water does to you. The answer to that is simple: don't touch it, use wine instead. Nevertheless, I have sampled water without incident in all the big cities . . . although one should be wary in small towns, as in Italy or Spain. Everybody drinks bottled mineral water anyway, both fizzy and not, and it is cheap. But if you should get a touch of what the Limeys refer to as "Bombay Tum" be forearmed by having some Entero-Vioform or Kaopectate along. Pre-race preparation is all-important. Mostly the trouble comes from a change of diet, plus unaccustomed rich sauces and wine, plus being jiggled about in the car all day, rather than any sinister bacteria. And if you are the ultra-sensitive type, better pack some extra Kleenex, especially for England. Remember too, it is wet here and bring a raincoat or folding brolly. I prefer the latter.

It would be a pity not to take pictures of your trip. Color film is cheaper in the U.S.—bring all you can fit in corners, but you can get it here if you run out. While Kodachrome gives the most "vacationey" slides, given plenty of sun, remember that the light isn't as strong here as in California, say. Also, you may find yourself at awkward shutter speeds or lens openings during one of the many rainy days.

I use Ektachrome a lot, and Super Ektachrome in difficult cases. Used to shoot a lot of Anscochrome which is better for *true* colors but not as festive, if you follow me. Gave it up because it is too hard to get processed outside Switzerland (Ansco-Berne). You should even be careful with Ektachrome . . . I can recommend Pictorial Service (17 Rue de la Cométe, Paris) and Studio 13 (Zurich, Switzerland), who both give fast and good service. You can take it personally to the former, but it has to go through a dealer in Switzerland. Kodachrome is no problem as there is a processing plant in every major country. If you have time, it is just as well to get a roll developed to see if camera and light meter are working. As far as a camera is concerned, if you want a new German make it is a good money-saver to get it here. Not necessarily in Germany, where they are very loath to give discounts, but a few of the big camera stores in other countries have tax-free prices and will wheel and deal as well. One that springs to mind is Photo des Nations in Geneva, but watch it! Add everything up and compare prices before you go in. You can also find Canons there, but they are cheaper in the U.S., I think. We could go on this photo lark forever, but I will content myself by cautioning you to get a *good* light meter and check it out before you leave home. I have a Norwood, but the editor uses a GE Golden Crown. And if you plan to take any photos at the races, have at least a 135-mm lens, plus shades for each lens you have.

But will I be able to get all this through the European customs? Yes, you will. With tourist plates on your car and your cam-ground Ammurrican passport, most border guards couldn't care less. In five years I have never had a bag opened, barring going *into* the U.S., that is. Some of these zollbeamters will ask if you have anything to declare. What they are generally looking for is merchandise that you might be going to sell. Each tourist is entitled to enough smokes, booze, etc., for his personal use, so feel free. It could get expensive if you had, say, three bottles of Scotch and 500 cigarettes and they got nosey, but they would have every justification. The Italian border men will try something once in a while but, after all, they smoke too. The only tiresome ones are the English who hold the whole line up to ask a bunch of stupid questions, not that they ever look at anything. The Common Market is putting this out of date anyway, so always speak English wherever you are, smile sweetly, don't cover things up madly as you roll up to the frontier, and you're in.

Next month, wheretogowhattobuy.

CLICHE CGT PHOTO

FRANCE

to my mind, is the heart of Europe. It used to be said that the French never traveled abroad because they had everything at home. On one side, the lovely countryside boasts Europe's finest highways, chateaux, restaurants, and vineyards, while on the other, there are some of the ugliest and most untidy small towns anywhere. This last does not apply to Paris, which is absolutely shattering. From a walk in the early morning, savoring the fragrant odors of Gauloise, something interesting cooking, and half-burnt Azur "ternaire," to leaning on the Pont de La Concorde at sunset, looking at the world's most civilized view, Paris can provide everything for soul and body.

And for those who like the cut-and-thrust of production car racing, Paris traffic will supply complete satisfaction without the formality of numbers and entry fees. Apparent absolute chaos reigns in the absence of the forest of stop lights and signs which strangle modern cities and enrich the magistrates; in practice, Jean-Claude coming from the right or Pierre in front have the right of way and the rest can all whistle. Phenomenal avoidances by the dozen are common, as some brave soul calmly barges out of a side street into the traffic stream. From the right, of course. Around the Arc de Triomphe, 12 main roads feed in spoke-fashion and I don't have to tell you what a mess that is as drivers try to get in or out at the street they want. Sometimes strangers go around for hours, rather as in the Sargasso sea. Rover P.R.O. Gethin Bradley, splendid in a large 3-liter with English plates, got tired of being carved up and just barged through. He was presently accosted by an indignant taxi-driver who said, "But M'sieu . . . *ce n'est pas* fair play!"

There is a very good chance that you will arrive in Europe at either Paris airport (Orly, in most cases) or one of the seaports like Le Havre. In that case, it is more than reasonable, especially if you plan to stay largely on the Continent, to take delivery of a French car. Formerly viewed with suspicion because of the poor assembly and finish of their products the leading French constructors now build automobiles as well as anyone. For those arriving by ship, it might be well to avoid Paris by picking up the car at a port agency; this way the all-important break-in period (for both *voiture* and *pilote*) will be spent in comparatively gentle country work and, at any rate, I think that Paris should be saved till the end. At this time you are more used to European ways and more receptive to her sights, and will have just so much money left to spend. Paris can be very expensive, and many journeys are spoiled through prematurely wrecking the budget.

To avoid extra expense in tourist traps like the Grand, I would recommend the hotels Victor-Massé, Grand Hotel Turin, and Duminy (in your Michelin guide); two reasonably cheap and satisfactory restaurants are Stes-Péres (corner Stes Péres and Blvd. St. Germain) and Lescure (7 Rue Mondovi). For a steak-what-am go to Chez Fred over on Blvd. Periére (reserve ahead), Chez Mercier is reliable (Rue Lincoln), and you can really do it up brown at Tour d'Argent or Laperouse, both of which are sort of tourist trappy, but you only live once. Naturally there are lots more!

If it's sightseeing you are after, buy a copy of the green Michelin "Paris" guide in English and follow its dicta. Shoppingwise, I will touch on gloves and silk scarves,

both of which are best (if expensive) at Hermés, where you will receive 20% off on traveler's or personal checks. Stinkum is all over, but for this as well as most purchases (female type) it is as well to go to a big store like Trois Quartiers, Printemps, or Galerie LaFayette, who will not only send an interpreter around with you, but send everything home if you like. The discount mentioned above applies in most reputable shops. For those who like goofy kitchen equipment like big copper pans (sold by weight!) and some of the most knocked out and baroque kitchen equipment ever, pay a visit to Dehillerin down by Les Halles, where you may also attend high Mass at St. Eustache and hear the best organ music in Paris. There are really lots of interesting clothes and oddments, so you may be tempted to augment your slender wardrobe . . . an interesting *nouvelle vague* place, if a bit pricey, is Puloinella, on Rue Vignon, near the Madeleine.

Your choice of car really depends on price. The DS and ID Citroens, whose ride and handling are as above reproach as Caesar's wife, are the most expensive of the passenger automobiles and will keep you very comfortable indeed. Equally favored by the ultra-conservative

French burgher as "serious" cars, the 403 and 404 Peugeots combine excellent handling with a good ride and perhaps, when the chips are down, would be a little easier for the corner gas station back home to deal with. Of the two, I think the 404 is the better car, even allowing for a little brake judder and bouncy seats. Next down are the Simcas, the larger of which will appeal to those who like compact 1948 American cars. The Montlhéry, though, with its new 5-bearing engine really travels and, although rather noisy and hard-riding, gives you that old vintage feeling in the best context. As far as Renault is concerned, if you can stand the price have a Dauphine Ondine Gordini, as the 3-speeder drives me, personally, mad, and the Gordini name will help you on eventual resale. Works car, *mon vieux*. Tuned by the Sorcerer himself. Otherwise, the Regie still makes the 4-CV if you want to save money and if there are only two of you the Caravelle is about, very handsome and better handling than the Dauphine. Citroen also makes the rather agricultural 2-CV, which I recommend heartily if you are a placid type and not in any hurry at all. Panhard, absorbed by Citroen, still markets its flat-twin sedan of amazing capacity and speed, but I would get it on a resale basis, which perhaps would also be more prudent for the 2-CV Citroen, big Simcas and 4-CV Renault, as you may have to eat them at home. I do not particularly say anything about the Facel Vegas, as the little one is a bit new and you can have a race-bred automobile for the price of the big one. Renault Alpines and DB's are also fun if you plan a little competition.

Looking at the International Calendar, there is the Monte Carlo GP on May 14, and if I had to limit myself to one race a year, I would pick this one. Not everywhere can you get wakened up at six ayem by a Ferrari at full bore winding in and out between the houses. Race cars, hot sun, blue Mediterranean, crumpet-covered beaches, cold rosé, grilled *loup* with fennel bush inside . . . aaaagh! Drivers stay at Hotel de Paris (expensive!) or Bristol, others at Mirabeau, Excelsior or Metropole (a tomb) or Palmiers or Balmoral, with view over Grace's harbor and for that matter, in Grace's window. Eat at the Bec Rouge (if open), a restaurant so good that one Prominent Journalist actually paid for his own meal. Try the *beignets de moules* (mussels) or practically anything else except the everlasting steak and cheeken which tourists freeze up on and order. Ask da boss. Of others, the English all eat at César's and have breadroll fights, so if you want to see the famous Cliff Davis (who looks like a raffish Teddy Roosevelt) in action, go there. But you have been warned about the food. We always stay at the Rome, but don't eat anything serious there. Nearest sand beach is at Cannes and unless Dean gives me more space I can't cover the Riviera or, indeed, the rest of France.

There are two more races, however: Le Mans on June 10-11 and the GP at Reims on July 2. The 24-hour go should be seen at least once in one's life, I suppose, but I have never been so wet, tired, and hungry in all my life as there. I don't know what to advise you for hotels, as everything gets ever so full weeks ahead. Pick one out of the Michelin and write well in advance. There is a camping place, but watch for thieves in the parking lots. It sometimes happens that one can get a press or photo pass of some sort by presenting a letter from a club saying that you are their official photographer or such jazz. All it will do for you, though, is get you in free. The pukka photogs have enough trouble staying ahead of the machinations of the little French press clique . . . last year our photo passes were good only till 3:45 P.M., the race ending at 4:00. Dirty pool.

I wouldn't bother going to Reims at all, as the race is invariably hot, very crowded, noisy in the extreme, and foreign press and public alike are treated with the utmost discourtesy. If you *have* to watch it, do so from the Thillois end where there is a pub and a hairpin. Either stay in the pub (Auberge de la Garenne), or where the drivers do (Lion d'Or), or ditto journalists (Welcome). Everybody gets gassed on champagne after the race to restore their water table.

Just a few last tips on touring. France is a lovely country and you should take the opportunity to look around. Start out early, go reasonably gently (gas is expensive, but you can get tourist tickets with traveler's checks for a considerable saving at any bank), and you can save yourself endless time and money by picnicking before noon. This, incidentally, goes for all Europe. Not only will lunch cost a packet that could be saved for dinner, but the roads are deserted during 12 to 2 and you can cover many kilometers while Jean-Claude stuffs his face for that time. And you would be stuck in the restaurant for a spell, too; lunch in France is a serious business. Stop in any town about 11:15, buy a wand-like *baguette* of bread at the *boulangerie,* cream cheese (St. Gervais double créme), fruit at the *epicerie,* pasteurized milk at the *laiterie,* fill your bottle (saves deposit!) at the wine shop at about 30 cents for a liter, some salami or *andouille* at the *charcuterie,* and chug off. Find a likely field out of town . . . there seems to be so much less fencing here . . . and eat. Look at the country and reflect that J. Caesar like as not walked down this road, doze, and when the 12 o'clock traffic dies down, charge on.

Especially in summer, stop early, picking your hotel from the Michelin or something like the Logis de France guide. Stay at the little ones. Have a cuppa tea or an aperitif (say "beer" when you want cough-syrup-like Byrrh and "Byrrh" when you want beer) at a sidewalk cafe, watching the ancients play bowls under the trees, and then sightsee. Take the Nagel or green Michelin guide and camera. Then, later, if you have wisely picked a hotel that has no restaurant, or one which doesn't ask that you eat there, go to your Michelin-starred (for cookery) restaurant . . . which is why that town was picked in the first place . . . and make a pig of yourself. Have the best fixed-priced menu with specialities. Don't be intimidated by the wine list; most places, except the fanciest, have open wine by the carafe in any possible color. Have a "fine maison" or liqueur. Stagger home.

ENGLAND

has probably the most beautiful countryside I have ever laid eyes on. Trimmed, carefully nurtured, boxed in by hedgerows, it is a joy to the eye. England is also the biggest pain to drive in, as far as the main highways are concerned. Everyone motors on the wrong side of the road for us, a road that twists and turns and wriggles, building up vast strings of frustrated traffic behind nose-to-tail trucks (limited by law to 30 mph) or pre-war incredibly diddly little soapboxes, chuntering along astraddle the white line. People park anywhere, causing the most annoying blockages, and there are miles and miles of 30-mph limits connected to towns, some of which boast the most modern speed traps and others, like Billinghurst, that still rely on drop-the-hanky and stopwatch. This is one country in which you don't want to stop where the trucks do as, generally speaking, roadside "caffs" are disgustingly filthy. Food hours are peculiar, drink hours even more so, and the hotels, taken as a whole, are among Europe's oddest.

So why does anybody go there? I dunno. It gets you. The people are as nice as any could ever be . . . and England creaks with character, history, and your ancestors' ghosts. Using the maps (Shell-BP sell good ones)

and trundling up tranquil side roads, you will find as you negotiate a variety of interesting corners that it is suddenly clear why the English build so many sports cars and every third motorist is an enthusiast. Where else can you get run over by a pre-1914 Rolls?

Nothing else is like the English race crowd, where bizarre long-haired young men in duffers and wonderful turned-up hats (called curly-brimmed trilbies) occasionally neglect the cars to speak with their young ladies. These are of two varieties: fresh-faced and horsey, and the languid societagh. But BOY! are there some beauts! And going home in open Lotus Sevens, too. But, generally speaking, race people are the same anywhere . . . some phonies and some not, although it is harder to tell the drivers from the fakers in Limeyland. The most im-

probable people, on looks, like John Surtees or Jim Clark or Peter Ashdown, go like the clappers and then you run up against some theatrical type with rolling eye, flowing hair, and quaint dress (like Innes Ireland!) and he goes just as fast.

As for races, England is lousy with them and, indeed, you could spend the whole summer there and probably see one every weekend. If you were going to do just that it might be worth investigating one of the clubs like BARC which, I think, gives a reduction on tickets to members. On *all* races it pays to get there early, bring your lunch (and tea), and eat something or fiddle around afterwards as the traffic jams are enormous. You can generally buy paddock passes.

The big events in '61 are the GP on July 15 (take your brolly!) and the TT on August 17. Last year both were on airport courses, albeit with permanent grandstands, which are easy to photograph and offer a pretty good view. Aintree is a little better spectatorwise, but you have to go to Liverpool. I like Brands Hatch, which had a GP last year, and I am told Oulton Park is the nearest thing to a proper road course. If you are staying in England

and want to do it all and make friends, best out is to buy a Jr. and enter it in all the races. Bags of pit passes.

I really don't know what to tell you about buying an English car, as there are so blasted many types. I don't know of any actually bad ones, although a few are unsuitable for extended Continental touring because of their gutlessness or fragility, or both. At the risk of offending someone, I will just report on those cars of which I have had personal experience and let you sort out the others at home.

Starting at the top, we have Rolls-Royce and Bentley; really the same car. It may sound silly, but this is a better driver's automobile than you think, and not just a dowager's carriage. Write ahead to the factory on your oilman's paper and ask them to arrange a test drive, preferably in the country. Take the wheel and never mind all the flannel about quality control; *no*body builds them like they used to. Very nice, and maybe you can write it off. If you can't afford the Rolls but want something plush, call Gethin Bradley at Rover and arrange to try the 3-liter. Leans a bit but you can weld on a roll bar at home. Ever so comfortable and if I needed that sort of car I should get one. Daimler (now owned by Jaguar) also makes a limo sort of thing that goes very fast indeed, and also handles. However, it looks very old fashioned, and

as little un-thought-out things drove me buggy on the Aston. Of course, that was some time ago.

Now there is a vast mass of two-door and four-door family cars, practically any one of which will do, keeping in mind your resale in the U.S. If you plan to stray onto the Continent for long, you should pick one of the bigger ones, such as Humber, Vauxhall (which belongs to General Motors), Standard Vanguard, etc., as, according to a frontier customs officer of my acquaintance, there is a higher percentage of the over-bodied, under-geared and under-engined varieties which come back on the end of a rope. That is one man's opinion, but it is true that even the English complain that their cars are engineered mostly for home conditions. The combination of long straight roads, a big load of people plus baggage, and Continental temperatures seems to put them off. Nevertheless, the Ford Zephyr (now with disc brakes on the front) has a good reputation in France for reliability and the Sunbeam machines are much improved. In any case, if you can afford it, fit an overdrive.

Of the little English stuff, the only one of which I have had any Continental experience is the Mini Minor. Although not yet completely *au point,* this is a remarkable car indeed, and bags of fun to drive, but it is happier in England. Above 60 mph, fan and wind noise is bother-

A "Divided Carriageway" in Surrey, England

why don't you try the V-8 sports? Feels like a TD with some transplanted big mill, but what a mill . . . lively and smooth.

Jaguars you know all about by this time, I assume, and very good value for the money they are, too. They used to have a reputation for being rather goosey in the wet . . . not surprising in view of the power available . . . but the newest 3.8 saloon is much better and you can get away with amazing things, as anyone who has seen an English production car race will agree. Just remember, in view of the high prices of European gasoline, that they are a bit thirsty if driven hard. There are rumors of something else jazzy in the works which might incorporate the big (4.5 liter) Daimler V-8.

If you like Aston Martins, it is just that you prefer them to Ferraris, Maseratis, and Facel Vegas, which are the only other things in their class, really. It all depends on what you are going to do with it and where you are going to be. The GT is lovely, but Ferrari seem to be quicker, if you are planning to race one. Otherwise, it boils down to whether you prefer the sound of a 6 or 12. I have owned one of each and prefer the Italian marque,

some and the very clever suspension, exceptional for competition, official or otherwise, is definitely vintage on bumpy Continental roads. Even so, I went to Portugal in mine.

However, it isn't any harder than most of the sports cars, of which England offers an unparalleled selection, and perhaps it should be classified with them. All are entertaining if you are willing to put up with their inherent drawbacks, such as rough riding, side curtains and limited luggage space, and most of the designs have been in production long enough so that they shouldn't give you much trouble; very important on a vacation trip. Speedwell, Alexander, and Sprinzel (to name just three) offer delivery of production cars more or less modified. This sort of thing should be approached with caution unless you have some valid reason—like production car racing —as, besides being expensive, it may make it unreliable or simply too hectic to drive normally. Also, you rarely get hop-up money back on resale.

There are Channel ferries but, unless you have bags of time to put up with the crossing and endless customs queues, I recommend one of the air services such as

Silver City Airways, which flies three cars plus passengers in vast Bristol freighters from France to England (or vice versa) in a matter of 20 minutes or so. The line I use most often is from Le Touquet to Lydd (Kent), and in summer one should book well ahead.

Staying outside of London (to watch a race or something) is not difficult as there are lots of pubs and small hotels about. One of the best, for Goodwood spectators, is the Norfolk Arms in Arundel. In London it is difficult, as there are too few hotels and they are either expensive, no good, or sometimes both. Try the medium range Green Park or Washington in Mayfair, or if you like old foo foo hotels, St. Ermin's near Buckingham Palace. Eating is a problem, but Postgate's Good Food Guide might help a little. Or try Soho . . . one I found superior was the Osteria Romana on Dean St. Or call up rallyist John Sprinzel and ask him. At any rate, London is a fascinating town and people from the East Coast will feel right at home. By the way, if your car falls ill or needs a good tuning, take it to Willie Griffiths, ex-Lotus boffin, at 18 Culford Gardens, SW 3 (actually around corner on Blacklands Terr.), near Sloane Sq.

Don't feel bad if you never get the money sorted out. And, speaking of money, if you feel need of female companionship walk around through Soho and watch the upstairs windows. They are all off the street now. Otherwise, for race chatter, go to the Steering Wheel club on Brick St. (near Marble Arch) and tell Peggy that you need a home away from home.

GERMANY

Scenerywise, Germany is not terribly interesting, except up and down the Rhine and Moselle, which are fascinating, being full of castles and vineyards. You will find the roads crowded and the *autobahne* even more so. These last are also very dangerous at times because of the German driver's conviction that he and he alone has the right of way. Not only that, he will take it even if a truck is about to shut him off, with the result that there are some super accidents. Hotels (which include the cheaper *Gasthause* and *Gaststatte*) are generally clean and good; restaurants are likewise safe, if not dedicated to flights of culinary fancy. You certainly will get enough to eat. Wines in carafe can be gotten everywhere and are habit forming; whites being better than the reds. You will be surprised at how nice they really are, as Rhine and Mosel don't seem to take to shipping, and don't be surprised if after two of those big glasses you are pickled.

Races are the 1000 km of the Nurburg Ring and the German GP. Where the latter will be I don't know, but if it is at Avus, don't bother, unless you particularly want to see Berlin. In this case, don't apply for a visa beforehand, as you won't get it, but just present yourself at the Braunschweig end (Helmstedt) of the *autobahn,* buy the visa, and drive in. Guaranteed to make your flesh creep. The Nurburg Ring is a sight not to be missed by enthusiasts (near Cologne, or Köln as the Germans call it), and at the 1000 km on May 28th you have time to drive around and see a lot. Best vantage points are the start, Brunnchen, Karussel, a bridge over the road to Adenau, Schwalbenschwanz, and Flugplatz. There will be lots of people there, so bring a Coke crate to stand on, plus long lens, if you want pictures. And get there early . . . the cops are a bit efficient, and in their long leather coats, boots and *wehrmacht* hats give you that old 1942 feeling. You can drive around the Ring for half a buck when the cars aren't practicing and look at all the interesting black marks. And then tell *me* how Fangio got around in 9 min. 17 sec.

Accommodation is tight at race time, but there are a few small towns around. Drivers fill the Sporthotel at the *Start und Ziel* but some are in Adenau, at the Wildes Schwein. Latter is also the best place to eat . . . if you feel brave, try the veal cutlet with nuts. Jenks and I stay next door where it is cheap.

There are not all that many German cars for serious touring and taking back to the States after. Mercedes makes very fine ones, if you want to spend the money. BMW produces the best looking sports model if it is still in production (507), but I wouldn't race it. Porsches are sort of an acquired taste, like chocolate cherries, and a lot of my journalist friends have them. But one sold his, bought a Mercedes 220-S, sold that, bought a Peugeot 403, and last I heard is contemplating a Volvo. The Porsche Super 90 does not seem to be an unalloyed success, several reports crediting it with being rougher, noisier, and harder riding than the Carrera, which seems to have gentled down a bit. However, Porsches have superlative finish plus performance and should be classed with the world's better sports cars.

There are medium-sized saloons like Ford Taunus, Borgward, DKW, and Opel (by GM), of which I have tried only the first one. However, it is near as not a Falcon and parts may not be imported to the U.S. The DKW

Cologne, Germany

750, yclept Junior, seems fun and there is a bloke in Stuttgart . . . which you will find a bit like Frisco . . . who guarantees a good hop-up within "inspection limits."

Then, there is the Volkswagen, which is a pretty hard value to beat on all counts. Reports from friends indicate that service is faultless all over Europe. The only rumbles are luggage space and poor visibility. No, I don't have one. Not sexy enough.

Some beer drinking types disappear into pleasant Bavaria and never surface again. The weenies are also good, not surprising, since they are supposed to have been invented in Deutschland. Dachshunds are being supplanted by poodles, some superior stainless cutlery (WMF) and knives (Henkel) can be bought . . . plus leather shorts if you are the type . . . and if you are a dedicated drinker make the pilgrimage to Bingen, which gave its name to binges. Night-life types go to Hamburg and visit the Reeperbahn, where there is allegedly night life as seen in those Cuban Mickey Mouse movies. So I am told.

Next month, many more countries to visit—plus some tips on buying/driving overseas.

MOTORING IN EUROPE   BY HENRY MANNEY III

PART IV

IN WRITING SOMETHING like a Guide you will appreciate that it is much harder deciding what to leave out than in. Therefore in this last shattering burst, akin to a dash for the finish line with all the rods rattling, we cannot possibly include all we would like about Europe, touring, cars, or races. That would be impossible without a lot more space and the best thing to do is just come over and see for yourself. Again, my advice is to plan for spring or fall; the weather can't be any worse than summer, often is better, and there is much more room for you as an individual without being swamped by swarms of excursionists. . . . And I quote:

> I ran into some trippers
> In my swift De Dion Bouton
> Squashed them flat as kippers
> Left them *aussi mort que mouton.*
> What a nuisance trippers are;
> I must now repaint the car.

ETHERLANDS

Lovely country, nice people, scrubbed clean and so orderly and quaint it hurts the eyes. They get out at six ayem and wash the house front with long handled brushes. Trés folklore, as the French say. If you want the distillation of Holland, pass by Delft going either to or fro the GP. Hotel Wilhelmina is where I stayed. Other sights to see are the long North Sea dike which is making it possible to pump dry the Zuider Zee, Amsterdam (didn't think much of the Central) and the Bols works, where all the manholes have gin underneath.

A friend shipped his VW to Los Angeles from Amsterdam with the very helpful J. T. Vervloet Co. in Rotterdam for $238.89, insurance not included. Arrived in good order. (Another you might write is Jacques Golaz, Suisse-Atlantique, 12 Ave. des Toises, Lausanne, Switzerland. He quoted me a price of $100 Dunkerque-NY for a Volkswagen.)

The GP is at Zandvoort on May 22, near Haarlem and it is a keen race to watch. As for all the GPs, get there early and bring food and drink. From the main grandstand you can see enough to make it not worth your while to walk around; just as well as the dunes are full of sand spurs. The North Sea beach is at your back, but in May it's not all that warm anyway. Biggest hotel is the Bouwes, but there are lots of little ones (Meyershof) and jillions of furnished rooms. However *book ahead* as this year the race coincides with Pentecost weekend, which is a big holiday. And the 22nd is *Monday,* not Sunday, so don't get caught out on travel schedules or reservations.

Food isn't bad but the best meal is breakfast, where you get boiled eggs, cold meat, Edam and Gouda cheese, six kinds of bread, and koffie. Lots of koffie. With luck and industry you can last till dinner. For afters, if you have a taste for such things, try Ould Genever, which is old gin, iced and straight. Pronounced ouwld gnhhheffer and after three you can make it, man.

As far as cars are concerned, the Dutch make a DAF, which is a very small belt-driven economy car. Very pleasant but there is a lot of ground to cover. If you are flying in via KLM to Schiphol, near Amsterdam, duty-free cars of all sorts can be picked up right there. I imagine KLM agents would know the details. The Dutch automobile club also gives a cheap course in submarine escape, for when your car rolls into the canal. Very amusing, I'm told, as it happens often. Other hazards include bicycles, of which there are millions.

Dutch girls tend towards the bovine, but there are exceptions. Night life is confined, really, to the big cities and it was there that I heard Willy Slopenjinger and the Cowboys sing Red River Valley in Dutch. But the language is really a camp, sounding like swish German and utterly incomprehensible. You have to see it printed before you realize that English is really a dialect of Dutch. At any rate, most everybody speaks some English.

ELGIUM

I always sort of press on through Belgium, as most of the roads are rough *pavé*, a good part of it seems to be one continuous town infested with tram lines, and everywhere you look there are red brick houses. Also, the last I heard Belgians didn't have to have drivers' licenses and we all know what that means.

The GP of Belgium is usually at Spa, out in the Ardennes, which is piney and therefore quite pleasant. Nevertheless, I almost died of hay fever there which should remind you to bring your anti-sneeze. If you run out, restocking may be done in Switzerland. Ah choo, where was I? The main grandstands are okay but it is a little better, I think, up the hill after the start. As for hotels, the Portugal in Spa is used by journalists and the food isn't bad. Vielle France is good to eat in, but very dear. Real France is just over the border. Lots of drivers stay in Stavelot where the Orange isn't bad. There is another bigger hotel nearer Stavelot hairpin as well. This also reminds me that practice is a good time to wander around at any course and try different vantage points. Stavelot is a very quick one and sorts out the sheep from the goats as does, oop, the hill after Eau Rouge. La Source hairpin, before the pits, has a restaurant-cum-hotel and is handy for getting gassed on beer and fried potatoes mit tartar sauce while you watch the race.

Getting back to practice again, it generally goes on for three days or so and regulations are much relaxed at that time about hanging around in the pits and paddock. You have time to try and fiddle yourself a pass or temporary job or at least buy colored paper and copy one. All I know is that the pits are always full of people who don't have any business there so loopholes must abound. Go make customer noises to Von Hanstein of Porsches or Tavoni of Ferraris. One I have seen worked is to wear a business suit like an English photographer, lug in a big Speed Graphic, and say "Go . . . . . off" in English to anyone who bothers you.

For Belgian girls read Dutch girls. Drink beer . . . wine costs more than food.

WITZERLAND

No races but a couple of chintzy hill climbs. Very pretty country and pleasant but expensive. Hotels all very clean, all ditto. One can eat surprisingly well, especially in the French section, and again you get a lot, but when in doubt try the RR station buffet. There are two classes; unless you are loaded, eat in the 2nd with the brakemen. Same food. Open wine is good, especially white Fendant or red Dole de Valais. Don't eat fondue, which is a melted cheese dip, or you may be blocked for weeks. If you are near Geneva, you must try the Café de Paris (near RR station) where all they have is steak with a special sauce plus praties and salad. Ever so good. There are many more near Lausanne. Ask the cashier in American Express, Fernand Demont, for a choice. If your car is ill, try mechanic Maurer, at Garage Villamont in Lausanne. If you feel like buying something better, you might cross horns with Baron de Graffenreid at Alfa Romeo (Il Rue Etraz) there. But watch it—what a character!

Switzerland is full of mountains and passes thereof. For the St. Gotthard and Simplon, you can take a train through the hole, if need be. Is generally quicker than going over the top, especially in the Season with hordes of sightseers about. Just drive your car on the flatbed, after paying and passing through customs (for the Simplon, at the Station at Brig; Iselle in Italy), just sit there and get yanked through the tunnel. If you drive over the pass be sure that you have a car in good condition. Some of the more jelly mold vehicles will boil or vapor lock, whereupon you get out, dip a rag in one of the handy roadside streams, and apply it to the fuel pump. Said stream is colder than all get out and you will proceed. A lot of the passes are not paved and some have

St. Gotthard Pass, Switzerland.

only rudimentary guard rails. If you hear a noise like Gabriel's trump, look around. It will be a yellow Swiss Postbus which has the right of way . . . even if you have to back downhill to a wide place.

It is just as well to include in your spares kit a plastic collapsible bucket for water, in case of boiling or splitting a hose. While we are on that I will observe that you should buy a good locking gas cap and keep the key on you. Also, don't leave anything loose in the car at any garage, whether for washing or repairs. Fling everything in the trunk, lock it with its separate key, and keep that. If a car doesn't offer you this convenience, buy one that does. You should not leave anything visible inside especially at night. Keep your petrol coupons, where applicable, locked in the trunk as well, as they will also be the first thing to disappear from hotel rooms. It is safer, at any rate with mass-produced cars, to stick a bit of adhesive tape over the number on the ignition lock. Sharp characters carry a ring of keys and binoculars!

And these precautions should be the rule pretty much throughout your travels. Switzerland doesn't have a monopoly on "disappearance acts," by any means.

Watch out for the Swiss drivers. They, too, have a God-given right of way and tend to speed up when overtaken. And you know who is at fault if there is an accident, don't you?

Lots of things are worth buying, including watches, and you can maybe wheel and deal by shopping around. Lay off the cuckoo clocks as they are cheaper in Germany . . . not surprising since most of them are made there. If you want a week of peace and quiet in the mountains, go rent a floor from Lillian Wellein at Chalet Haut-Talus near Barboleusazs/Gryon, near Villars. At the foot of Lake Geneva. Write ahead.

There are very many pretty Swiss girls and, from what I hear, the hunting is good. Geneva has many night clubs with one of them, the Bataclan, offering 18 strip acts the last I looked. As for all over Europe . . . possibly excluding England . . . don't drink whisky unless you want to get robbed. Drink the local wine, *eaux de vie,* or brandy.

Mentioning American Express back there brings to my mind that I have found Cooks to be much more satisfactory, except in Lausanne, for making any sort of travel arrangements, hotel reservations, or just plain information. Too, Cooks has many more offices in Europe than Amexco.

Tyrol region, Austria.

USTRIA

Friendly people, smiling country, food sort of heavy at times, especially the dreaded Lebernudel dumpling, which reassumes its cannonball form in your stomach with the last bite, and rolls about from side to side. *Haute couture* pastry was reportedly invented near Salzburg and I believe it. That town is very nice indeed and one look around will show you why Mozart's music sounds like it does. We stayed at the Goldener Hirsch there and were very comfortable.

PORTUGAL & SPAIN

The northern part at least is just like California and you will see why the Conquistadores felt at home in our West. Reports of Spanish roads being so vile are exaggerated, at least on the main ones I saw. However, gas stations are few and far between, only one or two evident in the biggest towns. Refuel even when you have a half tank left; it may save you a long walk.

For hotels and restaurants it is safer to confine yourself to the better places. Michelin's "Espagne" is very useful. We tried a couple of Posadas, which are old castles or monasteries converted into hotels by the Spanish government; the one at Ciudad Rodrigo was very comfortable. Its Portuguese counterpart of San Lourenço is 24 km straight up on the side of a mountain range, and I wouldn't bother.

The GP is at Lisbon and Porto alternate years. We have attended the latter and everyone is very pleasant and helpful. Stayed at the Infanta de Sagres, which is the best, I think, and very comfortable with pretty good food as well. Allow lots of time to get to Porto, if driving, as the road in is a hundred miles of rapid changes from right to left lock. In Spain and Portugal both there is lots of sun, which is often a contrast to the rest of Europe. Don't wear your bikini, nevertheless. They are still in the Middle Ages about some things.

ITALY

For some people Italy is the promised land, and others can't wait to leave. Everything is a bit on the disorganized side, there are far too many people and, taken as a whole, it isn't terribly clean. Roads are mostly narrow, twisty, incredibly slippery when wet, full of built-in hazards, cluttered up with every sort of obstacle you can imagine, peopled by a collection of drivers who would just as soon race you as not, and tremendous fun, if exasperating at times. Just when you are doing your nut trying to sneak by that Fiat there are always two ladies pushing baby carriages down the road. And the Fiat will go between them, given half a chance. On the other hand, Italians are still Italians, the famous light and architecture will surely please the eye, and if you have any sort of artistic sense at all, it deserves a long visit.

Getting the cars over with first, one will find with a little study that the big wheels are in three separate places. Turin is really the Automobile City because Fiat and Lancia are both there; besides that, it is a very pleasant and modern place that has a surprising variety of museums (Egyptian to Motorcar) as well as good restaurants (Cucolo, Cavallo d' Bronz, Gatto Nero) and hotels. All the Fiats are pretty good cars even if the 1100 sedan is a bit *demodé* now. We once had a 600 which was very satisfactory and its newer bored-out version (600-D) is a bit quicker. Owners of the bigger Fiats speak well of them. . . I would get only the 2100, as I don't know if the 1800 is imported into America and some parts may differ. As for Lancias, they are always satisfying by virtue of their evident quality and consideration for the driver. The 1100 Appia is a trifle sluggish but the 1500 Flavia, if you feel like risking one so soon after its introduction, is more the job. Also in Turin are speed shops like Nardi and Abarth, the latter of which also produces Fiat-based sportsters. I tried one of the little 750-pushrod Zagato coupes and was surprised by its silence and extremely comfortable ride, allied with a handy turn of speed.

Milan, besides having one of my favorite hotels in Europe (the Auriga), is an easy ride down the *autostrada* from Turin and plays host to Alfa Romeo. There are lots of things to see as well in Milan, but space forbids. Perhaps prejudiced, I would call the Giulietta range of Alfas well up in the world's more satisfying cars and certainly there are none safer. One finds absolutely no nasty tricks in the handling and the brakes are always there. A four-door Giulietta is perhaps not too good a deal to bring home, unless you are planning to do some production car racing, but in that case Conrero in Milan or Saurer (at Alfas in Lausanne, Switzerland) will administer a massive tweek. For about 500 bucks you can Velocify it, which makes a good Q ship. Alfas embody, in a most conventional yet refined way, the most needed attributes of a touring car over here; good road-holding, brakes, acceleration and delicacy of steering. Furthermore, Alfa dealers, especially in Italy, display a pride and knowledge of their line which does the old heart good in this day and age. A good example of this is Italo Gasbarri in L'Aquila.

Leap on to the Autostrada del Sole and go to Modena. There are always some American racing types lounging around the Palace or Real Fini hotels, or perhaps in the Fontana restaurant across the street from the latter. It is sort of an Italian Los Angeles, as far as go-fast machinery is concerned. Maserati has a factory right in town, as does bodybuilder Scaglietti; Ferrari has a depot down there too, but the factory is down the road at Maranello. Don't waste your time trying to get into Ferrari's unless you know someone, which you well might after moseying around the Palace. Of course, if you are thinking of buying a car just drop in. The people at Maserati, on the other hand, are very pleasant and if you liked both cars equally well why not have a Maser? The Ferraris have now gotten quite civilized and even a twitchy and rabbit-eared driver of my acquaintance allowed as how, with the overdrive, he might be able to put up with one of the coupes. Coming from him this was great praise, indeed. Also, Ferrari makes a little better car at the present time, I fear, for anyone contemplating a bit of GT racing. If you can't afford either, drop around with your Fiat to Stanguellini or you can buy Ferrari decals for about 10¢ each. Or Abarth, in Turin, will deliver your Fiat hopped up.

There are quite a few little piddly races, but the biggest is the Targa Florio in Sicily (around end of April), a big old-fashioned romp around the back mountain roads, and the GP at Monza near Milan on Sept. 10. Sicily is a long way down, but why not come early, pick up your Alfa/VW/Fiat in Naples or Rome and take it in? Monza is all very well if you haven't ever seen an automobile race, but being mostly a flat-out blind, it's as uninteresting as Reims. The other characteristics of the French event apply as well. The Mille Miglia, alas, is a shadow of its former self, but if you are around Brescia in May (better check), it might be fun to zip about inside the route and watch. Try not to get involved with Italian cops at these races. Ordinarily the soul of courtesy, they are generally too ignorant to interpret instructions about "keep everybody away from that corner" rationally and they also go ape about traffic circulation, operating in defiance of all logic.

Restaurants are much better than you would think, even if nothing like Italian establishments in the U.S. Cooking is very regional. Lots of strange things abound, among them ortolans on the spit, but generally any name you can't identify is veal. Service is tremendous; in fact, a little too much so, as the minute you sit down there are 10 waiters standing around at the ready. The drill is to order something easy like antipasto or minestrone zoop, everyone will vanish, and you can study the menu at your leisure. Funny places . . . a man in white coat comes, very proper with tongs and bread and napkins and all, takes the bread very gingerly and lays it on the clean tablecloth. Wines by the carafe are generally good; ask for Barbera or Valpolicella or Bardolino in the north, Chianti in the middle. Soave is a reasonable white. Desserts are the end, coming around on a special cart.

Something ought to be said about Italian coffee, which is the world's best. In immense shining machines, live steam is blown through great wads of grounds to give you about a double shot-glass full of black liquid. One cup is generally enough to give you a slight headache, but crikey, it is good. Two cups and you will understand why the Italians are so jumpy. But I could go on about the food for hours.

As far as general touring is concerned, gasoline is very expensive, but cut-rate gas coupons can be bought at the Automobile Club of Italy frontier office. If you are going to be in the country very long it is just as well to join the Club, as there are various perks about maps, towing, etc. They also have parking places all over which are supposed to be free for members, but in practice you are made to feel that you should tip the attendant, anyway. This doesn't hurt so much in Italy, as there are too many people and not enough money.

Again, on no account leave anything unattended or visible in the car. I have seen a very neat pinching job at a ferry where a bloke got out to stretch and a very neatly dressed passerby just reached in and took his wallet off the seat. This doesn't apply only to Italy, just as strictures about asking the price of the room before, adding up the bill, and so forth, should be observed all over. Even road maps, which one has to buy generally, or a half pack of cigarettes will vanish. Especially in the south, little boys do a lot of this.

As far as after dark is concerned, there are night clubs and stuff everywhere in the big cities. There are also B girls. Also watch out for Italian-made "Scotch" whisky. The seeker for non-professional female companionship might do some good around the resorts . . . Santa Margarita Ligure and the Lido of Venice are examples; the latter is about the only place you will see bikinis on Italian beaches.

In case you feel that the whining Vespa scooters are getting you down, along with the everpresent beeping and tire scream and massaging of gears, go to Venice. No cars, very few cops, and just a gentle urgle glurgle. Werry good for the nerves.

It doesn't seem that I have left anything out, but there must be. I'll see you at the races. *Buon Viaggio!*

Ed. Note: *The opinions and comments expressed in this four-part series are based on the experiences of the author, Henry Manney III, an American who has lived in Europe (London, Lausanne, the Riviera and Paris) for the past five years.*

A NOTE ON BUYING A CAR IN EUROPE

AFTER LOOKING into numerous programs for taking delivery of a car in Europe and hearing of buyers' firsthand experiences, I think that it is wiser to stick with those plans offered by the manufacturers. There are various private enterprises which offer delivery/repurchase/home shipment deals which seem reasonably kosher, but I would assume that manufacturers would have less to gain by exasperating hidden charges. The only ones with which I have had personal experience were a Morris in London and a VW in Paris. The latter was dead easy and, indeed, I have heard no complaints about VW deliveries in Europe. As for the others, go around and compare prices. Many times delivery charges are hidden in the bushes somewhere, or the cost of licensing plus touring documents is not mentioned. But Jaguar includes a Channel ferry ticket!

The easiest licensing setup is in France, where you pay your $15 for registration, *carnet de passage,* and TCF membership and are kicked out of the nest, licensed for a year. They generally just paint the numbers on, but watch out for people like Alfa in Paris, who charged a friend of mine $12 for a fancy chrome-and-red plate he hadn't ordered. This happens in England, too; just don't pay for it and they will take it off. The car is yours!

In England, it couldn't be much more complicated, as there is insurance to cover the purchase tax you haven't paid, RAC (or AA) membership for the touring documents which are quite dear, forms to fill out and hand in at the border, and the road tax. This is for a minimum of four months and if you leave and come in again, besides putting the border people into a paroxysm of paperwork, you have to shell out. But they are very sweet about it.

Germany gives you the first 10 days running free, as far as road tax is concerned, asking only $3.50 for documents. However, after that you are in for it; on the VW, $11 will fix you for three months.

Holland again is a bit complicated, as you get charged road tax (at the rate of $2 per 220 lb) depending on how long you want to stay. There is also a deposit of $52 on the carnet which is returned when you finally export the car from the Benelux countries. All carnets are good for a year.

Italy seems to be bound up with regulations pretty thoroughly and, indeed, I have heard only moans from those who have picked up cars there. There's a bond you have to put up, but the registration for one year costs $32, with the carnet on top, I think. Fiat operates under a system by which they give you 10% on the purchase price, plus the 3.65% sales tax back when you get home. I haven't been able to find out whether this is just Fiat or Italian regulations, but I do know that VW delivers its cars in Italy on German tourist registration. On the credit side, Fiat charges no transportation to any of its *filiale* or main agents throughout Italy.

I haven't been able to find out much about Danish registration for SAS fans, except that for a VW, transportation and document charges are about $50.

Notice that I have not included insurance on the car itself. Third party (the international green card) is required in most countries, and it is well to make liability limits high, because you can imagine what sort of chance you stand in a foreign law court in case there is an accident. Don't forget your fire and theft; a friend of mine did and he had his Sprite exactly eight hours. Deal with your agent at home and get him to send the policies to your pick-up point before you get there; the foreign agents are laying for you on short term policies.

CAR	DOLLAR PRICE	DELIV. & PREPAR.	CLUB REQ. CUSTOMS (1 yr.) DOCUMENTS
Alfa-Giul. Spr. Vignale	$ 2979	$ 195 (Paris)	$ 15
Alfa-Giul. 4-dr.	$ 1989	$ 195 (Paris)	$ 15
Citroen ID-19	$ 1995	$ 45 (Paris)	$ 15
Citroen 2-CV	$ 895	$ 35 (Paris)	$ 15
Daimler SP-250	$ 2995	$ 48 (London)	$ 15 (approx.)
DKW Jr.	$ 1187	$ 45 (Paris)	$ 15
DKW A-U 1000 4-dr.	$ 1691	$ 45 (Paris)	$ 15
Fiat 600	$ 1062 (Italy)	—	$ 32
	975	$ 35 (Paris)	$ 15
Fiat 1500 Convert.	$ 2730	$ 35 (Paris)	$ 15
Ford Anglia	$ 1236.06	$ 18.20 (London)	$ 40 (approx.)
		145.60 (Paris)	
Ford Zephyr	$ 1740.48	$ 21.35 (London)	$ 43 (approx.)
Hillman Deluxe	$ 1456 (London)		$ 40 (approx.)
Jaguar 3.8 Mk. 2—(overdrive)	$ 3667	$ 40 (Works)	$ 45
	$ 3765	$ 85 (Paris)	$ 15
		$ 50 (London)	$ 45
Lancia Flaminia	$ 4692	$ 105 (Paris)	$ 15
Lancia Appia GT Zagato	$ 2825	$ 105 (Paris)	$ 15
Mercedes 220-SE	$ 3570	$ 100 (Paris)	$ 15
		—(Works)	$ 24
Peugeot 403—Model E	$ 1650	$ 35 (Paris)	$ 15
404	$ 1644	$ 35 (Paris)	$ 15
(Am. sp.)	$ 1686		
Porsche 1600	$ 2885 (Wks)	$ 92 (Paris)	$ 20 (approx.)
			$ 15 (Paris)
Renault—			
Dauphine Gordini	$ 1135	$ 25 (Paris)	$ 15
4 CV Affaires	$ 715	$ 20	$ 15
Caravelle—4sp. convert.	$ 1747	$ 35	$ 15
Rover 3-liter	$ 3522	$ 17.36 (London)	$ 25.14
with o/d		$ 84 (Paris)	$ 15
Saab 96	$ 1360	$ 110 (Paris)	$ 15
GT	$ 2070	$ 110 (Paris)	$ 15
Simca Montlhery	$ 1300	$ 35 (Paris)	$ 15
Oceane Conv.	$ 2095	$ 35 (Paris)	$ 15
Sunbeam Alpine	$ 1971		$ 40 (approx.)
Triumph TR-3 conv.	$ 1995	$ 127 (Paris)	$ 15
		17 (London)	$ 67
		74 (Amsterdam)	$ 35 (approx.)
Herald	$ 1475	$ 124 (Paris)	$ 15
		17 (London)	$ 67
Vauxhall Victor			
Estate	$ 1778	$ 11.20 (London)	$ 30 (approx.)
Volkswagen Deluxe	$ 1181	$ 45 (Paris)	$ 15
		75 (London)	$ 28
		89 (Naples)	$109
		24 (Amsterdam)	$ 32 (1 mo.)
		50 (Copenhagen)	—
Volvo P-122S sport	$ 2145	— (Paris)	$ 15
P-1800	$ 3095	$ 40 (Paris)	$ 15

ONE OF THE CHIEF ATTRACTIONS of travel is the opportunity of varying one's habitual diet. With the current spread of Pleaseall Plastic Company's tinned goodies and frozen TV horrors, however, instant heartburn *à la mode* is now becoming available all over the globe. One can tour Europe without ever becoming separated from proprietary brands of plastic coffee, plastic cheese, plastic soft drinks, plastic cigarettes, and (supplied by visiting Americans) plastic sex, all just like in the good old U.S.A.

In spite of what the English are taught to think, American native cuisine is not necessarily the worst in the world. In all my rattling around Europe and after determined and repeated efforts to destroy my liver, I have never found decent (repeat as needed) spareribs, Mexican food, bagels or sour cream, fried chicken, hot bread, pizza, corn on the cob, or shad roe. America has practically a stranglehold on the pie family as we know it, as well as really good steaks, and bourbon whiskey is becoming *recherché*. In Switzerland, U.S. frozen chickens are not only cheaper but better than the domestic product, which apparently is offered for sale after being flattened by a Volkswagen. In some countries, beef appears in the butcher shop only after it is too old to give milk any more.

The key to true enjoyment comes in taking a careful look around, asking questions and most of all, having a lively interest in food as such. Those individuals who only eat that they may live can stop reading here, if they haven't done so already. *En voyage,* one should take heed of the traveling salesman's precept of avoiding such leftover-catchers as croquettes, *roulades* and stews (except in France), at least trying the speciality of the region except as hereinafter noted, and steering clear of obvious shifts such as Italian food in Germany, ocean fish in Switzerland, and French cuisine anywhere but its homeland. Logic is the answer. Rice dishes will be better in the north of Italy, where that grain is a staple, while *pasta* correspondingly is treated more sympathetically in the south, if one allows for the fact that it is liable to be in olive oil instead of butter. Those who like venison should know that the Germans make a Big Thing of it. Sandwich fans may well visit Denmark for the ultimate in open-face confections.

Danger signals may be flown, however, for the benefit of those who are a bit squeamish of stomach. Marvelous looking sausages may contain, on the Continent, various odds and ends of the beastie which are too intimidating for public view. A whole brain can be presented in clinical splendor, swimming in black butter. Octopi appear bathed in their own ink. The Scottish haggis has been known to cause fainting or worse. Tripe, the honeycomb lining of the cow's stomach, appeals to some tastes, but not to mine. Most odd articles, which also include snails, frog legs, and jellied eels, sprang from really serious shortages of more normal foods either during famines or off season—those spoiled Americans who are used to fresh fruit and garden peas all 12 months will find that the supply over here varies wildly with the time of year.

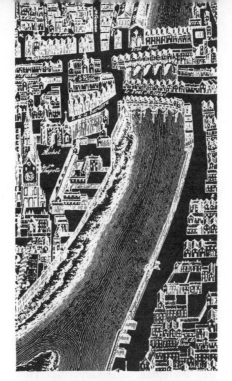

HOW TO
SUSTAIN YOURSELF
BETWEEN RACES
A GUSTATIVE VIEW
OF EUROPE

BY HENRY MANNEY III

The wine people stepped up their activities during hard times, refining the better growths of their product from something that just made you forget the lack of central heating to a bottled delight which caused duchies to change hands. And rightly so, as good wine (or beer), aside from its sometime modest alcohol content, has the virtue of making bad food bearable and good food better. It will, therefore, be treated along with food as we come to it, but there are a few things about wine which perhaps should be straightened out before you get on the plane.

There is nothing magical about wine in spite of attempts to buffalo you by merchants, headwaiters, and sexy advertisements in the glossy papers. It is, after all, only grape juice. In Europe it is taken as a matter of course by all and sundry, as casually as other beverages are provided at home. A French aspirin advises on the package, "Take with a glass of white wine." If you don't like it, rest assured that there are many Europeans who don't either and drink beer, bottled mineral water, or Chateau de la Pompe with the meal.

The rooty tooty restaurants will sometimes try to make you feel as if you have your cowman's boots on if you don't order a bottle of something expensive, but you can be sure that the bosses themselves usually drink the local squeezings and that 85% of the population of France has never tasted anything fancier than that. If you feel diffident about telling the *sommelier* to go to hell, simply point significantly to the region of the liver and everybody will understand why you drink water. This is because all Frenchmen have a Liver. Everyone has a liver, of course, but the Frenchman's is capitalized. As a catchall for bad humor, headaches, runny noses, lack of appetite, unexplained twinges, decreasing ardor, the fantods, and reluctance to write letters, the Liver can't be beat. It also, by localizing complaints, reduces crowding in the medicine cabinet. Bordeaux is supposed to be good for it, and *aperitifs* bad. But don't worry—it takes years to get one, but anybody can play.

If you feel like the cup that cheers, the drill is really simple. First off, forget all your worries about red or white or rosé. I personally find red a trifle unsettling and, like the Swiss, drink white with practically everything, as there is a vast variety of growths, ranging from dry Muscadet, which favors shellfish, to the astounding Montrachet, which complements most any dish. Only when something really ferocious presents itself, like my wife's *coq au vin rouge* or a steak with garlic sauce, will a hefty red be called for to make itself heard above the massive flavors.

On the Riviera, a local chilled rosé cuts the garlic admirably and chills the gullet as well. If you prefer rosé and are farther north, the Tavel or Tain varieties are the best; you have to be more careful with this color than any other, as a lot of really poor wine is tarted up by being turned into rosé.

You see, most wine is made originally from red grapes, as they give a bigger yield; the color is determined by how long the skins are left in the mix after the grapes are squz. As the skins, besides containing tannin, also carry fermenting bacteria, it naturally follows that the longer the skins are left in, the "rougher" it will be. These extra substances are gentled by aging, fining, and other mysterious processes and of course the vineyard, grower and shipper have a lot to do with it. The Bordeaux reds are a bit more gentlemanly if your liver is acting up but the good Burgundies are hairier and thus more fun. The ubiquitous Beaujolais is also a Burgundy and, as it is quite well known, is the subject of more abuses than any other wine. In its home country it is a common garden-variety table red, served from bulk more often than not, and definitely meant to be drunk fairly young. "Vintage" Beaujolais is a lot of poppycock, especially when brought in one of those reclining baskets meant to preserve the crust and sediment of really vintage booze. Four or five years old is about the limit. In addition, outside France the *appelation controllee* laws about trademarks carry little weight and Beaujolais can be and often is something else.

If you are looking for something modest, ask for the *vins ouvert* or *courant* (from bulk); these will generally be a cut above the *vin ordinaire* which the Frenchman drinks and which is grown in Algeria or the Midi from the high-yield Gamay grape. If you don't feel like boning up on a book like Lichine's "Wines of France," ask the waiter for suggestions. Most natives do.

A GUSTATIVE VIEW OF EUROPE

ENGLAND. To the visiting Continental, English markets present mouth-watering displays of the very best meat and vegetables. It has always been somewhat of a mystery as to what happens between that point and being presented at table. Both home and restaurant are pulling up their socks now, though, as a result of the growing popularity of vacations on the Continent.

The safest way to eat in England, especially London, is still to search out some likely Italian or Chinese restaurant, but there are some English ones like Wheeler's or Kettner's which do nice things with the English specialties such as Dover sole or a mixed grill, which are almost always safe. The good domestic restaurants, however, tend to cost the earth, the cheapest wine (a vinegary "Beaujolais") runs to $2.80 or thereabouts, and the service is not what it should be when the prices are considered. There are also little establishments tucked around in which, as I said, the standard is improving, as well as some rather grand pubs out in the country which have local fame. Best move is to buy a copy of Postgate's "Good Food Guide"—which will at least steer you away from being poisoned —or get some English friends who like to eat. If you fancy roast meats, you might do worse than call up Grease Gun Charlie Leibman in Fleet Street, who is a pub-rel man for a chain of this sort of restaurant. I personally am not mad about the famed English rosbif places, possibly because they follow the prevailing English fashion of serving all the food lukewarm.

[Two excellent restaurants in London are the Connaught House—in the hotel— on Carlos Pl., and the Guinea on Bruton Pl. The Connaught is very expensive—but very good—with a large variety of delectable dishes to choose from, while the Guinea features steak only—excellent and at more moderate prices.—Ed.]

I remember a cellar joint (Fiddlers Three) on Beauchamp Place in Kensington, Cleo's near Gloucester Road tube station, and a very nice fish place starting with O (I'm sorry) across from Victoria RR station. As for Italian, Osteria Romana in Soho is very good and the Roma is cheap, anyway. Pere de Nico (near Sloane Square) has very good food even if the waiters camp a bit, and the Paramount Grill near Covent Garden is much frequented by the ballet crowd. If you crave curry, an Indian friend likes the Shah on Drummond Street. Photographer John Ross knows more nice little places than anyone else, Douglas Armstrong (Shurlock Row 204) does an eating column for the Rootes house magazine and so is fair game to ask. For that matter, practically any of the automobile public relations people (especially if you are picking up a car there) can make suggestions. The Good Earth in Chelsea is a fine Chinese place (Plawn clackers), Petite Etoile and Escargot Bienvenue in Soho have good *prix fixe* meals if you aren't going to France, and if

you get homesick for cheesecake you can go up to Golders Green and eat at the Madeleine with the Speedwell boys, hearing the latest hop-up gossip at the same time. Assuming that you have motoring interest, I will mention that the famed Steering Wheel Club near Hyde Park Corner is the best food value in London; your sports car club card will get you in at least the first time, and you may possibly see somebody who looks familiar.

This slops us over into pubs, which are English drinking houses dedicated to warm beer and weak gin. As I don't appreciate either, and the rapidity with which they open and shut at different times of the day to accord with local ordinance befuddles me, I will report only that the Cheshire Cheese on Fleet Street is very old and, as the French say, *trés folklore*. If you have any English friends at all you will get drug into one or more and then you can make up your own mind. You can also eat in them but it isn't recommended. Also not recommended are any roadside restaurants, cheap joints, or "caffs." The food is either nowhere or the place is filthy.

Some of the hotels out in the country are interesting, especially the Trust Houses, and you can even eat satisfactorily in a few. The Norfolk Arms in Arundel, near Goodwood, pleased us as did Rowton House near Chester, where we stayed for Aintree. Gethin Bradley of Rover knows about a good place between Solihull and Coventry and the Bell at Hurley is highly recommended. There are others, not always expensive. Write to the *Sunday Times* or *Observer* eating men.

As in the U.S., breakfast is often the best meal of the day, with bacon, eggs, etc., but avoid the sausages. Afternoon tea is an extra added attraction and one which should replace the barbarous custom of belting down one or more highballs before dinner. Low, or "dainty," teas feed maiden aunts and you should search for high ones which include sandwiches, cookies and fruit cake, and may make it possible to avoid lunch and dinner altogether. I highly recommend the Four-and-Twenty Blackbirds on the way back from Goodwood at Petworth, which gives scones, clotted cream and the lot, even if they do use tea bags. In the country, keep an eye on the clock, especially in summer when the days get very long, as after 8 P.M. you are out of luck as far as food is concerned. Up in Scotland you can eat very well on salmon, etc., and fresh shortbread is very jolly. Innes Ireland advises to look for some "single" or unblended Scotch. The country of Ireland itself, I am reliably informed, is a gastronomic desert but one can always drink.

GERMANY. Whatever else happens, you will get enough to eat in Germany. The accent is on potatoes; wursts of various sorts were all invented here, and breads are really good. After trying a large variety of places, I can state that you will get a poor meal only in tourist traps like the Nurburg Ring Sporthotel. Small hotels called *Gästatte* are numerous and with a judicious eye toward the number of cars lined up outside you will find many satis-

factory indeed. In this quest, it is as well to invest in a "Varta Guide," which lists hotels and restaurants in the manner of the well-known Michelin. As the Varta is still rather new, it isn't quite as reliable but will save you anyway from international plastic hotel cooking. To save money, frequent the smaller hotels and restaurants mentioned, as the more renowned ones are apt to be dear—all you will get in the fancy places is liable to be their idea of French cooking. There are two good ones in Heidelberg, one right down at the corner and another up on the mountain behind, but the best place to eat in Heidelberg is *chez* Sloniger. There is another fair eating place at Bad Wimpfen on the Neckar, where you may also buy your sweetie a suede coat very economically at the works nearby. At the Nurburg Ring, the Wildes Schwein is very good indeed for game and trout, the former, however, coming with some sort of sickening jam. Down the street, the Blauer Eck is a good bet even if the service is slow, the herring in sour cream being a specialty.

Surprisingly, much German cooking tends to be a bit spicy and so it is just as well that the beer is so good and wine tasty and abundant. As far as the latter is concerned, there are no great growths such as one finds in France, if one excepts the expensive sweet *spatlese* variants. The name of *Liebfraumilch* has suffered almost as many abuses as Beaujolais and thus it is better to avoid the question entirely, unless one has done some previous research, and simply drink the plentiful open wine. The white, both Rhine and Mosel, is served chilled in glasses which contain a quarter of a liter; sitting on the banks of the Rhine hand in hand with some salmon, two or three of these disappear very shortly and you may find that when you get up to go to the Herren that you can't. Many are the bows in the direction of *Bernkasteler Doktor* and other more expensive Mosels, but inasmuch as it all tastes so good that it goes down in a rush, I say plump for quantity. There are generally five or six varieties of open white and why not try one of each?

For afters, the Germans also make a form of brandy but you might as well go the schnapps route. Better for the liver. Steinhager is a charming form of this and the various geists (himbeer, erdbeer, etc.) also are fun as they are dry *eaux-de-vie*, rather like fruit-flavored vodka, for want of a better description.

Photog Gunther Molter shot me down in flames before for not mentioning the specialities around Stuttgart. His number is 67149, and it serves him right.

AUSTRIA. Read as above but generally more countrified. Wine is a bit more expensive, so drink beer. In the proper season, look for green branches above pubs and sample the new wine. In Salzburg the Goldener Hirsch and Til Eulenspiegel [within earshot of Mozart's home —is one of Europe's best—Ed.] are very nice and, of course, Vienna is like any other big town with good ones and bad ones. If you are desperate, call Martin Pfundner (642543) for suggestions, but just following your nose and avoiding the big hotels should see you through. While we were avoiding one, we looked all over for the famous Viennese coffee which, at least in the rest of Europe, is a sort of mixture with ice cream. When we finally found some, complete with whipped cream and Japanese parasol on the top, it was called *café Parisienne*. Austrian coffee tastes better than German (but then almost anything does) and in any case should be consumed with pastry which is the best in Europe.

◆ ◆ ◆

BENELUX. The admirable Michelin people make a hotel and restaurant guide for this region and you should have one, bearing in mind the same cautions as with the Varta. You can eat very well indeed in any of these countries but, especially in Belgium, it can be more expensive than anywhere else in the world, except maybe New York or Caracas. Try the small eating places unless you are on a flying visit or an expense account. The fancy ones I have tried, which include the Old Dutch in Rotterdam, Vielle France near Spa, a castle near Maastricht in Holland, and another "one star" about 20 km from Spa, had pretty good food but suffered from poor service, small portions (not the usual complaint in these regions) and too much fla fla. For something different, you might try one of the numerous Indonesian restaurants in Amsterdam — there was one big one we liked right beside a canal.

Breakfast again is a good bet, with lots of cheese, salami, boiled eggs, and other extraneous articles including a linoleum-like black bread. As in most of the European countries, bread is very good indeed and you can see why it was termed the staff of life. It is tasty, nourishing, and suitable (as it was intended) to be the focal point of the meal, carrying soup and cheese along with it. Unlike plastic nearfood as found in the U.S. and England, it lends itself to a really solid picnic lunch which will save you more time and money while touring than anything else. To this end, there are a lot of snacks about including herring permutations and Dutch Edam or Gouda cheese which, on its own ground, is a very different thing from the pallid stuff at home. These can be gotten young, and carried around for a sufficient length of time to achieve a lovely orange color and pungent taste.

In Belgium, anyway, you can combat that sinking feeling between times by visiting one of the numerous *friture* fried potato stands. You get a sackful, which can be eaten with tartar sauce, mayonnaise, or several other non-fattening but tasty combinations.

Drink beer (some Belgian cafes list as many as 30), as all wine must be imported and is both expensive and chancy. I don't have to tell you about Holland gin, either, which is better straight, chilled, and occasionally old then when mutilated in Martinis. Stock up on cigars here as well as in Germany. Try the 40 pf Mountain Union from the latter country and any of the Schimmelpenninck tribe from Holland. I prefer the light Sumatra.

SWITZERLAND. In the German parts, cooking is pretty much the same as in the country of origin but a little more staid. Also, the portions are bigger. You should try the famous *rösti*, which if memory serves me right are boiled potatoes hashed up and refried with onions. Cooking in the Italian section around Lugano is not as Italian as one would suppose as it is heavily influenced by the Germans who pour down there. In Lugano, Bianchi offers local specialities and there are small pubs in Morcote, for instance, where one can dine on the edge of the lake. As in all tourist regions, watch the prices.

Around French Switzerland, one can eat very well but the choice tends to be a bit monotonous. A big specialty is *entrecôte* steak with a garlic/basil/butter/oregano sauce which reaches its apogee at the Café de Paris in Geneva, which in fact serves nothing else. The French Michelin covers Geneva but again watch the expensive places. Around Lausanne, Café de Mousquetins (Chez Charles) does excellent steaks and frogs legs in butter sauce; Chez Pitch at Port de Pully features steak with sauce and very good small filets of lake perch; Pomme de Pin has excellent if expensive chicken upstairs and cheap student leftovers downstairs; and Chez Felice (?) in Morges has a good chicken in brandy. Ask M. Domont at American Express for more. For a blue plate while watching the exotic female scenery (best in Europe) try the City or Centrale.

Beer is okay but the cheap and good Swiss white wines are the thing to have. If one seems too thin (they vary from year to year), try another. They come open in "deci" or tenths of a liter and it isn't worth your while trying the expensive bottled stuff. The best Swiss red is Dole de Valais, which has a high alcoholic content and tastes faintly of raspberries. Most of the open reds, such as Algerie and Beaujolais (which is really Algerie), are okay anyway and cheaper. For tapeworm killing, you really must try a bottle of Williamine, a clear eau-de-vie made from pears, preferably made by the Valaisan firm of Morand. Try a shot in the restaurant or café first. An amusing pub is the Café de Vieux Ouchy down by the lake, where country ham (*jambon a l'os*) or air-dried beef are good for snacks. Swiss cigars are a good value and the Rossli 20 are cheap.

The national dishes seem to be *raclette,* in which a large melting wheel of Bagne cheese is scraped and poured over boiled potatoes, and fondue, where a pot of melting cheese (Gruyère and vacherin, with kirsch, garlic, and white wine inside) has bits of bread dipped in. He who drops the first bread buys the next bottle of wine and, if female, gets kissed by all and sundry. As one runs the risk not only of burned mouths (from the fork), bruised lips (from the smooching) and a hangover, but also of financial destruction as well, it is as well to warn you that only white wine should be drunk with this; otherwise your insides will be replaced with one long congealed snake of cheese. There is also Fondue Bourguinonne where one dips bits of raw meat into berling erl and then into various condiments. For the indigestion resulting from these, as well as

other unwise excesses, I recommend the old standard paregoric and/or an English pill named Disprin or Dispril. For in-between times, Swiss chocolate is the real stuff, and not the brown wax encountered elsewhere.

In Lausanne, everybody worth looking at (or staring at, in the case of the Swiss) has coffee at the Escale. And if you can't find anywhere else to eat, the railway station buffets are better than you would think. As a matter of fact, even if you're not desperate, give them a try.

◆ ◆ ◆

ITALY. The first thing you must get out of your mind is that Italian restaurants in Italy are like the same thing at home. In the mother country, local specialities are featured much more according to the region and the fried sparrow's toes you had in the Abruzzi, for example, you won't see anywhere else.

On the Continent, Italian restaurants are just about the only places where the tourist will get fed quickly. It isn't that they want to get rid of you, the natives simply like to get in and out at speed. As you enter the average pub, a cloud of waiters will descend on you and divest you of your coat and hat, if any, and bear them away to a far region where a young lady in sateen smock hides them. No hat check—if you don't like the clothes you get back, you ask for others. Having been swiftly seated, you will regard an enormous menu filled with millions of things you have never seen before and then, panic-stricken, lift your eyes to meet those of the headwaiter and about six assistants. They are all watching you and waiting. Emulating the aplomb of the stout Florentine at the next table, you order the first thing you can think of, which happens to be antipasto, and they all disappear with the speed of light. You are left with the menu, a lone waiter who adjusts the breadsticks (get the Turin sort) and then asks you if you want *rosso* or *bianco*, of which more later. The menu itself is divided in several sections, headed of course by the name of the place and how much the *coperta* (linen and bread) will cost you. The first category is usually labeled *Minestre* and includes various things in *brodo* (broth), *stracciatella* (scrambled egg soup), *minestrone* (vegetable soup but sometimes almost a stew) and various hors d'oeuvres called *antipasti* (literally, before the pasta). These range from vegetable salad through odd objects in oil to pickled octopus, which is very good; the whole business is presented on a rolling cart and is priced (SQ) depending on the quantity you eat. You may also find *prosciutto* (raw cured ham) and melon or figs in this category—I don't think real *prosciutto* can be imported into the U.S., so do have some.

Next up is *pasta,* which of course includes spaghetti, *maccheroni,* and its various forms, stemming mostly from the same dough but somehow tasting differently on account of the shape. The spaghet' may be Napolitana (with tomatoes), Bolognese (meat sauce), *con vongole* (clams), *Carbonara* (bacon, ham, mushrooms), *con funghi* (mushrooms), or with garlic etc. etc. Noodles (*tagliatelle*) also **show**

29

A GUSTATIVE VIEW
OF EUROPE

continued

up green or white, the former in the tasty but heavy Lasagne and the others as above or in Rigatoni. Rice dishes will also be found here, like the Venetian *risi e bisi* (rice and peas), Milanese *risotto* (saffron and various objects), and the corn meal mush *polenta*. There are also *gnocchi*, rather heavy potato dumplings. Most of these, unless taken in moderation, leave you no room for the next course.

One of the waiters, passing by on the dead run, removes your plate, the head-waiter approaches to take the order for each course separately, and a little man appears with white gloves, tongs, and a strange doughy roll on a plate. This he removes with great ceremony and lays it on the tablecloth.

The meat course is next, or fish if you prefer, and there is a wide and puzzling choice of the former, which turns out mostly to be veal. Vegetables are ordered separately, and just as well, as they are not a strong point and take up much-needed space. The dreaded veal cutlet abounds, of course, and ranges from the modest one with lemon to *saltimbocca* which has ham and bay leaf stuffed inside. Beef also appears *(manzo* or *bue)* and is best around Florence; otherwise it is liable to be thin and rather tough. Fish is a big thing with the Italians, although not necessarily on Friday, and it is wiser to avoid it in the smaller places of the inland regions. It is nice grilled *(alla griglia),* and one of our favorites is fried *calamare* (octopus) and scampi or *gamberi* (shrimp) mixed together. Indeed, the *fritto misto di mare* (mixed fried seafood) is nice or you can have that grilled as well, as the Italians are ready to cook anything any way you want it without even raising their eyebrows. Chicken is also very common, especially around the faster highways, and a sickening variation around Modena is the breast fried with cheese.

As far as cheese itself is concerned, real Gorgonzola is always nice and then you can go on to the fruit or any one of the variety of deadly desserts which will sometimes arrive on a cart. Most of the cakes seem to be loaded with maraschino or some other liqueur; there are good fruit tarts or just cooked apples or pears; and in some localities the chocolate-frilled Tarte St. Honore rears its fattening head. After that comes espresso coffee, engineered by a bloke at a Roxy organ who produces mad sounds blowing live steam through the grounds, and perhaps *grappa* in it, if you are not drunk already. Add up the bill if you can—it will almost certainly be in their favor.

Most Italian wine that is any good, as in Switzerland, doesn't get exported. Most places have open Chianti, Barbera or Valpollicella which will satisfy the red craving —none of these is very heavy, and all sit well. Whites are less satisfactory and you will probably have to buy bottled Soave to get something decent. The bottled stuff in reds isn't all that dear anyway, if you stay away from the sweet and fizzy Asti Spumante. When around Modena, try the slightly bubbly and light red Lambrusco. You will also notice the Italians drinking large quantities of Boario or San Pellegrino mineral water for their *fegatos.* Nobody thinks the worse of you if you have that instead of wine, but milk is not such a good idea. Also salads, while good, are not always clean.

For further research, better have a copy of the "Michelin Guide for Italy" and, if your bank manager doesn't mind, Sam Chamberlain's "Italian Bouquet." With them, you can avoid hotel food, which is usually dull except in a few special cases, and extend your knowledge besides. As in all countries, books of this sort are a better bet than the "guides" printed in various glossy mags which lead one invariably into the expensive credit card palaces. These have no compunctions about impoverishing you, and then consider you a sucker.

Although hotel dinners are usually indifferent, the comparatively inexpensive Jolly Hotels (where you should consider staying in any case) put on a good feed, which is just as well, as they are deliberately sited in areas needing good hotels. The ones in Palermo and Cefalù, Sicily, are a case in point. As far as a few other recommendations are concerned, the Michelin is reliable but not so much so as in France, especially in big tourist areas where cupidity gets the best of the owners. In Milan, the excellent Auriga Hotel sees to the inner man as well but watch the specials—such as the macaroni left over from lunch. For snacks, there is a big mad sort of joint right around the corner behind the Pirelli building which may have the sort of thing you want. There are many excellent places in that city, including Abetone (the eggplant fried with mozzarella), and the Firenze or Savini around the Galleria Vittorio Emmanuele. I *don't* send you to the aptly named Biffi, which rooked us in the most cold-blooded way. In Florence, we really like Sabatini's but not Doney's; Alfa PRO man Bernasconi recommends L'Abbondanza (which everyone calls Troia or Sow).

In Modena, both Fini and Oreste are good—if you go to the Fontana, across from the Reale Hotel, you may even see sundry racing personalities. We used to like the Cucolo and Cavallo di Bronz' in Turin but standards have gone down and prices up since the Exhibition. The Zagato people recommend the Gatto Nero. The famous Pappagallo in Bologna we found rather tired, a complaint which seems to affect many big restaurants around dinnertime, as the noon meal is the main one. In Venice, we preferred the little *trattorie* (like Al Gambero) better than the more expensive places, as the art of cooking seafood is pretty well down pat there. The Quadro, on St. Mark's Square, had one of those mysteriously multiplying bills and the Graspo de Va and Da Nane seemed to be out for the dollar as well.

As a snapper, if you are in Pescara, drive south down the main drag across the "river" and at the café immediately afterward, have a *granita de caffé.* This little monster, shown to me by Bill Hughes, consists of very strong espresso coffee frozen, shaved, mixed with cream and sugar, and refrozen with whipped cream on top. You won't sleep, but it's worth it.

Next month, Spain, Portugal and France.

A GUSTATIVE VIEW OF EUROPE   PART TWO   BY HENRY MANNEY III

SPAIN AND PORTUGAL. In our limited experience on the Iberian peninsula, we followed the *Guide Michelin* faithfully (that name again!) and weren't disappointed. The cooking is better than you would think but the mealtimes are odd, being much later than is really necessary. However, there is a well-developed trade in snacks (shrimp and suchlike) which will tide you over. Many of the dishes seem to be cooked in olive oil, which is never changed in the cheaper joints—with disastrous results to the digestion. You can get around this by sticking to grilled items or sea food; the beef is good but a bit fresh, as refrigeration is not all that widespread. For this reason, too, finny friends are hurried to the table. The famous *paella,* mishmash of rice, mussels, shrimp, chicken, and anything else that is leftover, is worth a try but only in a decent place; you might also like the *gazpacho,* a cold soup of tomatoes, onions and whatnot.

Local wines are surprisingly good and cheap, especially the reds like La Rioja. No point in drinking the imported stuff, really. A lot of people who turn up their noses at Spanish wines have been drinking them for years under another name, even in France. Beer is okay but not as good as Mexican, I think, and mineral waters are widespread for good reason.

We tried a couple of the *Posadas,* old castles turned into hotels by the government, and at least the food was hot and didn't give us Montezuma's Revenge. In Portugal, the cuisine was more interesting, perhaps because it was based on peasant cooking, and the very nice Infanta de Sagres in Porto laid on a good spread. Generally,

though, if you try the upper middle-class restaurants and choose carefully I think you are in for some rewarding eating.

There are a million varieties of sherry to go with your shrimp and you had better sort them out for yourself. As in all foreign countries, beware of local imitations of whiskey. Ugh.

FRANCE. I have talked to quite a few people who don't like French cooking. Too many funny sauces hiding God-knows-what, they say, and the meat's always underdone and everything smells of garlic and those cheeses are like somebody's old socks and meals always go on for so long and I always get indigestion. And snails!!!

They may be right. There are people driving Ferraris who would be far better off in Chevrolets and there are people whose needs are met perfectly by the common or garden variety hamburger steak. This is not to say that they are in any way inferior to those of us who like to waste our money on our stomachs instead of a slot machine; conversely, it doesn't necessarily follow that we are headed for Hell in a handbasket, as our friends of the nut cutlet brigade would have us think. Those who are destined to turn purple and drop dead at the news of the State Department's latest fiasco will do so whether they lived on mock rissoles of veal or *coq au vin jaune d'Arbois.* Just the same, the liking to voyage in the vast hinterland of unexplored tastes is a highly personal thing (as anyone who has two or more children can tell you) and is best left at that in spite of the accelerative factor imparted to the proceedings by

a hungry and convivial party of six.

To enjoy yourself at a table in a foreign country (and you never realize how foreign it is, really, until you pick up a menu you can't read) takes a little time as well as a fundamentally relaxed attitude. Due to the language barrier and the capriciousness of waiters everywhere, you won't get what you thought you ordered 80% of the time anyway. By the end of your stay, when you can read the *carte* without having to say Whassat? in a stage whisper to every entry, you will have a pretty good cross section of French cooking inside of you. Above all, don't panic. In France, restaurants are there to feed and serve you, not to provide Today's Painful Experience as in some parts of the U.S. and England. They are in a highly competitive business and it is in their interest to attend to your satisfaction and have you come back.

There is no ju-ju to French cooking, at least until you get into the Curnonsky class. Mostly it is just plain, straight work with attention to detail and taste. French fried potatoes are served hot and fresh on heated plates. The bread is fresh. Omelettes arrive comparatively light, tasting of egg instead of crankcase oil, as they have their own special pan which is never actually washed, just scrubbed out with paper so the raw material floats on a film of cooking fat. The vegetables have special seasoning to set them apart from other vegetables. As a step further, to combat the sameness brought on by seasonal shortages, various simple sauces from stock to cream, or whatever was leftover, or pickings from the herb garden were introduced. Most of them add to the taste and none will kill you. They may have

A GUSTATIVE VIEW OF EUROPE

all these strange names . . . *bonne femme, madriléne, remoulade* . . . just so that one can order the same thing twice in a row. Good raw materials are the secret and your own sauces including wine (*coq au vin rouge,* for example) will be all the better for having some of the bottle from which you will be drinking and not that vinegary abomination called "cooking wine." Try some of the things you don't know about and lay off the ever-present steak and French fries.

I T IS again essential, I think, to have the restaurant and hotel guide put out by the Michelin tire people. (No, my Alfa doesn't have Michelins!) This guide also gives a lot of other extraneous information, including quiet hotels, where to get a specially good meal for a buck fifty, ferries, opening and closing of mountain passes, vintages of wines, local specialties, glossaries, when to tour various regions, town and road maps, and what pressure to blow your (M . . . . . n) tires up to. It also lists restaurants on four basic categories. First, and largest, is simply a recommendation that it is fit to eat in; this is followed by gradations of one, two, or three stars which mean "good meal in its class," "worth a detour," and "formidable!" There are only ten of the latter. Michelin also, by the awarding of numbers of crossed knives and forks, indicates the fanciness of the service. One-forkers, and their cousins the knife and goblet, are the modest little places where the boss waits on table, so to speak. Five forkers have everything *flambé* but the bill. You pay for this service and uproar; obviously what you want is three stars and one fork, right? There ain't any.

Therefore, we do a little research. One soon learns, from the map in the front of the book showing where the starred restaurants are located, to seek out one and two stars having the minimum number of forks, compare their prices, and include them in the itinerary. Some hotels have starred restaurants—that a hotel is included at all is supposed to be evidence that its restaurant is up to par but I don't always

find it so—and other places list themselves as restaurants with rooms. Because hotels of a certain class can charge only so much for their rooms and the deficit is usually made up in the restaurant, unless the hotel is particularly well known for its table I prefer to stay in one without a formal eating department. This saves trouble anyway if you have your eye on a certain bistro, as some hotels require that you eat in the house restaurant.

Driving down the road, you will also see hostelries displaying a red-and-blue sign with *"Routiers"* on it. As this means roughly "truckdrivers," there will often be several heavies and private cars parked outside. These places draw on the fiction that where the truckdrivers stop there must be good food. This isn't necessarily so, but there are some which are highly spoken of; at least the food will be palatable, cheap, copious, and the joint will be full of characters.

Most travel-cum-food articles go into rhapsodies about Paris restaurants Tour d'Argent, Laperouse or Grand Vefour but for the average bloke (which includes me), it is my formal opinion that the full expertise of French cooking will only burst upon one out in the provinces while touring. There are some tremendous places, like the Cote d'Or at Saulieu, which many regard as the best in France, but I am speaking more of the one or two star, one or two fork, which one will find scattered here and there across the country. Of course, if your tastes are elevated to those of the great Curnonsky and your bank balance is sturdy, by all means make the pilgrimage to the Parisian marbled halls; it would be a crime not to do so and if I were researching this on R&T's money I would too. Just the same, you will get more satisfaction, as well as more mileage for your franc, out of places like the Balance at Arbois, Chabert at Tain l'Hermitage, Auberge Bressane at Bourg-en-Bresse, and Bec Rouge at Monte Carlo. The atmosphere is better and more sociable, they have more time to help you with the menu, and there is not that business atmosphere so stultifying to digestion.

On that horrifying subject, I find that I can't eat a big lunch and big dinner, no matter how tempting the opportunity. Neither can or do the French. And if I eat a big lunch, as

seems to be more natural to the French, I go to sleep or get the vapours all afternoon and evening. Accordingly, while touring, the thing to do is stop before noon in a convenient town, buy a flute of bread at the *boulangerie,* fill your wine bottle (top with cork—the plastic stoppers leak and stain clothes) at the wine store or pick up a fresh local, get whatever paté or cheese you need, and go picnic while the traffic thunders by. Nap a bit if you like while others are commencing their two-hour meal, and then set out again on deserted roads. Stop early in your interesting town like, say, Arles, pick your hotel before the mob, go see the sights, and have dinner at your leisure while the others struggle on into the dusk till the last light. This is especially true during July and August when all France takes to the roads. After dinner, if you can still see straight, go to the local café to have coffee (always expensive in restaurants) or a brandy, sit outside under the plane trees, and watch the passing parade. It's a good life.

T HE French meal, like the best architecture, is constructed as a whole and not in bits and pieces. Each dish is meant to complement the others and it is folly to order the garlicky escargot, for instance, and follow it with poached turbot. Your stomach won't necessarily be upset, but the fish will have no taste at all. Consequently all except the most high-falutin places will have one or more *prix fixé* meals in which, for a certain listed price, you will be served three or four courses (none of too great a quantity) which lead up logically and gastronomically to the end. The object, need I add, is not to make a pig of oneself but to savour the man's work. There will be, usually, one or more specialities of the house and region included in the *prix fixé.* Unless they strike you as absolutely revolting, it is a good idea to try these for the same reason that you go see the local Roman arena. Likewise, try the *vin du pays* and don't always stick to Chateauneuf de Pape.

If all the goodies you require are on a cheaper *prix fixé,* why not bust a bottle of really good wine? Much cheaper than at home and really an experience. Don't worry too much about vintages, good years, and all that jazz unless you are an expert. Many of the better known names like Chablis and Nuits St. Georges are over-publicized and are in the wine list for people who only know those names or are determined to look like connoisseurs, but that doesn't mean that you won't get a good bottle of either. The same goes for the Pouillys—the French even like to confuse their own people between Fuisse, Fume, sur Loire, and several others. There is a big difference, the first two being definitely better.

Do try the white versions of big Burgundy growths like Mersault, as well. Really smashing. Most restaurants of any standing have a reliable cellar and if you need help to find a wine sweet or dry enough for your tastes, just ask the man. That procedure is safe enough except for tourist traps, which you will soon learn to avoid. In these places anyway, be very cagey about a bottle which is opened in the kitchen and brought to your table—it may have been too sour for some discriminating patron, sent back, and saved for the first pigeon. Sourness, or flatness, is about the limit of evils on poor wine. Very, very rarely a bottle is corky, when air has gotten in past the stopper, and then it tastes as if someone had washed his socks in it. Most restaurants will take it back with no trouble. A few reds taste sour anyway on first acquaintance and will improve as the wine warms up in the glass, so be sure of what you are doing. Also, some, meant to be drunk young, will go "off" if kept too long; they taste musty and the whites are very yellow. For a finisher upper after the cheese, some of which is supposed to be odoriferous, try some marc, which is white lightning made from the stems, seeds and skins after the wine fermentation. Just like Clorox. Or for that matter, what's wrong with brandy? Try the dry Denis Mounié.

Michelin (or Sam Chamberlain's Bouquet de France, as well) is not infallible, mostly by reason of the chef being off duty, sick, drunk, or gone to a better-paying establishment. So don't blame me or M. Bibendum if the meal is poor, just reflect that his batting average is very high indeed. If you get taken pricewise you have nobody but yourself to blame as most restaurants have the menu posted outside. Don't forget to include the cover (for tools and bread) and the service, from 10 to 15% generally, which will be added to your bill. Add it up as well—everybody does. Coffee and extras of various sorts also cost, as that is how they make their profit, not on the food. Speaking of coffee, the French variety tastes like ground up rubber tires (M . . . . . n?) to some people and in places it probably is. This is because during one of their earlier wars, when this commodity was in short supply, the authorities had to roast the heck out of it to get rid of the bugs and mice and also were forced to adulterate the beans with chicory. The French have got used to coffee that way, what with three wars since 1870, and there you are. You will find it isn't bad with milk in the morning for breakfast, but straight—have your fillings checked over. If you have any say in the matter, get the after-dinner coffee from a machine or pot and avoid the diabolical *filtre* machine. This miniature drip pot perches above the cup, filled with hot water and grounds, and has certain affinities with the Chinese water torture as, if it doesn't block up, thus insuring burned fingers, it will deliver you a cold cup of coffee in 15 minutes or so. Fortunately, the espresso machine cometh. There is no hope for French tea.

IN SPITE of being the capital of France, which is the capital of food, Paris is a very tricky place to eat in and get complete satisfaction. Prices can get very high, and remembering some of the cheaper and satisfying meals you have had in the past, you wonder is it worth it? Every now and then, though, there is a really goofy dish which obviously took talent and you can see where the money goes. Further down, there are also a lot of restaurants which charge much more, really, than the repast warrants, and then there are a bunch which give true value for money and that is where the mining is. Even the lousy ones are full of Frenchmen, so what is a body to do? Taking someone else's word isn't good enough, as tastes vary widely, so you just have to get out and slog it. That's what we did and you can try these if you like.

A Burgundian pub and steak place, but don't expect it well done, is Chez Fred, over on Blvd. Perière, while, if you like baby lamb and the real concentrated *foie gras*, Chez L'Ami Louis is really good if a bit expensive. One of the sawdust-on-the-floor places, reeking with atmosphere, is the Grand Comptoir (country sausage and lentils, snails, try the house Fleurie) down by Les Halles, the market of Paris. Another classic place is Roy Gourmet, on Place des Victoires, where the somewhat gamey andouilette sausage is a specialty. A typical sort of place we often go is Rest. Sts. Pères on the corner of that street and Blvd. St. Germain—food is good, house wine ditto, a painting in the little inside room is marvelous, and the parade of weirdies from the student section is better yet. Diagonally across the street, the Relais St. Germain is well spoken of by a knowledgeable friend but I am afraid that Calvet nearby has fallen on evil days. Chez Mercier, over near the Champs on Rue Lincoln, is a big bustling place which is always a safe bet as it has an extensive menu, and for a cheap lunch (although the meat tends to be a bit gristly sometimes), Rest. Lescure right near Place de la Concorde is fun. Get in early for this one. My wife and Brooke Burwell like Chez Papille. Telephone ahead to all of 'em.

The more rooty tooty ones I don't go to much (cheap skate) but Allard is very good indeed (I had frogs legs), Roger le Grenoville is hilarious and, if you want to be intimidated, you can go to Chataignier. There you are seated in low leather armchairs by a baroque waitress and eventually the chef, complete with white hat and knife, comes out and recites the menu off on his fingers. Nothing to look at, no prices, nothing to hide behind. Confused? Crikey. Best thing to do is to pick something at the tail of the recital you like, such as chicken with water chestnuts, and ask him to compose a menu around that. If you fancy sea food you can try Prunier Traktir over near the Etoile but if you just like ersters, clams and sea urchins, there are shellfish stands dotted all over Paris in the season. Go into the nearby cafe for two glasses of wine (one for you, one for the man) and toot sweet he will open you a dozen of the best, which may be consumed on the spot. Or, if you are a secret picker, you can buy a bag of periwinkles to take home, complete with pin. Marius & Jeanette also do seafood near the Place d'Alma and you can look at the Eiffel Tower. If you want to look from it, there is a pretty good restaurant on the second floor. After the bill, you may jump.

By no means the most expensive place in Paris, Tour d'Argent has a marvelous view of Notre Dame which is almost better than the food. You will get treated better in the off season when it isn't so full of tourists. Don't let the ladies take fright, as only the gentlemen's menus have prices on them. A nice touch, and also they will let you pinch their handsome ashtrays. Laperouse, down the road, is a little more *intime* and we have been twice; once was great and once we were shuffled off into a back room, but what can you expect. Had a pale green pea soup and then something called Delice des Gourmets, which was chicken livers and other oddities in one of those non-fattening cream, butter and wine sauces. Great taste. We also expected great tastes at Escargot-Montorgeuil but perhaps for that reason were disappointed; also the service, food, plates and reception were all chilly. Relais Bisson is highly thought of by our publishers, Auberge du Vert-Galant is nice on the Ile de la Cite, and anything else you want to know will be by your own legwork.

There are few pleasures more excruciating than driving through the beautiful French countryside knowing that a slap-up meal is waiting for you at your destination. It may be taken in the midst of that New French Modern (of

A GUSTATIVE VIEW OF EUROPE

which nothing is more ghastly, as their famed chic too often embraces red and yellow paint with cubist light fixtures) or more luckily a valiant attempt at French Provincial, but at least you know that your money goes into the kitchen and not reproducing Cleopatra's powder room. Sometimes the decor of hotel and restaurant both are just right, antiquey and restful, and the kitchen is good as well. A place like this, for example, is a stage jump south of Paris at Sens called Hotel de Paris et de La Poste. The refreshing aspect about touring in France is that there are really so many of these superior establishments around that they aren't jammed to the doors. A few are, of course, but at any rate most of these provincial inns offer such a fascinating choice that the evening stop becomes a subject for discussion all day.

There exist individuals who find one of these sympathetic hotels and settle in for a few days, sampling the full range of the chef's art and only emerging to trundle gently about looking at whatever modest tourist attractions present themselves in the town. The Cote d'Or towns of Avallon and Saulieu, both of which possess three-stars, and both of which are in lovely rolling country, would be good for that sort of thing. This is Burgundy, and of course a minute inspection must be made of the vineyards. That the French government appreciates the value of the region is plain, for soon after the massive castle of La Rochepot the generous main highway necks down to a miserable two-lane road when it passes through the precious vineyards of Chassagne-Montrachet, with the communes of Mersault, Puligny and Aloxe-Corton hard by.

THERE is bound to be a small hotel around here, boasting only local fame, where M. le Patron presides over his coal stove and copper skillets in the kitchen. His nose is red, as it should be, the bottles have no labels, and the resident dog or cat spends most of its time sleeping in the vine-shaded courtyard below your window. The roofs are pointed, in Burgundian manner, and have patterns in colored tile. Your bed is brass with a white spread and many pillows and from it you can see the vine-clad hills behind the Saone. When you shut your eyes (frequently) you can see nudding but you can smell interesting things cooking. So can the resident dog/cat, who periodically gets booted out of the kitchen. Dusk is coming, the strawsuckers are wandering back into town, and the quicker ones are already sitting out in front arguing the virtues of their favorite football team over an *aperitif* or *coup de rouge*.

It is almost suppertime. You were going to take a walk. Might make you too tired for supper. After all you drove 22 miles today. Making a few laps of the typical French wall switch, that lights each (15-w) bulb in turn but never allows more than one on at once, you struggle up and comb your hair over the white ewer and marble-topped commode that your Aunt Mamie would give her left arm for. You look at the picture of Gaston Toudouze, dead for his country in the 1870 war, and he looks at you. Finding the blackout combination on the switch, you descend.

The ground floor front is two rooms. One is the bar and is colossally ugly with too many mirrors, poisonous *aperitifs,* a 1932 radiogram, a rather flyblown Panther Pils beer calendar and numerous sacklike types in berets propping up the bar. They all look. You smile and say *bon appetit* or even drop dead and they all smile too, showing an interesting collection of snaggle teeth. Their noses are red too. Madame la Patronne, who would give Hoss Cartwright to think any day, also smiles (see above) and indicates that the dining room is next door. And so it is, a whitewashed room with paper tablecloths on small tables, from which one may look out onto the courtyard or street. A map of Bourgogne on the wall. Somebody's mother. A diploma for something—food, you hope. The strikingly good-looking daughter of the family gives you the eye as she places the bread and tools on the table, including the wine glass, which would be a chopped-top brandy snifter anywhere else. She may want to go to Paris or then may just be amiable. But you remember Mama. About this time, M. le Patron advances from the kitchen in a coat which was white yesterday. The dog/cat follows at a discreet distance. Chef is smoking a Gauloise. Filter, naturally —he is a man of the age. He nods to three plump gentlemen at a corner table, who have alighted from a Citroen with Lyon registration and who are making a grave survey of the wine list. *Bon soir* he says, scattering ashes down his front. It is that M'sieu would like to try the speciality of the house? A bit of *paté* before, perhaps, and the bottle of the patron is very good? A sign on the wall catches your eye. "Don't ever say to me; patron, I won't drink your wine." Repeat as needed. It's a good life.

It is well known that the Human Body cannot stand speeds

in excess of those delineated by Nature: to wit, that of a spanking horse & carriage. Consequently

it was with some Alarm that we received an invitation to

make the Long and Arduous London to Brighton run on board a Powerful 6-hp Motor Carriage, which would certainly carry our Mortal Shell to velocities never before attained.

O, we stood in Fear and Trepidation at the Prospect, as this invention of the Devil had been constructed by the Ancient Usines of Panhard et Levassor, whose Similar examples are well known as Chicken Killers and General Scorchers in their homeland, having even participated successfully in various contests of speed to distant points. Egad.

We were assured by the Intrepid Pilot, a gentleman masquerading under the unlikely pseudonym of R. Bensted-Smith to fox the ever present Peelers, that he himself had exceeded 25 mph on many occasions and was none the worse for it; accordingly, we screwed our courage to the sticking-point and, armed thoughtfully with a small bottle of Medicinal Spirits, betook ourself to the Dark and Misty recesses of Hyde Park where, unbeknownst to us, a Large Number of similarly Afflicted individuals had gathered with their Machines.

This was no chance gathering, but the 66th anniversary of the Emancipation Run, which was held when the hardy Motorist was freed of certain Crippling and Onerous legislations relating to speed limits.

O! It was a Marvelous Sight to those enamored of machinery, as the most Intimate Details of the motorcar were osten-

BY HENRY N. MANNEY III

DECORATION BY LEO BESTGEN

tatiously visible. For those jaded with modern and inaccessible tinware, the sight of a proper de Dion axle (on a de Dion, for once), the exposed innards of a drive train, or even a crankshaft and rods revolving lazily in the open air holds a considerable fascination. Even more attractive were the sounds; a sibilant popping of automatic inlet valves, the gentle swish of driving chains, eldritch shrieks from vintage clutches as the drive was taken up, and a steady *poing poing poing* from large-bore exhaust pipes. Like Mr. Toad, I was immediately smitten and straightaway set out to explore among the strange and wonderful bodywork surrounding us on every side.

The Vintage movement is especially strong among the English, perhaps because they seem to keep their cars so long anyway, and the fostering VSCC and RAC are hard put to whittle entries down to the regulation 250 for the London-Brighton run. This is even more remarkable when one considers that only cars manufactured in 1904 or earlier are admitted and most of these have been certified as to date by the Club. Reflecting on the unreliable state of machinery at that time and the haste with which the human race throws out anything not considered useful, it is a miracle that so many have survived, and even more so that they have been lovingly restored to running order. Collectors like Lord Montagu and the Shuttleworth Trust have, of course,

London—the start of the long and arduous run to Brighton.

MAX LE GRAND PHOTO

The 1904 Cadillac, with its spare tire perched on the roof.

PHIPPS PHOTO

LONDON TO

contributed to this, but the largest percentage has been resurrected from some barn or coach house by private individuals slightly crackers about old motor cars.

Owning and running a vintage machine, even in these days of decent tires (mostly provided by Dunlop), is no pursuit for the lazy or ham-handed. Our mount, a 1902 Panhard, is a case in point. Lent by Lord Montagu's Motor Museum, it is a 6-bhp water-cooled vertical twin of 1652-cc capacity (91 x 127 mm) which drives through a 3-speed *non*-synchromesh gearbox and via chains to the rear wheels. This car is fairly modern in that it owns a foot throttle; evidently a later factory mod, as twist-grips for throttle and spark occupy two of the steering wheel spokes.

The spark itself, so important for crank starting, lives now on a separate little quadrant, alongside a battery of sight-feeds which insure that oil is reaching the total-loss sump as well as halfway down the bore (127 mm is a long way), gearbox, and anything else moving down under there. Besides keeping these reservoirs topped up, at regular intervals the driver must see to oiling the chains, screwing down the sprocket shaft greasers, refilling with water and benzine, and giving the odd dribble with an oil can to anything that feels dry. In addition, bouts with the grease gun before setting off are recommended.

There *are* brakes, the foot pedal operating a transmission device and the outside handle (in brass, as is the gear lever) working on an external contracting affair on the rear axle. As owners of Model Ts will remember, this sort of thing was all right when *nobody* could stop. As the Panhard was a 1902 model and descended directly from the 1898 racing cars to boot, with our starting time of 8:20 ayem we were assured of reasonable leeway on the 50-odd miles to Brighton before the portcullis dropped at 4 P.M. Many of our number, though, were of considerably older vintage and, allowing for the usual fuel, coffee, food, refreshment, maintenance and derangement stops, the cushion of eight hours would not be too much. For others, like the magnificent 1903 De Dietrich racer

One candle power.

PHIPPS PHOTO

capable of 70 plus, the obligatory 20 mph upper average was something of a restriction.

An increased murmuring and pattering of little cylinders brought to our notice that eight o'clock was approaching, and with it the departure of the first 22, the Methusalah of the entry. The traditional first runner, Captain Colver's 1896 Arnold dogcart, was late because of the breakdown of its tender vehicle, but most of the others, which included examples of Lutzmann, Léon Bollée, Benz, a Panhard and Delahaye from the AC de l'Ouest, and Californian Helwig's Peugeot, got away somewhat hesitantly on time, barring one unlucky type who broke his crank on the first bang. As subsequent groups formed up to depart at 5-minute intervals, including such choice items as the belt-drive Menon from Italy (driven by ex-Maser crack Count Castelbarco), rafts of de Dion Boutons, an enormous 1902 Mercedes two seater, a hissing Serpollet steamer, and Warne's Royal Enfield Quadricycle, our Panhard was made ready to go. This involved setting the spark to semi-retard, turning on the fuel tap, making sure all the drips were dripping, swinging the headlight bar out of the way, and giving a healthy pull on the crank. *Teuf teuf teuf.*

Unlike Keystone Kop Model Ts, the Panhard keeps teufing, but at such a relaxed rate that one initially fears it is going to stop. Driver and passenger (in that order) mount to their seats, the spark is regulated once more, low gear gingerly selected, and with alacrity we shuddered out to take up our position by the blue RAC van in company with our peers. With the estimated 35,000 eager spectators, it brought back memories of what the old town-to-town races must have been like, although a modern note was struck by the approximate ratio of two cameras per person.

Consulting his watch, the august starter eventually dropped the Union Jack and with another lurch we were away, selecting second gear as we rounded the bend toward Hyde Park Corner. The big Mercedes crew, togged out in white crash hats, powered past us right away but aside from that "ricer" we were more than holding our own. Past Buckingham Palace, down the Mall, round the corner (guarding against

A veteran ploughs through a modern sea.

Bill Harrah's 1904 Knox (left) passes a 1904 Humberette.

DAVID PHIPPS PHOTOS

Gardner Serpollet steam car.

No Dauphine this, but still a Renault; vintage 1904.

Edwardiana; photo might have been taken 60 years ago.

the Dreaded Sideslip as it had rained during the night), past the Horse Guards Parade, a couple of wiggles and then across Parliament Bridge under the eye of Big Ben, our way marked by the route card and by the legions of bobbies.

On the bridge, racing driver Henry Taylor's 8-bhp Peugeot came by us with a rush, but later on we came upon him stopped with water pump maladies, which much later resulted in a blown head gasket. Then commenced the endless crawl through South London, choked with thousands of cheering viewers and Sunday traffic. Negotiation of this block would have been impossible except for the cooperation of the police, who cheerfully waved us through red lights, on the wrong side of traffic islands, and up the outside of the winding queues of modern automobiles. In spite of lowering skies and the mammoth congestion, all London had turned out to have a look.

On the outskirts, we stopped to have a cuppa tea and sandwich at a friendly Ford garage, hard by a church whose pastor had foregone his sermon that morning for obvious reasons. The chance was also seized to have a look around the Panhard, which was running perfectly but accepted a few essential fluids anyway. That done, we set out once more and soon were in the green and pleasant English countryside where . . . Zounds! . . . we finally selected top gear and bowled along at a rattling 29 mph. The passenger, sitting on his hard seat, is by no means a supercargo on these excursions as besides keeping watch for overtaking cars, he must rest an eye on the drip feeds, check that no importunate cyclist is caught on the nearside, take photographs, and depress the sump and gearbox feed plungers from time to time.

The driver is far too occupied to attend to everything, as the small round wheel takes only ½ turn from lock to lock and, with the bouncy ride afforded by cart springs, he can ill afford to be distracted. Gear changing as well is something of a project, as there is no familiar gate on the outside handle. Depressing a rather stiff button, the chauffeur must move the lever until he feels a sort of high spot; there, with any luck, lies the desired gear. The primitive carburetor is not terribly flexible, the clutch drags, and engine revs while shifting down

BRIGHTON

are largely a matter of guesswork and fiddling with the spark. Nevertheless, our dashing conductor achieved a few noiseless changes which were duly rewarded with a round of applause. As M. Levassor himself remarked about his gearbox, *"C'est brutal, mais ça marche."*

Speed is relative. Accustomed to the normal 80-mph cruising gait of my Alfa, I nevertheless felt that the 15 mph "town" second gear of the Panhard was plenty fast enough when I was driving. For long straights, though, a higher gear is called for by braver spirits and also to avoid overrevving the engine. This is disastrous, as the automatic inlet valves bounce on their seats, lose the cotters, and fall gaily into the cylinders —to the great anger of the Ancient Usines of Bonehead and *Laissez-Faire.*

Therefore, when faced by an open, very flat, stretch of road or a moderate descent, Dick fiddled with the levers (gritting his teeth), there was a moment of silence for those pinions that might depart, and then we leaped forward to a queer slapping of the chains and the engine giving four plunks to every telegraph pole. To be sure, any moderate acclivity caused us once again to take to the second speed, but this proved more than adequate for handling all but the very steepest, or when we were balked by crawling columns of sightseers. This was no real tragedy, though, as we had plenty of chance to wave to the crowd (including a small, solemn girl with a Union Jack in her hand) and look about to see how our competition was faring.

There seemed to be quite a few cars that had fallen by the wayside since we left Hyde Park, including Lord Montagu himself and his restorer, Mr. Warne, who had endless trouble with the Royal Enfield. Many were just carrying out routine adjustments in some quiet spot and 220 of the 230 starters reached Brighton on time. The later numbers were now starting to catch up, and many majestic saloons sailed by on the hills, including the beautiful Knox Waterless of Wm. Harrah and an even more stately White steamer with a sort of baby railway compartment at the back. We also liked the odd but advanced Lanchester, with outboard radiators, which slipped past in dead silence and then there was a fascinating Renault coupe sporting tubular spring housings which took the place of spokes in its wheels.

England is full of hedges, and the modern motorist can only guess at what lies behind them. Perched high on the Panhard, we had the most extraordinary view of the rolling countryside and thus discovered yet another attraction of vintage touring. It does have some disadvantages, though, and one of them is being totally exposed to whatever elements may present themselves. Teuf teufing along above the endless rows of spectators, we had plenty of time to inspect the bank of clouds forming ahead and to prepare ourselves for J. Pluvius' several onslaughts. Anyone who knows about English weather comes dressed like a deep-sea diver and we were no exception. Withal, the first drops seemed to penetrate into the usual unexpected places, perhaps because I had to secrete cameras and road book underneath my voluminous parka. The rain came, it went away, came, went away, and we understood the early motorist's preoccupation with the weather, even if we had not to cope with a smeary windshield wiper. We passed a penny-farthing bicycle, going strongly, then the intrepid Colvers in yellow oilskins, then a vintage Rudge-Multi passed us as we were negotiating the French Panhard 1899 wagonette with crew in Breton costume.

Onward and onward, with thoughts of a soft cushion and a cuppa running through our heads, now leaning forward in best wind-cheating fashion to gain that elusive 1 mph uphill. Brighton finally came up and ever-increasing cheering crowds . . . was this the Paris-Nice or the Mille Miglia? Traffic, traffic and around the outside, dodging some red-faced nit in running shorts, through the bus stop, third speed down the avenue in defiance of the 30-mph sign, and finally the smell of the sea. Doctor Brighton and the pier, cockles, winkles, Brighton Rock, a cuppa.

Follow the blue RAC man, round onto Madeira Drive, and down through a seething wall of people to the signing-in caravan. Rec'd, one medal, one pennant. Thank'ew. Teuf teuf to the numbered parking lot, select reverse, back in. Hi to Annie and Dick's wife. Food. Cuppa. Dick switches off and one last teuf. Good old Panhard. Must come back next year. Now for that cuppa.

"Hot baths will be available free of charge to competitors wearing their official lapel badge at the Aquarium, Brighton." . . . extract from regulations. ⬡

The finish at Brighton, from the flying bridge of the Bensted-Smith/Manney Panhard et Levassor, with eager crowds closing in.

MANNEY PHOTO

An Incompleat Guide to the

ILE DU LEVANT

*Or, where to park your car
while investigating
the bare and the beautiful
of the Golden Isles*

BY HENRY N. MANNEY
ILLUSTRATIONS BY RUSSELL BROCKBANK

A GOOD PERCENTAGE of France's population goes every year to the Cote d'Azur (loosely called Riviera) simply because there is sun. The northern Atlantic beaches, while charming indeed, suffer from an abnormal tidefall, and thus large quantities of mudflat may be exposed most of the day. Furthermore, there tends to be a constant wind and while this is great for sailing or seagulls, it tends to be a little too bracing for lying on the beach. On the other hand, the wine-dark Mediterranean suffers little variation in level, what breeze there is comes as more than welcome, and even if the beaches tend to be both over-crowded and rocky, they are at least warm. Also, for the male segment of the population, much better sport than seagull spotting may be indulged in, as the Riviera is the birthplace of France's national costume, the bikini. The sun is there, a tan is smart, why not indulge?

As Europe is an extremely northern continent, sun-worship is much stronger here than in the U.S. At the least feeble ray, large numbers of people are to be seen sitting in the parks with faces upturned. Consequently, there are those for whom even the bikini is an obstacle to full enjoyment of this precious gift and one hears of colonies of *naturistes* all over Europe. I used to have a friend who was a practicing nudist and I must say that they were on a par with vegetarians and other crack groups. They made too much of a Thing about it to be relaxing. Tea dances in the nude may be all very well but when there is a sort of a beadle around

to tap you on the shoulder when impropriety nudges . . . well, who needs it? Consequently, it was with some indifference that I learned, when spending a week or so with my family at Le Lavandou on the Cote d'Azur, that one of the larger islands offshore harbored a thriving resort for naturistes. You know what to expect; fat old men, ancient ladies with spaniels' ears, earnest middle-aged librarians with spectacles and wooden beads, the lot.

The beach at Le Lavandou is sand, not bad at all, but far too cluttered up with people and especially children, who seem to divide their time between throwing buckets at each other and screaming. Consequently, when a really sparkling day came around and I remembered that Loulou le Corsaire, among other wherrymen, ran boats out to the Ile du Levant every hour or so, I collected a clean towel in a string bag and set forth for the docks. The round trip ticket cost 12.50 francs for the 45-min. journey *chez* Loulou and, whereas others may be cheaper, he boasted the largest and more seaworthy-looking boats. A considerable number of passengers came aboard and took their seats on the benches along the sides; they didn't look in the least like sex maniacs, but generally like a cross section of any excursion trip anyplace else in the world, except that there were rather less of the ubiquitous middle-aged American "girls" in tennis hats, bobby sox, and drip-dry skirts. There were children, a baby or two, young couples, (mostly with camping equipment), older people, a sprinkling of single men of all ages, and even a dog. There were also a few remarkably pretty girls

ILE DU LEVANT

whom I hoped I would see later. Nationalities seemed to be a European assortment with the accent on Belgian and German, I supposed, as the French were already in residence. Most seemed as if they had been there before and were coming again, and most had the start of a good tan, except for one remarkably pale English couple with whom I spoke.

After a rather bumpy trip, we drew close to the Ile du Levant and had a good look at it. Rocky, precipitous and arid, but with a good furnishing of green shrubbery and trees, it rises out of the blue sea just a little distance away from its sister island of Port-Cros. Almost four miles in length and rising to 450 ft at the highest point, a large part of it is occupied by the French Navy as a small-boat and rocket base. Free access is permitted to most of the island, though, and as we drew near to the port of l'Ayguade on the western end, we could see pinkish and brownish splotches on the rocks, rather like a seal rookery, and small figures winding along the cliff paths. The port itself is rather modest and little more than an indentation, shelter from the mistral being provided by a small promontory and a beached trawler, while Port-Cros holds off the wind from the west. Quite a few small sailing craft swung at anchor nearby, their crews behaving exactly like boat people usually do, except that they wore little if anything besides a yachting cap. As we drew into the concrete dock, we could see a sizable crowd awaiting us,

mostly for provisions, friends, or mail (as it turned out) and one felt rather like Columbus approaching the West Indies, as there was an awful lot of suntan showing. Nobody, though, seemed to be actually naked, which was rather a relief as there had been some discussion in my mind as to what actually was the drill. Did everybody on the boat, or some given signal, stand up and take off his/her clothes or were there bath houses or did one wear one's clothes or what? The sight of the local cop, in shorts and his kepi somehow was rather reassuring.

Once we stepped ashore and looked around, everything became clear. Most people seemed to be wearing a sort of G-string in various fanciful colors, and indeed there were two or three booths selling these as well as bikinis (the tie-on sort), postcards, suntan lotion, shell or medallion necklaces, which a great number of girls were wearing, and the usual schlock to be found in souvenir stalls anywhere. Most of the first timers gravitated to these booths and, not without a certain amount of giggling, purchased one of the "minimum" bathing costumes, retiring to the back of the shop to don it. Nobody took the slightest notice. They are sufficiently large, of triangular shape, to hide the more private portions of the male/female anatomy but, as there is nothing at the back besides string, offer full scope to those in search of a comprehensive tan. No bra is worn, as a rule, but I did see some on young ladies who hadn't gotten over the shock yet or who had suffered sunburn on a hitherto protected area. There were also abbreviated "grass" skirts in various hues, which seemed to be popular, and something may be worn under them or not, as the customer chooses. As the island is well out in the sea and a brisk breeze blew most of the time, one can understand the feelings of Fletcher Christian's mutineers. While we were all standing around getting our bearings and trying not to stare at each other too much, a statuesque young lady rushed down the hill to meet some friend, clad only in the local costume, everything possible moving briskly up and down. Every male present promptly turned around and had a good long look, which made *me* at least feel better.

From the port, an unpaved and rather steep road leads up to the village of Heliopolis, which is a collection of hotels, restaurants and shops. To facilitate the movement of the clients, a collection of war-surplus vehicles meets the boats and runs up from time to time, thus saving all and sundry a 15-min walk. In these regions, a notice in several languages informs, the "minimum" must be worn. To each side, and along the coastal regions, the same sign states that there is no restriction in clothing but begs cooperation in matters of dress, also noting that photography is expressly forbidden except by permission of the subjects involved. All very clear, so taking my "bathing suit," I proceeded up through an open gate in the wire fence, following the path to the Plage des Grottes and, finding a convenient bush, changed and stowed my clothes in the string bag. A large number of the new arrivals had preceded me, and while many did as I had done, even more shucked off their clothing entirely and strode off in search of a convenient sunning place. This was not all that easy, as already, though early in the morning, most of the infrequent flat bits were occupied. The only thing to do was carry on to the Grottes area, where the rocky path opened out into a pleasant woodland shaded area and, just the other side, a proper beach. This was sand, all too rare on the Riviera and even rarer on a rocky islet, and practically every inch was occupied with reclining couples or groups. Men and women were swimming, engaged in skin diving with flippers and mask in the clear blue water, or just talking, but most were just doing what people do on the beach anywhere, broiling themselves absolutely black. Practically all were as nude as worms, to use a French expression, and the main difference from the normal French *plage* was that there were no transistor radios, many fewer squalling children, no young hoodlums kicking sand all over everyone, and little heavy necking. All very relaxing, and finding a convenient spot on the side of the hill, I settled down to do likewise and watch the new arrivals.

These were an exercise in comparative psychology. The men, as one would expect, cared little about what state they were in, but a good percentage of the young ladies hung on to the bottoms of their bikinis (or in several cases, only the top!) until they got used to the idea. Even then, they only removed the last garment when lying absolutely flat, in the odd belief that it was somehow less revealing that way. The more relaxed types flopped about in any old position, or gallivanted to and fro and, while I won't say that none of the men refrained from looking at the more toothsome specimens (which numbered about 25 per cent of the population), there was nothing like the stares which greeted a young thing who appeared on the beach at Le Lavandou in an extremely brief bikini. As Flo Ziegfeld discovered many years ago, to his pleasure and profit, the sizzle sells better than the steak.

After a while, I bethought myself of lunch and walked back and up the hill to the village. There are numerous hotels scattered around, bearing such names as "Le Minimum," "Pomme d'Adam," and so forth, and while these are rather small they do have a number of bungalows which they rent out to couples or groups staying for some time. These vary in price, generally including full pension, from about $8 a day upwards and more accurate information can be gotten in the booklet available from the Chambre d'Initiative (Chamber of Commerce) in Le Lavandou. As far as I could tell from looking on the menus and on peoples' plates, you get pretty much what you pay for, although cooking is probably permitted in some cottages (a large group is at the far end of the island), which would naturally be cheaper. The advantage of the eastern end is that there are less day trippers about who tend to stare a bit, the main disadvantage of the port area. You could also bring your own yacht.

Anyway, I found a table under the trees at the "Minimum" and was duly brought the daily menu (about $2) by a charming if somewhat homely young lady clad only in the bottom of a bikini which was in imminent danger of falling off. In this she kept her change purse, as the only available receptacle, and it reminded one somewhat of Life Among the Kangaroos as she kept diving in her front to fish out this object. As she was anything but flat-chested, the actual service itself between the rather crowded tables tended to be more exhilarating than is normally the case, but I kept my wits about me enough to report that the repast was both copious and tasty, while hardly up to Michelin 3-star standards. It was most interesting, in the intervals between courses, to observe the passersby and reactions therefrom. The normal parade of young crumpet in minimums produced no great turning of heads, but a demoiselle in a pair of red nylon underwear pants, rolled tightly to approximately the same dimensions, occasioned much interest. The favorite, though, was a sweet blonde thing (accompanied by an older lady) who sported a gold-colored coin necklace around her shapely hips with an orange chiffon scarf worn Sioux-fashion. My two German neighbors, who had been drinking beer, almost fell out of their chairs at that one but cooled off on hearing, in clearest Kensington tones, "And then, Mothaw, we went around to Harrods and ordered the game pie . . ."

There were a couple of bar-cum-night-spot looking places around as well and I inquired about these. Apparently young people are the same everywhere and must have something to do at night besides go to the cinema, of which there isn't any. There are evidently Miss this and Mr. that competitions put on from time to time, as well as the usual sort of peurile parlor games one finds in resorts, but apparently one mostly sits around and drinks pop or beer and talks. A large area is given over to camping and, as these people are chronically short of money, night life must be cheap. Two of the shops showed the usual narrow silk trousers and blouses for ladies common on the Riviera (even if there wasn't a great choice) and I assumed that these were worn in the evening as at any beach. At St. Tropez, for instance, skirts are rare in the extreme. An even better variation was a smashing long-haired girl in a blue and white Tahitian-style sarong but the hotel-keeper told me that these were all right for walking but not so good for twisting. Apparently a lot of dancing to the ever-present jukebox goes on and, upon being pressed about costume, he cheerfully said that if the weather was warm

ILE DU LEVANT

people wore mostly what they did in the daytime ... if not, sometimes a sweater on top as dancing got you rather warm. Twisting with one of those creatures in a minimum ... I should think so. On reflection, it must be the ideal outfit.

After lunch, I shouldered my string bag and walked down to have a look at the other side of the port area. The verge here is considerably steeper but as consolation there are several tiny coves and, above them, flat individual sunning places formed by cement poured into the crevices of the rocks. Reluctantly passing one cove which seemed to be filled with long-haired golden girls like the better sort of cheese-rarebit dream, I walked along and eventually found a comfortable flat bit down by the splashing sea. My neighbors, at least those that stirred from time to time, seemed to be Dutch and profoundly interested in skin diving. I must say that it was very relaxing; there were no crowds, no scooters, no cars, no dust, no squawking children, and the soothing effects of the sun and breeze on usually covered parts of the body was pleasant indeed. I don't intend to become a nudist, you understand, but I could certainly understand why even people who didn't care a hoot for that philosophy could profit by a visit. All very unwinding, but not dull for those who are not too TV-spoiled just to look at the ocean. For a while I watched the Hollanders skin diving and then we all watched some bloke in shorts taking movies of his girl friend capering about on the rocks, and then she went away so we all went to sleep. When I woke up, the sun had not slid all that many degrees and a couple of the frogmen/ladies were still getting bashed against the rocks at intervals, but movements attracted my eye from a hitherto vacant place only 10 feet away. It was now occupied by one of the most attractive girls I had ever seen, with snapping blue eyes and

Brockbank

inky black hair cut in a dutch bob. Notwithstanding the fact that she was already a deep briar pipe brown everywhere, she was meticulously applying suntan cream to such portions of her anatomy as she considered in need of it. As her tan was extremely even, there must have been considerable single-minded work like this already accomplished, and she proved it by continuing to butter herself with the complete unconsciousness of a Siamese cat at its toilet. Eventually she got up, stretched, and made her careful way down to the sea where she dabbed about in the tide pools before coming back to lie on her towel, rotating herself luxuriously by degrees under the broiling sun. She kept a sharp watch on the cliff path, smiling and waving from time to time to friends and eventually one of these came down and joined her. After the usual French kissing on both cheeks, he lay down with a good book whilst she attentively applied lotion to his hide; that finished, she went back to her own moutons. Needless to say, this performance did not go totally unobserved by me (nor my neighbors, one of whom woke up from a deep sleep to watch), although

42

to you, dear reader. They both turned out to be terribly nice, he confessing that he was about to ask me for some matches for his cigarettes and after a pleasant 15-minute conversation during which I am proud to say that I didn't disgrace R&T in any manner, she finally decided that being in print wasn't really her cup of tea. I bade my adieu, and shortly afterward she rose, donned bra, sweater, headscarf, and minimum in that order, and departed up the hill in search of fire for the boy friend's weeds. Gentlemen, it was nice.

Well, it was getting about that time if I was going to catch the 4:30 boat and besides I had turned a pale but nonetheless unmistakable shade of pink. Wending my way back to the port, I stopped to put on the minimum once again and in doing so was passed once more by the same young lady, who gave me a flashing smile and unself-conscious hello. At the port, those who were to take the boat back to the mainland stood around gossiping, reluctant to abandon themselves to conventional clothing until the last moment, and I had an interesting conversation with a busty and tanned young creature and her fiance about the number of people they had seen sneaking pictures that afternoon. One corpulent German fellow had secreted his Minox in a box of baby cigars and there was considerable merriment when I described, the loss in enlargement being what it is, what he was going to get out of his long range shots. Generally speaking, everyone seemed to be extremely sociable, much more so than at the normal resort.

In summing up, I can say that it was a very interesting day and not altogether for the reasons that one might think. The greatest attraction, at least after the first visit, would be the utter tranquility and lack of hurry, combined with the relaxing effect of getting a tan in an extremely thorough manner. For those who plan to include this stop in their vacation plans, it is as well to remember that the weather is better in July and September, although June and August are quite nice, but that all of France is on vacation in the two middle months. Accommodation on the island is limited and should be reserved well in advance, and this caution also applies to the whole Riviera, although in June and the latter part of September it is a bit easier. Best method is to bring your own girl friend (unattached females seemed to be few and far between), book one or two of the bungalows, and enjoy yourself. You can leave the car garaged at Le Lavandou, along with most of the baggage. One suitcase will do.

it was difficult to keep from staring in the interests of common politeness. After getting a cramp in the eyeball from looking out of the corners, I finally had to adopt a rather oblique position with my head pillowed on my arms but this had to be abandoned as my glasses kept misting up. The only way to get around it was to take the bull by the horns. As I had brought my Rollei, with which I had taken a few general views, I got up and went over to ask if I might photograph them (not that I was terribly interested in him!) in ever-living color as a service

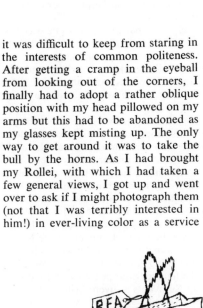

Manney's Selective Guide to the Emerald Isle

Manney and friends drive the Ford Corsair in Ireland and find
the country a delightful contrast to their normal routine

BY HENRY N. MANNEY

"WOULD YE BE after fastening your seat belts and refrayne frim smoking?" caroled the hostess of the Paddy Hopkirk Pig Sty, Driving School, and Air Line Co.'s Viscount (hereinafter referred to as Air Bejabers) as we lowered down over Ireland's green and checkerboard fields to touch down at Cork. And it wasn't even raining, which rendered the question of why we had spent an extra two hours drinking plastic tea in London airport even more puzzling. "Well, it must have been the weather, y'see," explained the taxi driver. I suppose in winter they ferry the passengers across in coracles.

Anyway it was better to be at Cork ("a town of tirty tousand people") a bit late than the subject of intense search by the local offshore seiners, so we directed our Mr. Flaherty to the Ford Motor Company's Irish assembly plant on one quai of the River Lee. There we picked up a Ford Corsair with automatic transmission, this model being the Cortina variant introduced last year with different body and de luxe trim and, after denuding Mr. Mahony's office of maps and tourist flack, set sail for Killarney.

"We," to explain further, were the most complete road test crew I had ever carried—my wife, her sister, her mudder and her fadder, and we came to be in Ireland because Ford had incautiously stated at the Corsair's introduction that if anyone wanted to test one, he could pick it up in Cork. Pronounced Cark—and don't we all have a little bit of Irish in us?

As I had fond memories of Killarney, we stowed our mountain of junk comfortably in the Corsair's capacious boot and set forth on the road to Kerry, giving Blarney Castle a miss partly because none of us felt like hanging upside down after the plastic sandwiches on the airplane. We took the southern route to Macroom to avoid the notorious Boggeragh Mountains, which must be pretty fearsome as the English use "boggeragh" even more than other derivate words like "boycott."

Macroom proved to be a market town, and one of the nearest things I have seen to movie sets of midwestern towns in the early 1900s, except that there was a distinctly Eastern

seaboard touch on all the shop fronts, with O Flaherty, O Malley, O Banion, Hanrahan, O Sullivan and so forth. As we have been saturated with Dupont and Dupond for all too long, this was a little bit of home.

An interesting sidelight was that the apostrophe was missing and also that some of the shop signs were in Gaelic; the road signs in that part of the world tend to be bilingual as well so that Killarney looks something like Cil Arhné, and Dublin Baile Atha Cliath. But Airport is Aerophort, Guinness is Guinness, and Bar is Bar, so we wouldn't starve to death anyway.

The rocky road to Killarney winds over a sizable range of old ground-down hills and, while the Corsair pulled and handled well, the shocks were dead tired, the rear seat cushions way too springy, and I had to moderate my speed to little better than 30 mph to avoid the sight of three rhythmic jack-in-the-boxes appearing in my rear vision mirror.

On arrival, my navigator went into the Great Southern Hotel for a looksee, but returned in fear and trembling that it would be 70 shillings (abt $10) per head bed and breakfast; after some discussion, we then betook ourself to the Mountain View b and b, a private home really, on the west side of town where we got the same thing for 15 bob, just over $2. That formality over with, the females disappeared with loud screams in the direction of O Sullivan's souvenir shop to buy Irish hand-knitted sweaters (about $20) for everyone down to third cousins. They eventually found that Michael Moriarty (Draper) down the street had a bigger selection and there were some cheaper ones to be had (the good ones were the same) as well as a stack of interesting tweed, bawneen, and many other articles useful to the female soul.

Fadder (the celebrated baseball player Jigger Statz) and I disappeared into the nearest pub for a draught Guinness, which I suppose I will get used to some day. It must be good for you, in all its thick brownness, as the natives look so healthy. We were in some doubt about the pubs being open,

there is rocky in the extreme, undoubtedly presenting a forbidding appearance to those sailors of the Armada who were shipwrecked there, (cf Valencia Island nearby, where the Atlantic Cable starts), but around Darrynane on the tip of this peninsula there are several good-sized coves with big hard sand beaches and rolling Atlantic breakers.

We had our picnic lunch at one of these and it was really nice to be next to the sea again. There were very few people about and Derrynane, say, which is a well-known lobster port, would be a good place to take the kiddies. Weather? It didn't rain more than a sprinkle the whole time we were there and, in any case, it is much clearer on the Atlantic coast. So I am told.

As it was getting late in the day, we cut up the glens at Waterville (where one may follow the beagles [!] or fish) to Killorglin, passing through some lovely scenery and seeing an authentic peat bog. As trees are in short supply, this semi-fossilized material, on its way to becoming lignite, is cut out of the ground with special spades and set out to dry. It feels dry, spongy and rather light. How the perishing stuff ever burns is beyond me.

Anyway, from there we motored across to the pretty seaport town of Tralee, into Listowel, which had two fantastically painted hotels on the town square, and then to Tarbert, where we followed the broad Shannon past the Lord of Glin's castle to Limerick, where we got lost. Part of this is due to Limerick being a rather unattractive industrial town but also the Irish seem to run out of road signs when they get inside the city limits.

After swilling about a bit, we headed out for Killaloe, farther up the Shannon, but our navigator got us wrong-slotted on a road which led straight into a farm. A man appeared on a tractor as we were backing out and gave us proper directions but inquired why we didn't go to the farm anyway, as "they were very nice people down there." In Killaloe we holed up in the local resort hotel which, besides some good grilled salmon, provided us with first class Irish coffee and the sight of Irish waterskiers falling flat on their faces trying to take a water-jump. I gather it's not done to point the skis down on landing.

Next day we fired up the Corsair, which was accepting all this stop and go work without complaint, and wandered down the back lanes toward Dublin. The back lanes are really much more interesting than the main roads, as Ireland is essentially a rural country. The main drags are quite a bit wider,

CONTINUED ON PAGE 52

having had sad experiences in England, but a copper assured me, "Sure and the back door's always open."

Next day we beetled off on the so-called Ring of Kerry, past some beautiful lakes in the direction of Menmare, passing on the way one of the horse-drawn gypsy wagons that you can rent in Cork for about $1.30 a week. The country around here, especially when you get up in the bare rocky bit, reminds one more of Scotland than Ireland or even the country around San Simeon.

Under the shadow of Magillicuddy's Reeks, we cut across towards Parknasilla and Sneem [Ed. query: Is Manney making up these names?], where we were astonished to see palm trees even though the Gulf Stream is close by. The western coast just

ECCO LA MOOSTANG!

*Our man in Paris tells how it is to
drive a Ford Mustang in Europe*

BY HENRY N. MANNEY

PHOTOS BY GEOFFREY GODDARD

WE GET SO used to driving those funny little furrin cars over here that we forget what U.S. iron is like. Our only contact is with enormous vehicles bearing Belgian plates and towing caravans or else transporting some Levantine gentleman with his expensive popsie, this last of a quality that we could never hope to attain. Nice looking cars (road test ones) never helped *us* to get any crumpet so the Marquis de Matelas must have been right when he observed that women need money, lots of it, and accordingly will do anything to get it. As any married man and/or father of a small daughter knows, rationalization of a high order is second nature to females.

At any rate, the only time that we really think of American cars is when the f.l.f.c. falls to bits inside 20,000 miles and one remembers gratefully the '54 Plymouth wagon that ran for 55,000 without much more than a change of plugs. But since that time the American cars have gotten far too large and furthermore are as alike as English machinery. The advent of the compacts raised a hope that we might bring the Truth to the heathens, but then they got too big too. We have tried a 2-speed automatic Corvair over here but it went like a stone and the brakes and shocks were poor; the only other domestic product under test was a Monte Carlo Rallye Falcon in 1964 but, the fervent avowals of the Ford Motor

Co. notwithstanding, it was a trifle removed from showroom stock. In fact, it was a great grumbling fiberglass mutha that one could have started the Mille Miglia with and had some hope of finishing.

In the last year or so we have seen a lot of enthusiastic comment about something called a Mustang and have even seen a few in auto shows and the Tour de France. As we are always looking for a decent GT car to cart our family around in, we approached George Trainor of Ford International in Brussels and arranged to borrow his hardtop, a 289-cu-in. V-8 without the performance tweaks but with 4-speed floor shift and front disc brakes. Not only were we to borrow it, we were to take it to the Targa Florio. On receipt of this intelligence, our various colleagues either fell over laughing or promised to light candles for us, telling us all about how horrible American cars were but not about how much advertising English cars took in their newspapers.

We picked up the Mustang from James Kuhn of Ford over rather too good a lunch, and as a consequence I don't remember much what he said about it. Driving home, it did seem bigger inside than outside but evidently taxi drivers thought otherwise, as the too too solid flesh and substantial bumper caused them to sheer off when threatened. It was just as well as, frankly, visibility seemed lousy to me with a tank slot to peer through, the fenders miles away, the hood actually rising upward toward the front, and sizable posts and trim at the corners of the windscreen. More than once an anguished peeep warned me that I was about to crush a 4-CV underfoot, but unless the peep came from the right they could go to hell. Driving in Paris is fun, isn't it? Anyway, the steering, if a trifle low-geared, wasn't as woolly as I had been warned and the engine was lovely. Used to watching the temp gauge like a hawk, I stared at this one fixedly during a prolonged traffic block and it never moved, nor did the plugs become fluffy on pickup. The gearbox was equally good, even if the clutch was rather sticky, and enabled me to shut the gate resoundingly on a cab or two, the rats, at places where they normally try to take advantage. REVENGE!

The next day I flung my stuff into the trunk (big enough but not as good as my Lancia—could do with a dent so the spare could stand upright) and rumbled away to get Geoff at Orly airport. Not being used to driving such a big wagon, I charged off up the motorway at a reasonable rate through the gears and straightaway found that I was murdering all the Citroens and Peugeots up that long hill without using more than a whiff of throttle. In 4th already and they were all massaging their gearboxes like mad. Once the road became flat, the basking sharks went whistling past in time for me to move over and force them to take the fork for Orleans when they really wanted to go to Orly too, but until I had some flying time I wasn't going to go fast. And where was the redline? There was a small tach and matching clock, called nauseatingly a Rally Pac I believe, but no redline. And Sicily was a long way away. At any rate, Geoffers was duly collected and, while he sat there memorizing the slightly gaudy decor with his eyebrows on top of his head, we discussed the road to take and so forth. This was to be a perfectly straightforward run down the N6 to Tournus, cut across country to Bourg en Bresse, Amberieu en Bugey (where the bugey men come from), through the Gorges de Fier to Belley (oh stop), through the Tunnel de Chat to Chambery, and then over the Montcenis pass into Italy and Turin, which afforded us Varied Driving Conditions.

There was a certain amount of sidewind that day, and once we got a bit of speed on we became aware of considerable difficulty in maintaining the correct course. In fact, we were all over the road. At the first gas stop, we put two kilos in the tires (abt 32 lb), which helped some, but there was still a lack of directional stability at, say, 140 kph (abt 90 mph). The front sort of waved around like the arms of a praying mantis and it was more a matter of aiming it than steering it when passing the larger trucks. I suppose that the usual Stateside shocks were fitted and it needed a good set of Konis badly; in addition, the front seemed to be needlessly up in the air to give the Young America Dragster Image and a coil lopped out of the springs would have been appreciated. The back seemed okay aside from rubbery damping and was even a trifle stiff. A GT car loose in the front and stiff in the back doesn't sound much as if Ford was applying what it has learned with the Prototype coupes. In spite of all that, the smoother corners could be taken without slackening speed, although we weren't as brave as the Citroens on the tighter ones. Generally speaking, though, the car was giving us a lot of enjoyment and we hadn't found anything yet that couldn't be ironed out.

A thundering good rainstorm hit while we were negotiating the Montcenisio and, although it didn't leak, we straightaway found out a couple more areas for improvement. The Goodyear tires fitted were diabolical in the wet and I can't think how George drove it around Belgium on the pavé without getting shunted. The least slick patch would give wheelspin or a sidewise attitude and Geoff thought I was just being a clot until I handed it over to him. Additionally, the front wheels would lock under braking with the least encouragement and/or wash out from under on corners so that we had to slow right down while Renaults and things beetled past. Our carefully developed mountain technique of point-it-and-squirt came to naught as the squirting was liable to lead to the Dreaded Sideslip. The front discs were efficient enough in that they didn't fade or rumble, but a bit more work needs to be done on the servo balance as the car had that feeling of not really stopping even in the dry and if much pressure was used, one front wheel, or perhaps both, was apt to lock and stay locked. I would recommend wider-based wheels with Cinturato braced-tread tires for a start and then perhaps harder pads.

On the long autostrada run to Naples, mercifully in the dry, we had a chance to check over the livability and found it pretty good. In spite of the pedals being offset toward the center, the driving position was just right for me, as my arms didn't get paralyzed nor did my legs go to sleep. Coming back alone, I flogged on for long distances and the seats suited me better than the Lancia's. On the dark side, the door handles are poorly situated and I kept hitting my knee while changing gear, the fat lip over the glove box intimidated Goeffrey's face, the central flat bit on the gearbox tunnel could have higher edges (and perhaps partitions) to keep glasses and things from sliding off, the glove box was only fair, and there were no pockets or shelves to keep maps plus the usual impedimenta of travelers. We didn't much like the lap straps, especially since the seat backs fold forward without hindrance to cut you in half, and the control positions are good, but a column-mounted light flasher is badly needed. Mechanical noise of all sorts was very low up to about 4000 rpm when it started to zizz a bit, but we couldn't find any combination of windows to cut down wind roar. The fresh-

air feeds under the dash were much appreciated, as was the formidable heater, but most of all we liked the instant horsepower or *"chevaux minute"* as a Swiss friend called it. As we were not sure of the correct cruising speed, redline, or the tires, come to that, we ran mostly 140 kph (86.8 mph) on the autostrada, with an occasional sortie to 160 (99.2 mph). At this the Mustang was doing a lousy 3500 to 4000 rpm which didn't seem to have any effect on the engine. Just as a passing note, over about 3000 mi it used less than a quart of oil and no water. Anyway, at these speeds we would gradually be overhauled by the quicker sort of 2300 Fiat saloon or an occasional Alfa TI. Sooner or later there would be a traffic block and we would accelerate out with them in top while they rowed about inside and simply kill them dead. After one or two bouts of this they quit trying. Such nice
CONTINUED ON PAGE 79

Manney's Incompleat Guide to Tunisia

and some new Fords as well

STORY & PHOTOS BY HENRY N. MANNEY

WELL HERE WE were, beetling along out in the middle of this limitless waste—Blyne the transplanted Tasmanian, Dickie the ever-so-English gent (with invisible bowler and umbrella) and me, the Thing from the lower 9th Arrondissement. Strung out ahead and behind us in the Tunisian desert were similar groups of English journalists, some of them decked out as if representing the British Raj even if the temperatures weren't all that warm, and all driving new Fords.

To most of them the typical clear air, barren mountains, dry washes and scanty growth were as different from Surrey as the Tycho Crater, but to Blyne and myself it was home. Just like that bit between Deming and Las Cruces I said, and Blyne claimed it was like out back of Bourke. I said what about Death Valley and he said no that was more like Beyond the Black Stump where there wasn't *anything*, not even gum trees where you get bimbye fahlweb spiders. I said no that was more like Possum Springs with Joshua trees where you got Gila monster bit but Dickie piped up about that time disgusted and said that the whole thing looked liked the Romney Marsh compared with his rosebed but just at that moment we came upon a herd of camels. Big ones, little ones, all a sort of dark camel hair color (they aren't keen on washing), except the babies which were a sort of fuzzy grey and, if possible, less attractive than their mums. Regardless of my first cigarette ever being a Camel, the real thing is sort of off-putting as there apparently are too many joints, odd parts are covered with calluses, the face reminds me of my Cousin TC's Aunt Pearl (she was afflicted), and a strong smell is evident at a distance. In short, they look like Martians or perhaps Venusians and if I were those astro-nauts I would quit now before discovering anything worse.

The Bedouins, however, don't seem to mind, perhaps because riding makes a change from walking. These independent folk, not a bit like the skulking Algerians seen in Paris or even the normal Tunisian townspeople, don't seem to mind walking at all and in fact are often found striding along briskly miles from anywhere. Or else they just stand motionless in the middle of a barren 20-square-mile plain and when you come back that way three hours later they haven't moved. It isn't from concealment motives either as sometimes they are all lined up walking down the road and give a wave as you go by.

The Bedouins (if that is the correct term) in those parts are a cheerful bunch and not at all like the movie sort. A trifle dark and of a different facial configuration than the normal Arab, they seem to be nomadic herders of some sort and since we saw mostly women, brilliant as courting birds in their purple cloaks, orange underdresses, and kinky silver jewelry, I suppose that the women do the work while Dad is drinking mint tea with the boys. These females, while interesting enough looking with big white-toothed smiles, are hardly the veiled and seductive harem beauties of stage screen and radio but perhaps they look better after a good wash and in a dim light. In any case the optimum age seems to be around fifteen as I think they get toothless pretty rapidly after that (the men have terrible teeth, probably from chewing Pot); however, as Dickie said, I am no prize either, even to a Bedouin.

Anyway we were all in Tunisia to try a new Ford, the vehicle in question being Dagenham's reply to practically anyone you could mention in the 2-to-3-liter class. The present Zephyr,

while still selling well, was not as modern as every buyer would like and in addition Detroit thought that it might as well be included in the performance V-image program like the present German Taunuses and the Corsair GT. To this end a range of 2-liter V-4 (out of the Corsair GT), 2.5 V-6, and 3-liter V-6 engines were put in hand to be installed in a new chassis-body design. In appearance at first the Zephyr really doesn't look very Fordlike but rather an amalgam of Avanti and Zagato Flavia. After a spell, however, it begins to appear *very* Fordlike indeed with even traces of the old Zephyr shape in but fortunately brought up to date with convex sides and lots of glass area.

Technically speaking the new series is right up to date with engine specs including an alternator (ray!), "ashtray" pistons with combustion chambers in the crown, pressed rockers for the row-of-nails valves, four mains, weir-type fuel feed, and Fordomatic if desired. The real snapper though is the inclusion of a trailing-arm independent rear suspension system that is set up to require no sliding splines in the half-shafts.

Taken overall, the Mk 4s seemed to be a very nice car with good stability in sidewinds, a comfortable if hardish ride (export suspension), good driving position, nice seats (even the bench), and on the bigger engined ones a longlegged cruising speed of about 85 miles an hour. Performance is quite lively even if it is hard to tell with three people and luggage aboard but the twin-Webered Zodiac is rated at 144 hp. Wind roar at higher speeds was considerable, attributed by an engineer to poor sealing, but then these were the first cars off the line. Other black spots were the very slow steering which was also stiff in the extreme for parking, possibly as a result of the front-end geometry, and absolutely the worst column shift I have ever seen. This "concentric" change was possibly forced down their throats by Dearborn to get a slimmer steering column but the result is like throwing the baby out with the bathwater.

All these comments are purely academic as it is unlikely that the Zephyr-Zodiac will be sold in the States but for you who might be coming over to Europe, the Mk 4 is one of the best cars that Ford has put out and barring the slow steering and comparative lack of power, is a lot better than the Mustang. Yes a V-8 will go in. The value of the irs is illustrated both by our standing starts, when it became impossible to spin the wheels much under 4500, and also when we went up some accursed goat track covered hub deep in mud and camel droppings. Most Fords I know would spin themselves to a standstill straight off with normal tires but aside from winding furiously to get enough corrective lock, we plocked away very comfortably up some hills that I would hesitate to try without snow tires.

As many of you won't ever get to Tunisia and for that matter I probably won't ever again either, I might as well deliver myself of a few words about it. Tunisia lies in the latitude of lower Sicily on the north African coast between Algeria and Libya, being considerably smaller than either of them, and is mostly desert fringed by the green and fertile Mediterranean littoral. Up to quite recently it was a French colony, I believe, as most people speak French but is now a republic led by M. Bourguiba, whose picture smiles down at you from practically every business establishment. Politically speaking they are non-aligned as while a lot of German money goes into building hotels and holiday resorts, the Bulgarian and Russian trade ambassadors had just been there and Moscow Dynamo soccer team was playing at Sousse.

Americans can get in without a visa but the currency problem is rather sticky as no dinars are allowed to be imported or exported. All money must be changed and recorded on a currency declaration, and while prices of normal things are fairly cheap I have a feeling from looking about that the dinar is pegged artificially high to gain foreign currency. For instance, the government has put money into building large hotels like the Tunis Hilton plus a few other luxury ones through the country and the prices in these vary around $10–15 per day per person full pension. As the help can't be very expensive to hire and the food, to say the least, is indifferent, they must be a good source of foreign exchange. No matter, as the visitor otherwise might be forced to stay in older hotels that don't look all that enticing and thus probably never come.

Tunisia in any case is enjoying a tourist boom, largely from Germany which is always on the lookout for sunshine and exotic places at a reasonable price, and most of the really interesting places like the Island of Djerba (where Krupp is putting up a monstrous holiday village) are booked solid for 1966 anyway. You can get there via most of the usual European airlines like Air France, Sabena, SAS, and of course Tunis Air (Caravelles) or else via the Tirrenia Napoli-Palermo-Tunis boat. This last is probably the best out for those with time to look about Europe as rental cars are both expensive and regardless what Mr. Hertz says (judging by my experience in Sicily), apt not to be up to snuff.

Driving is no problem as there is little traffic but there is a 50-mph speed limit (cops are mostly in towns) and it is well to remember that camels, goats, Bedouins, sheep, and local drivers tend to be unpredictable. All vehicular traffic is rather enamoured of the "*priorité à droite*" rule and cheerfully charges out under the wheels of rumbling oil tankers. As far as the roads are concerned, these are mostly straight asphalt and diabolically slippery in the dry, let alone wet; back in the desert one also finds dirt roads which are pretty good ones of their sort and will let you look at villages or other sights off the main road. There, however, a good road map is needed as a lot of the signs (when present) are in fretwork only. The Michelin map No. 172 (Algerie-Tunisie) is better than nothing but it is out of date and the tourist office has a later one.

The tourist office for that matter is a fount of wisdom and has lots of interesting flack about hotels, old cities, ruins, etc. As far as hotels were concerned, we stayed at the plush Tunis Hilton and the Jugurtha Palace in Gafsa, taking meals besides at the Cilium at Kasserine and the fancy seaside Skanes Palace near Monastir. The first and last of these were very comfortable indeed even if they missed the chance to be a bit more oriental palace folk-lorey. The other two were nice and clean but the paper doors, etc., reminded one of modern Italian resort hotels. Food in all of them is pretty nowhere, i.e., International Hotel Plastic, with the Skanes Palace a little more enterprising. It might be worthwhile to ask some reliable local for a good clean Tunisian restaurant.

The cuisine reminds one vaguely of rural Mexico with fried-up taco-like objects called "briks," hot sauces with chili peppers, and a sort of stew-cum-paella with mutton and semolina as the main components called *couscous*. There are, naturally, many others but our Ford shepherds didn't want us to come down with gyppo tummy. In fact, I trod a careful path about veg, water, salad, etc., just as I would in Mexico and had no trouble. The wines are quite good barring the whites that are sort of insipid. We can recommend the Rossel red and Thibar rosé as being as good or better than 90 percent of the French "table" wines which probably come from that part of the world anyway. For finishers there is Boukha fig brandy that smells like nail polish remover but actually is quite nice.

With horrid memories of the Algerians in Paris, we weren't looking forward to meeting the Tunisians all that much but in actual fact they are quite friendly and leave you strictly alone if you want to be left alone. Even in the crowded native *souks*

of Tunis they do their best to keep from bumping into you which is more than one can say for the Parisians. Naturally enough in the back of beyond you get stared at but then you are doing some staring as well at ladies all wrapped up in white veiling, either with or without a small black yashmak, three Bedouins on one donkey, or practically any of the desert dwellers with their odd costumes are worth à look. Likewise even in the smaller stores or sidewalk cafes everyone is quite sociable and even the shoe-shine boys don't look particularly put out if you tell them no thanks. It helps to be polite and relaxed as they are polite and relaxed.

Shopping isn't going to take up too much of your time as there isn't too much to buy apart from old Arab silver jewelry, handwoven carpets, and the odd amphora (unless you go to the central handiwork store in Tunis) but prices are quite cheap in small shops. Anyway you can use the money driving about and if nothing else, enjoy the sunshine (avoid July and August as too much of a good thing), clear air, lack of crowds, moseying around in the native markets, swimming, or visiting one of the desert oases like Tozeur.

After a long drive through bugger all you can understand why a bar could be named "oasis" for after all that dryness there is greenery, drooping date palms, grass, running water, and an immediate drop in temperature of about 15 degrees. This is at the edge of the Sahara and inevitably one finds the usual German tourists having their big thrill and just as inevitably the squalid little men who tout for camel rides and souvenir shops. But you can ignore them as it is a real boot to be in a real oasis and there is even a hotel or two.

Better try it now as one of the Middle East hands said, "They're enjoying making ninepence a day now instead of herding goats but in a few years they will be like the other developing tourist countries—all standing around with long faces and their hands out for money." Perhaps he is right; already dayglo socks are beginning to sprout beneath the calf-length Tunisian robes, plastic sandals in hideous colors are replacing the turned-up slippers, the belly dancers all have stiff nylon mesh veils instead of supple silk, the white-clad females now have plastic tablecloths wrapped around them on rainy days, little men are commencing to materialize out of the ground at the frequent and unattended Roman or Carthaginian ruins, and the next thing you know some smart Oriental will start selling transistors. Better get over there quickly . . . it's keen now but it can't last. 🜨

AT LARGE

WITH HENRY MANNEY

DUE TO THE unexpected confluence of the New Year, the Mid-Winter Equinox (hereinafter referred to as the party of the second part), Auntie Dollie's birthday, the anniversary of Lloyd George's speech to several Ffestiniog railwaymen, St Finian's Day and a tide of 4.2 ft over MLLW in certain parts, our Editor has decided to make a few changes in the magazine. One of the less attractive ones is that I am supposed to do a monthly column, as if I am using up their ink in the flannel panel I might as well be in evidence, right? You have been warned.

Not all columns will be as scrappy as this one, as we are sloping off to Europe in a few days to get my Christmas pudding, see a couple of auto shows, try a couple of cars and get stuck into a few good meals. Another recurrent aim is to see if we can find out why Englishmen really talk like they do, not that they all sound alike of course. A famous writer said he felt that if one kicked them sharply in the shins they would stop making those funny noises at once, not that they are any funnier than the nasal neighing of some American babes. Anyway, all will be reported in due course.

Motorcycles have been intruding into my ordered existence recently, partly because my wife always seems to have the car (leaving me with the Yamaha) and partly because I fell in with a Kawasaki press do to introduce their new line. The scheme was to be toted to Catalina on the hydrofoil around noon, lunched . . . er, given lunch . . ., given the bikes and returned around 2300 to San Pedro. Actually it didn't quite work out like that; largely because of Murphy's Law, but the *histoire* is worth mentioning to still the murmurs of those who feel that we are always getting invited (expenses paid) to the plushest bordello in Marrakech to meet the new 6-cylinder Comatose, the bejewelled bints taking our notes to neatly slice out any criticism. Anyway the hydrofoil ran over a bagel or something in the channel, rendering itself unserviceable, so we were directed on to an ancient banger which had clearly been to Manila with Adm. Dewey. It was a good thing that most of our complement were either motorcycling bods or else radio and TV drongoes as our caravel over the mile-deep Catalina channel was clearly held together with many many coats of war surplus paint. If we had run into a paint thinner slick instead of one of UN**N O*L's crude-oil ones we would have joined the beer cans on the bottom quicker than you can say   a
in Japanese. Be that as it may nobody worried   v
very much, partly because of the lashings of booze   a
for those who partook and partly because *Cycle*   s
World's Ivan Wager and I never strayed very far   t
from the lifeboat, meanwhile taking constant   !
bearings on Point Vincente light with our pocket pelorus.

Eventually we were decanted Port-Said fashion into bumboats at Avalon and proceeded to the Country Club to meet numerous exceedingly polite Japanese brass, a buffet and the bikes in that order. Unfortunately Kawasaki's pleasant and efficient Mr. Masek had not reckoned on the capacity of certain freeloading members of our select company and within short order the highly potent 3-cylinder had been dropped by some clown, two other bikes had been slightly bent, two more had been "erked" because of an excess of rpm on new engines and our kind hosts were looking a little fraught. In fact the whole affair was called to a halt just in time to prevent a mess as Scotch on the rocks, winding tree-bordered roads and motorbikes don't mix no matter what you may see in the movies. More's the pity as Kawasaki makes very nice motorcycles and it was all over a bit quickly to do them justice. Two I did get to were the indecently fast 100-cc Green Streak TT bike which seems to have all its ends around 9000 and the new orange-tanked Big Horn 350 motocross. This last one had a lot more power than it was prudent to turn on at short notice but when I get back from Yurrop I intend to try it again.

We will draw a veil over the return voyage, as not only did everyone barring yr fthfl svnt seem a bit boozed or asleep but our Captain, hereinafter referred to as the Ancient Mariner, took about an hour trying to get the hook out of the ground. The electric anchor winch shuddered and blew fuses and made the chain hop over the gipsy and emitted strange odors, while we still remained swinging around the moorings putting the fear of God into those innocent souls anchored nearby. Eventually the AM made a run at it backwards and broke the chain off short so we were away, but not without an odd circular shot at the breakwater which had Ivan and me poised in our starting blocks ready to go over the blunt end. About three ayem, after an interminable but fortunately calm run broken only by melodious technicolor yawns over the side by some of our party, we got back and made it to the slip with only six passes at it; not so bad when you consider the tide sluicing out, only two crew members, monster freighters appearing at our elbows, and an avalanche of

Our Friend

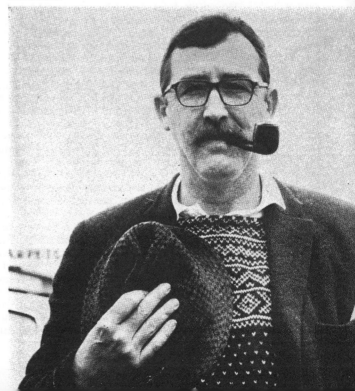

MANNEY AT LARGE

home-goers over the rail when we got close to the dock. Marrakech indeed.

What this is all leading up to' is motorcycle races. Apparently the half-mile Championship was to be at Ascot speedway in Gardena the next week and CW's Dan Hunt prevailed upon me to go with him, promising all sorts of derring-do. Now it is a long time since I was at a proper dirt-track motorbike race as we have been Engaged Elsewhere (as they say when one has been in nick), the last ones being short-track JAPs at now defunct Lincoln Park. After collecting my pass from one of Mr. Agajanian's little men without incident, I wandered down to the track gate to find a sociable policeman who warned me that "they" were still on the track and to zip across after the "yellow one" shot down the straight, doing about 100 mph with his elbow three inches from the wire fence and I was turned loose like the hunted hare to scurry across the dirt to safety in the infield.

Quite frankly it was a bit of a shock over there and I wish that some of the highly vocal but bubble-footed drivers I know could have seen it! The infield itself was a pretty good grade of plowed field laced liberally with humps and bumps while the track wasn't all that much better, the only section able to be called smooth with any accuracy being a narrow groove on the best line. Anyplace else looked as if a cultivator had been at it or was covered with marbles. As it was now approaching 8 p.m., the lights were on but these were of such power that any well trained firefly could have got himself a job as a headlight. Furthermore, barring a coffee-cum-hot dog stall (well protected by a brick wall) and presumably a privy there was nary a covered shed—or for that matter even a clean paved surface —for any one of the 50 cyclists to take his racing machinery apart on. Really, Aggie, must you be so parsimonious?

About that time Dan Hunt, carrying a camera no less, fell across my feet in the dark so we went to watch the first amateur heat. For those unacquainted with the sport; all hands qualify, those too slow are tossed into outer darkness and the favored few are divided up into heats in some mysterious way. There seemed to be separate heats, four each, for experts and amateurs although I couldn't see much difference, really. The fastest three (?) of which go into the main main. Got it? Anyway we beetled down to one corner while a rising mutter filled the air and Christ! Out of the Elysian darkness this pack of mad buggers, all elbows and feet, came piling down the track in a mad seesawing bunch. At once they all seemed to fall over halfway and drift around while holding the bike up with their teeth, then continuing the same act down the backstraight. After a few rounds my eyes focused somewhat and it was apparent that the drill was to come charging down the straight as close as close to the fence, cant the whole plot sideways while shutting off momentarily (brakes don't appear to be used much), and then power through in the groove while using a steel skid shoe on the left foot as an outrigger. It quickly became apparent that considerable skill and not a little mutual confidence entered into this as anyone who fell off was going to get a Harley up his back.

In between *repechages* I was toted around the infield by Mr Hunt and filled my ears with homely witticisms "Why you wearin a Yamaha tee shirt?" "I'd wear a tee shirt with ******* on the front if somebody give it to me.", tried some of the brick-house's good coffee, looked at some of the wondrous machinery, talked to Lt Jody Nicholas USN having a night out, looked at Mert Lawwil's special twiddle knobs and generally enjoyed myself not taking pictures. We had a long conversation with Mr Lawwil who seemed to be the favorite here and an even longer one with his head mechanic Jim Bellard who is as knowledgeable as good head mechanics usually are. He had charge of Mert's racing Harley, a highly developed 750-cc flathead twin and I was astounded to realize that Harleys must be the only successful flathead racing engines left winning today. This is mostly because of the machinations of the Harley-oriented American Motorcycle Association but they do have for competition 750 overhead machinery like BSA threes, Triumphs, etc, although the most successful on this sort of track seems to be the oldish BSA Gold Star. Apparently a certain amount of modification is possible with frames, etc, as most of them didn't look like any BSA I ever saw, not to mention a racing Yamaha and Kawasaki 3 with what looked like a tractor frame. Anyway I was told enough about the science of weight distribution, choice of tires and so forth to realize that whereas the whole business looks a bit casual, lots of work goes into it.

It was a very interesting evening, all in all. The races were run off promptly, not too many folk fell off and surprisingly few dropped out with mechanical ills, the agility of the announcer calling places was only matched by the agility of the riders stripping successive layers of goggles off as they hurtled past inches apart. Our friend Mr Lawwil won, to receive a monster trophy from a smiling Aggie plus, I hope, a large bag of gold for his efforts. From my point of view this is a lot spookier than doing Indy and yet one leading rider recently, after winning heat, trophy dash, main and for all I know the race queen, reportedly went home with something like $145. Wonder what the Grand Prix Drivers Association would think of that?

Emerald Isle

CONTINUED FROM PAGE 45

and perhaps for that reason the pigs, cows, chickens, farmers and jarveys give them a wide berth. The pccf and j are what you've come to see.

So we bumbled along, stopping to take pictures every five minutes, until the terrain began to flatten out. We passed first the gigantic horse-racing track (field would be a better word) near Kildare before we got to Dublin itself. Where we got lost.

Frankly, I was a bit disappointed in Dublin, as it is just a big country town without the country town's atmosphere. We ate rather poorly, and the famed O Connell St reminded me of any town's E. Main St with its junky stores, and the shops were not all that red hot. True, we saw some pretty lightweight tweed (for lydies) at the Cottage Industries' place, in stores on Dawson or Grafton Sts, and there was a very nice department store, but I thought the rest of Ireland much more interesting.

On the way out, we passed that well known shrine devoted to the Irish Hospital Sweepstakes and then set course for Cork once more. The road down through Cashel is a fast one and, in common with most of the main arteries, there is little traffic. In one small town we were stopped for a license check (there was a drive on at the time) and the copper took time out to tell us the *prettiest* way to Cork.

From then on it was harry flatters to make our plane, using the kickdown of the Borg-Warner transmission to eat up short straights, most of the hurry being because we wanted to be in time to have a few jars of the hard stuff at Cark Aerophort. But we will always be puzzled by a sign we saw in Fermoy on the way down: P. O Connell, Floor Covering, Linoleum, and Tintawn Specialist. What could that be, do you think?

All in all, I can recommend the trip highly to anyone, whether they be of Irish extraction or not. The mellifluous Irish brogue falls ever so easily on the ear, the blarney the same, and the people are absolutely the nicest that I have ever run across. The only black spot is that the cooking is really indifferent, except for breakfast. For a change, in Europe, the Americans are actually popular, and every so often one comes across a sign that one of the Kennedys stopped at such and such a house. The automatic Corsair, with its fussless habits, helped make it an extremely de-contracting holiday and if just talking and walking and looking in the beautiful countryside doesn't do it for you, well, will you have a drop of Paddy?

SEEING THE SHOWS AGAIN

AT LARGE

WITH HENRY MANNEY

THE CELEBRATED Cyril Posthumus, bless his little steel-rimmed spectacles, has been busy documenting the Turin Show for you elsewhere —————— so you mustn't feel that you are seeing double; he has got all the precise gen and those who want to check out the latest Rivolta may immediately pass on there. In fact, this is nothing else but what it feels like to return to the Show scene after a couple of years' exile in Tapioca Beach, USA.

Frankly it feels keen even after ten and a half hours on one of TWA's flying daycoaches, packed in so tightly that my kneecaps haven't recovered yet. At any rate it wasn't raining in London for once which lets you get a look at the birds who are the best looking anywhere and not just because they wear the shortest skirts either. Nice to see some lean legs with muscles instead of the almost uniform fat ones on local young dollies. Er . . . the cars. As far as I could see London traffic was still a shambles as formerly with the exception that there were rather fewer of the Princess R sort of Managing Director's transport about and rather more of what Detroit calls personal transport like Sunbeam Alpine coupes, Ford Capris (the later sort), hotted up Austin 1300s and the like. Sports cars per se seemed to be pretty thin on the ground, probably because of insurance rate increases, even if you always see more of them in the U.S. while the number of imported cars, especially Fiats of the 850 coupe and 124 size, had jumped sharply. Shoals of Minis you always have with you, like the poor. In spite of the low cotton act put on by various English papers and the reports of shaky currency, some of it must be percolating down to the masses as it is pretty rare now in central London to see any of the terrible little tin boxes like Austin A35s, Standard Pennants, those horrid 2-tone Vauxhalls, and the early Triumph Heralds, let alone the immediate post- and pre-war *cartons de savon*. Likewise there are many new motorcycles, medium Japanese sizes and not the big British ton-up types, which must put an awful crimp in the local bog-wheel journals. Strangely enough quite a few brand new Morris Minors are running about: they are still in production and much prized by a certain set as they not only handle as well (it is said) as a Min but don't fly to bits if something falls down through the mangle. I don't think that Morris Minors really work anywhere else but then we over here tend to lose sight of the fact that not too many English cars work well anywhere else. The Channel is every bit as wide as the Atlantic, y'know, and the English have been making goods for their sweet selves since Boadicea painted her hermans blue with woad. If all your country, and a densely populated one at that, is made up of winding roads (always a little damp) with less motorway than there is in Southern California, I think, has a moderate climate, boasts indefinite miles of 30-mph limit to be covered in top gear, lets 60 percent of the country's goods move about at 40 mph or less by antiquated truck, and boasts that any occasional straight bit of road was built by the Romans, you are bound

to build peculiar motor cars. However, long may they wave as where else can you get a proper Tea with all the trimmings including watercress sandwiches, sticky cakes, Thud, and three ladies sawing behind the palms on selections from "The Student Prince?" God grant that they stay peculiar.

There is such a thing as being too peculiar, though, and Earls Court, often referred to as the Blue Mosque of the British Motor Industry, is really the oddest of the lot. Part of this atmosphere is due to the average Englishman's attitude toward his car, i.e., to make it a member of the family. This is a hangover from horsey days in the case of the uppah classes but you must remember that until quite recently (historically speaking), for both sociological as well as purely monetary considerations, the greater part of Britain's population could not aspire to personal transportation. Thus, as distinct from the vintage movement, you still see old bangers on Sundays, polished within an inch of their lives and crammed with family, trundling gently down to the seaside at a speed calculated to make Old Dobbin last out the century. At any rate this gives the motor merchants a chance to put on the halls of ivy bit at Earls Court with fraffly refained stand attendants flourishing real feather dusters, lots of cutaway mechanical bits for Dad to peer at, and a refreshing lack of hard-sell messages being delivered by types with microphones although there *was*, at Press day, a topless dancer on the Lamborghini stand. Mr. Photographer Goddard was mad that he missed that one but reportedly Comm. Lambo was even madder as none of the newspaper photos showed the cars. There is a lesson for Detroit there someplace.

Aside from that the London Show was the same dim, airless tomb with the cars all jammed together, looking just the same as when I last walked out the door in 1966. Same ex-Regimental Sergeant Major commissaire, same scrubby little men in white coats tidying up, same potted plants, same poisonous tea, same relaxed looking bobby, same Birmingham gents in wide trousers and slicked-down hair, same dull club, school, or factory ties (there is even one for a homosexual society!), same dusty smell and freezing cold, same hordes of schoolboys in those dreadful shorts collecting wads of brochures; all was preserved in amber with the only really marked change being the absence of those itinerant "take-your-piksha-at-the-show" photographers with no film in the camera, presumably chased out by the cops after a half century of fiddling the public.

There is really no figuring the English. Who else would go to vast expense setting up their own national automobile show and then allot the two stands slap by the main entrance to foreign makes, namely GM and Volga-Moskvitch? What with the Prime Minister's desperate efforts to get into the Common Market, it was to be expected that many foreign firms would be represented, including a much stronger Japanese contingent than formerly, but really. In actual fact the foreign representation is like the well-known iceberg with 9/10 of its bulk below the surface as Ford, Vauxhall and Rootes are either partially or wholly owned by Ford, GM, and Chrysler respectively. All of them are betraying very strong evidences of Detroit thinking now re bodyshells and rationalization (for which read cost) engineering; Rootes is lagging behind a bit and suffering as well because of heavy losses from labor trouble in the Imp plant that the Gov't made them put up near Glasgow, Vauxhall makes the sort of cheap tin boxes that GM does so well and would make something newer if it weren't for labor trouble, while Ford has come out of it the best in spite of labor trouble. Probably because of the prevailing labor climate they are phasing stuff back and forth so that the 4-cylinder Cortina engine is gradually being eased out and the handier V-4 and V-6 seen formerly in the Ford Köln Taunus range (and before that intended for the Cardinal) are now seen in various ramifications of the Mustang-styled Capri which is doing very nicely thank you. The racing/rally image doesn't hurt their sales one little bit but the engineering department hasn't been asleep either; they have managed to make the rough-running Taunus V-4 downright civilized in the Capri, something neither Ford Köln nor Saab could do.

Manning the ramparts against the wogs (anyone east of Calais or west of Offa's Dyke) is the hard-working Lord Stokes, whose Leyland truck firm first swallowed up Standard-Triumph and then gigantic BMC with all its ramifications including Jaguar, Innocenti, Uncle Tom Rover and all. All these stands now have tasteful signs saying "British Leyland" on them but apparently for the moment all the tentacles are operating more or less autonomously even if some strange bedfellows have been slung together. I wish him luck with BMC, the despair even of the English, as its snakepit of conflicting models, brand engineering, outmoded machinery, and stodgy management couldn't last for a minute on a free market. However he is lashing around a bit with his patented headsman's axe and if anyone can make it work he will. For details see Cyril but a lot of dead wood such as Farinamobiles, jellymold Jaguars, and the like have already been cut away, presumably to make space for more exciting things . . . even for Auntie Rover! I don't think he got to BMC proper quickly enough as they succeeded in making the Mins even uglier by raising the grille and adding a few inches, presumably in the latter case to get them into the USA. Their latest real effort, the Maxi, is laying somewhat of an egg in spite of an ohc engine (seen at Harry Weslake's over five years ago), five speeds, five seats, and as an unkind journalist friend of mine says, five hours in the garage en route to Monte Carlo. It is at present on 3½-days production a week, I am told, probably because it costs a thousand quid more than the larger but equally dumb 1800.

Happy to say that the British interest in sporting things is increasing as practically every car can be seen with racing stripes on the rocker panels and one of the pretty series of Dunlop mag wheels, even with the horrendous rise of insurance for anything even smacking of GT. The same specialist builders like Morgan, Gilbern, Marcos, Lotus, etc., etc., are still going strong and more or less modernized although some are pretty odd. We noticed in passing the Dreaded Jim Endruweit, dirty-fingers days behind him, all cityfied and mit carnation chez Lotus and also Coventry Climax had a lightweight 4-cyl diesel on their stand, based on the small ohc, which of course (being British) they have no intention of making. The formerly great bodybuilders plow the same furrow following Rolls-Royce, who took a tentative step into the 19th century with their Silver Shadow, and the only ones of that sort looking ahead are Jensens really, AC and Bristol being dead for all intents and purposes. Pretty depressing but it is nice being back in London just the same; we love it for all the sour comments and you will read about it in The Near Future.

So it was then into a borrowed Capri across the Channel, and across France with a few stops for food and drink towards Turin. God it was nice to get off the ferryboat in Le Havre, turn into the Hotel-Cafe Wossisname opposite the RR station, and have real croissants and cafe au lait. God it was nice. Anyway back to Turin which was as different from Earls Court as chalk is from cheese, the Piedmontese show fizzing with light and life and characters waving their hands about and real espresso coffee in spite of rumors of the Workers marching on the show with brickbats as Italy has labor trouble too. There were truckloads of carabinieri out front limbering up their finger-wagging right wrists in the morning chill but then anything in Italy down to and including the dedication of a new espresso machine is attended by truckloads of carabinieri. I suppose that they try to give

them something to do; for a start they might sort out the parking around the show which is a real disgrace. Anyway there were no journalists about when we arrived in the middle of the afternoon as they had all been scooped up by Fiat's Mme Rubiolo for a press conference but there were lots of cars barring Fiats which presumably were at the press conference too. In the morning it had been exactly the reverse . . . no cars at all and lots of journalists which is standard show procedure. At any rate we amused ourselves by looking at Young Italian Youth which has finally discovered mod dress. Naturally when you are off behind the Alps there are a few oddities and we noticed a strong trend to the Little Beaver bit with fringed buckskin headbands, and so forth and also to a peculiarly Italian version of the double-breasted suit, viz one in Orange Julius with a blue and yellow windowpane check. It almost came off as Rich Young Italian Youth, especially the sort who have managed to stay away from the pasta, are probably better looking

GEOFFREY GODDARD PHOTO

Our Friend.

with their marvellous complexions and striking features (if you like noses) than any equivalent bunch on earth. They have really nice clothes and they carry themselves well, but their cackly chatter, like Louis XV's courtiers, is something else.

It is something like a miracle how Fiat, in a charming but disorganized country like Italy, can keep going from strength to strength even when it doesn't care all that much about its export market and has a nationalized automobile company competing with it in the shape of Alfa. The answer is I suppose that Fiats get on with the job of making good cars and profiting from everyone's mistakes. They just snapped up Lancia to save it from being et by an American firm, allegedly for one lire a share as poor Lancia was a long way in the hole from trying to produce 20th century cars by 18th cen-

CONTINUED ON PAGE 71

AT LARGE

WITH HENRY MANNEY

YOU WOULDN'T THINK it after all these years but one of the greatest joys in my life is going to a race when I don't have to report it. Keeping track, not to mention taking photos, is such a 4-star bind that when Mr. Editor Crow says why don't you go out to see the Rex Mays 300 practice just for funsies, I am off like a shot. Conversely nothing would make me go to the race itself if I didn't have to; as the Dook of Wellington observed after Waterloo, Gad Sir the Noise! and the People! Not to mention the freeway afterwards full of nonagenarians driving camper trucks at 0.05 mph.

Actually practice is always the best bit as in spite of its being the usual shambles everyone is much more relaxed. Racing drivers do tend to become thoroughly worked up on race day to the point of incoherence; the incompetent ones because they are going to get blown off before x thousand people, the merely good ones because they are afraid of making a mess of it trying to keep up, and the experts because (1) they know something ghastly wrong with the car that may or may not last, (2) whether they will get blown off by the other experts before x thousand people, or (3) whether some clown will make a nonsense of it and let them in for x months in hospital. Contrary to what you see in movies very few racing drivers ever think about the suspension etc falling off as if they did they wouldn't go race driving. Illustrates really how good the human mind is at shutting off unwanted segments rather as baby daughters are poor at hearing such comments as go to bed while simultaneously twigging a candy wrapper crackling four rooms away.

Historically speaking there were not that many changes really from last time I was there as the USAC evolves just a little faster than Galapagos tortoises (cf Darwin), with which they have a lot in common anyway including lumbering gait and a fine display of neck wattles. As before most of the machinery in competition, not to be confused with competition machinery, seemed to be powered with great big mutha-lovin' Fords, turbosupercharged or not. One of the mysteries of the age is why the Can-Am races are full of successful Chevies while the talented Mr. Donohue seems to have the only quick stovebolt on the USAC circuit. Perhaps it is really Mr. Donohue or then perhaps Mr. Penske is right in leaving very little to chance as regards preparation. Just putting a new set of rod bearings in now and again is not preparation but on the other hand if Mr. Penske has access to special goodies that would explain a lot. At least the remaining half is explained by the fact that there are very few experts around and Mr. Donohue is one of them. Then of course there was Mr. Andy Granatelli's modest little backup spread to Andretti starring Messrs. Sam Posey and Geo. Follmer in what looked like the Indy Turbo Lotuses with Plymouths installed. Mr. Posey seemed to be enthusiastic about the Lotuses even with their automatic transmissions, as according to him they gave you more spare time to concentrate on driving. That may be true on the straights but on the corners poor Sam looked as if he were conducting a Buick Dynaflow, the thing whirring busily but not much power getting where it was wanted. Then again the Plymouths, not having the benefit of that much F super One alky road racing ex-

perience, may be a little short on power; put these all together plus the power losses inherent in 4-wheel drive and they spell frustration. The celebrated Mario Andretti on the other hand was thumping into the gear he wanted when he wanted it and therefore was able to hold a proper tight line through the hairpins, thus accelerating away at a great rate of knots. Now he is the USAC Champion and shows it but there isn't that much difference in one hairpin.

Watching Andy Granatelli, the Diamond Jim Brady of the Mezzogiorno, at work is always fascinating. He has my greatest sympathy in his battles against hometown decisions but like so many folk perpetually engaged in battles he brings a lot of it on his own head. According to another source (not Sam) he is a charming chap but has the fixed idea that everyone else in the world exists to serve him in some way; if they cannot be of some use they don't exist. You can imagine how that goes down in some quarters. Jack Early tells a funny story about how shortly after WW II when California was the speed capital of the world that Andy *e fratelli* came out to Los Angeles to buy a couple of fast cars. Somebody loaded them up with a load of old junk at premium prices but the laugh was not on Andy; his little men stripped them to find out why the cars went faster and then built better ones. Keith Duckworth, or maybe it was J. S. Bach, once observed that the main difference between millionaires and lesser folk was that the millionaires took pains and never got tired. Losers are always tired.

One of the more humorous things going on was USAC vs the Women. Apparently there are a few lady journalists in the racing racket and naturally they ran head on into the USAC proviso about no women in the pits. Now as an old crusty reactionary I will go on record as saying that there are precious few journalists to be trusted in the pits at all and even fewer lady journalists, the serious ones of which (as distinguished from *m'a tu vus* and photo-snappers) can be counted easily on the fingers of one hand. USAC is right in a way as there may be a good deal of coarse language thrown about in the frequent pit stops not to mention the danger factor; quite frankly the refueling setups with cars booming in and out at high speed give me the creeps. Long lenses and lots of room is my motto. Anyway one of the charming ladies was moaning to us about it and of course we suggested that she paint herself with Man Tan as then it would be Discrimination, a powerful word these days. Eventually USAC's Henry Banks bowed down and let them in for race day. I hope that he lets in wives/girlfriends as well for chartkeeping etc.

USAC also let itself in for another lot of ill will when they started mucking about with signaling arrangements. In the recent reconstructions at Riverside, the track level was raised up a bit so that certain parties considered it possible that cars touching on the pit straight might just project one over the barrier fence, usually lined with frantically wig-wagging pit men. This fence usually looks rather untidy anyway as far too many people are out there but they do have to signal, after all, and they are the ones providing the entertainment. The upshot was that Tom Sawyer's famous chalk line was drawn at a distance back from the fence and pit men were forbidden to cross it. This immediately provoked some discontent and a certain local driver and men took it upon themselves to ignore it which provoked even more discontent. The usual superannuated track policeman, wearing his uniform like a suit of armor, was just about to cast the fat in the fire when Don Ricardo smoothed everything out. Actually the fence there is a highly dangerous spot but the whole strip, or come to that pit area, is not safe from a cartwheeling car. The obvious remedy is a decent angled high wall (which of course would block some of the grandstand view) with a step behind or better yet, signaling from a slower part of the course with communication by telephone as at Le Mans. I don't know what it is about racing that brings out the chicken-feathers in organizers but it surely does.

Adventures in Rentaland

ANYBODY WHO does a lot of traveling runs into the boring problem of how to get to the airport. At home you can always prevail on Auntie Dollie (if your nerves are strong enough) to take you in the Terraplane but in strange towns, unless luck has been with you in forming a temporary liaison, you are faced with more or less public transportation. Some locales run a mammy bus or "limousine" to the airport from a hotel that you are inevitably not at, others require that you go to a town terminal and board some sort of charabanc; the whole affair harking back to the Army in the humping about of baggage plus the hurry-up-and-wait atmosphere. Taxis of course exist but aside from the usual problems of supercharged meters (Las Vegas) or just native cunning, many airports are just too far into the boondocks to make taxis economic propositions. For example anyone fool enough to take a taxi into town from London Heathrow without careful inquiry is going to be lighter by about $20 and I am told that Los Angeles is almost as bad.

At any rate on this last trip we tried the gambit of renting a car whenever applicable, the first shot being from here in Newport Beach to LAX. Now getting there from here usually involves either (1) asking someone to drive you the 50 miles on the freeway, or (2) driving to Orange County Airport, ditching the car for someone to pick up, taking a helicopter or rubberband bomber to LAX, waiting the hour-and-a-half necessary for your baggage to be transferred, or (3) buy a junker and leave it in LAX parking as the charges will be more than the car is worth after a week. Anyway, the easiest way seemed to try Mr. Avis' protestation that he really did try harder and so:

L.A. Enormous Plymouth. Clean enough. Engine in poor tune, power brakes extremely grabby, front wheels way out of balance, front end odd with no shocks, seats well sagged. Mileage low but looked as if it had done service as taxi in Athens. Getting rid of it easy; put in slot past TWA terminal and hand papers to pleasant young lady at desk inside. Cost about $22 roughly; bit fierce for 60 miles driving approx in mere Plymouth but probably cheaper than helicopter, not to mention less likely to crashland on Mickey Mouse.

London. Avis in Headfort Place mews, behind Palace roughly (ahem). In spite of having booked ahead, some 20 min. delay to do papers and produce car. Usual luck as Linda (first day on job) was left to do it while all hands shoot smartly out to tea. Car Vauxhall Viva. Clean enough but almost worn out at under 10,000 miles indicated. Front end very loose, steering v. sloppy, tires out of balance, clutch chattery, strangled noise from engine at anything over 50, moan from back end. Someone stabling horses in boot. Seats shocking. Doors rattly. See reference to taxi above only Mexican. Haven't got bill yet but was quoted one pound sterling for four hours plus sixpence a mile and insurance. About fifteen miles to airport at most. Getting rid of rather complicated as after off-loading Anne plus bags at BOAC, obliged to do the GP bit around looking for Avis. Eventually found by No. 2 parking lot. Chap pleasant, swift, gave me Bengali gentleman (goodness gracious!) to drive me back to terminal. Remind me never to ride in a Bengali taxi.

New York. Picked up vast Plymouth at 76th St office after booking by phone. Monosyllabic clerk in charge was efficient but knew nothing whatsoever about getting out of New York. Neither did his associate at the desk. Car vast Plymouth which looked as if it had been washed in kerosene every day. Pretty tired at indicated 6838 mi with odd noise in engine, lumpy running, front brakes pretty near worn out, steering sloppy, seats sagged. Delivered to us with ¾ tank. Wonder who gets the other quarter? Hood blew up twice on freeway onto safety catch. Boo, hiss. Flat spot in front tire, distinct moan from back end. Stalled twice (in front of JFK airline terminal) and was difficult to restart. Fuel consumption ferocious. Was glad to get out of it but even that was difficult. Due to usual jam on freeway arrived Newark air-port with little time to spare. Off-loaded Annie, usual GP around strange airport to dump car. Found place to do so but two languid laddies in charge didn't want to know. "Put it down udda end." All very well but 5 min. to catch plane. GP down other end into another full parking lot. All Hertz slots full, all Avis slots full, all other slots full. Rousted by usual charmin' NJ cops for not moving fast enough. Really helpful, educated accent. Eventually found slot belonging to airport manager or somebody. Dark figure appears at window and says Avis? I says yes and he takes the keys but not papers which he doesn't want to know about. All very well but no time to pass by Avis which is (naturally) the other end of Newark terminal from the car. Pretty hectic, especially at airport where the customer is usually in a State anyway.

You can draw your own conclusions of course but my opinion is that whereas Avis may be trying harder to hire girls with toothpaste smiles, that the effort sort of slacks off after that. You get the feeling that the only thing that is ever done to the cars is to wash them and put gasoline in. Obviously the car rental business is a highly profitable one as otherwise they wouldn't be able to pour vast amounts of money into TV and magazine advertising; the loot it takes to put in one of those Sunday shots while Namath is thinking up a new pass would buy quite a few shock absorbers. I know all the arguments about getting the product's name in front of the public etc but it is a fact of modern life that many of the products most heavily advertised on TV are perceptibly poorer than those who don't advertise so much. It just boils down to the fact that you can't spend all that money and still make a good product for a reasonable price. This applies just as much for a service like that of Avis. Still, the advertising theory must be sound as it got us!

Our Friend.

PAUL CROSSWHITE PHOTO

56

AT LARGE

WITH HENRY MANNEY

EVERY NOW AND then you get one of those hot flashes that knock you straight into the reverie of Former Days. For instance, not too long ago in the space of an hour Tschaikovsky's "Mozartiana" came over KFAC, the postman brought a back-ordered record of the Strauss-Desormiere ballet "Le Beau Danube" and I uncovered a MacRitchie pastel of Ballet Russe's Yvonne Chouteau. All nice schmaltzy stuff 20 years back, bringing memories of many smiling faces, but out of print now, even Yvonne who is married with kids. At least one can see her in the flesh again by traveling back to Oklahoma U. but the two romantic ballets are gone in favor of nameless writhings on the ground in body tights, collecting splinters the while. That isn't quite fair really as there were always body-tight affairs (was ever anything uglier) but aside from the usual kiddies' "Nutcracker" or wossisname's latest version of Petipa's "Swan Lake," armpit ballet seems to be the only sort taken seriously today. The wooden-bead-and-furrowed-brow set always did of course because they felt that it was expected of them, even though ballet skates an extremely fine line between magic and ridiculousness even as opera, baseball, stag movies, and the Le Mans start. I rather like the story of the rube, confronted with toe-dancers for the first time, who observed that if they wanted tall girls they should have hired tall girls.

All this has some relevance, you may be pleased to know, as today was one of those *neiges d'antan* affairs as well. First off I saw a prewar Packard 4-door convertible, the sort I always coveted for its snogging possibilities in the rear seat. Then by a drive-in rested the ultimate in stylish sports cars, a gray BMW 507.

And then as we were all waiting for a stoplight, a nice clean Triumph Mayflower scuttled past. You may well ask what in Tophet a Triumph Mayflower is to which I will reply that it was one of the more misbegotten efforts of the British motor industry, ranking with the Flying Standard and the Austin A 90 as (1) a reminder of the days when the world map was mostly pink, (2) an exponent of the British attitude that they could sell anything to the colonials because it was British, (3) one of the chief shovels which dug the grave of the British motor industry in the States. To be sure the intended recipient isn't quite in it yet but there would be a lot fewer VWs, Fiats, Opels and Toyotas if the titans in Coventry, Birmingham, and Oxford had really stopped to think. As a matter of fact perhaps they did as Rolls-Bentley razor edge styling was very big among the posh classes and furthermore carried definite advantages in the use of interior space and glass area in what was in reality quite a small car. Unfortunately for the prospective customers it also offered definite advantages for the manufacturers getting rid of some minuscule and gutless flathead fourbangers plus a shopload of leatherette-covered cardboard (held on by three pk screws) masquerading as interior trim. Those who were not put off by the packing-case effect soon found that the Mayflower was a typical British prewar small sedan selling at postwar prices. with sloppy suspension, tootsie-roll sized shocks, an encyclopedic selection of Industrial Revolution thread sizes, and a

roll center as high as Brighton pier. There were a lot of them around Bermuda due to the regulation barring anything above 25 actual hp, I think, but my heart has always bled for the poor wights who bought them over here for economy cars and then were presented with the necessity, after some 8000 miles of out-to-the-Valley-and-back commuting up the then-new Cahuenga pass freeway, of a full overhaul with valves, pistons, rings, the lot. Part of this was due to the highly leaded gasoline still prevalent here, part to driving it at 60 when it was designed for 30 mph in top, and part to the poor quality of British engine parts at that time. The Mayflower really was lots of fun if you had a fatalistic turn of mind; several of us including the late great Ernie McAfee, Bill Pickrel, Murray Nichols and myself went for a drive down the pike in one and were rendered helpless with laughter on even mainroad corners by the attitudes it would get into. You may inquire like the rube above, why if they wanted tall girls, etc., but there was a mad drive on then to get anything on wheels into the marketplace for hard currency. A bit of looking behind all the flossy advertisements will tell you that there are still cars being made like that to trap the so-called economy car buyer, the one who is looking for a cheap first cost and supposed low running expenses before all else. This attitude is what keeps carnivals, Las Vegas, and con games going as it is very very rare when you get something really good for little money. There are two ways to approach the problem; either by obtaining a car which has a good reputation but is not as cheap as it might be or else by buying a decrepit but sound model from a reputable factory . . . which doesn't necessarily mean an old Bristol or Borgward. .

Dean Batchelor and I, on a trip to Greece or someplace, played a game entitled "If I Were Dictator." Most of the suggestions were outside of the compass of this column but one was that three models of every car put on sale in the U.S.A. should annually be thrashed around a road circuit for 24 hours, said circuit to be a judicious mix of mountain and highspeed work. Any car which utterly failed to finish would be banned from sale for the next calendar year but successful models would be given liberal publicity. As all the world loves a winner, there would be no official overall slot but lots of classes; likewise to avoid the usual fiddles which stud Le Mans history there would be plenty of nosey supervisors. Naturally the cars would be As Sold with stock seats, stock brake linings, stock 2-ply tires and the lot. The first year we wouldn't allow any spectators as the carnage would be terrific but after that they would shape up.

SOME OF THE best lines you ever hear, good enough for starting one of Mr. Henry Gibson's poems in fact, sort of fly in over the transom like Marty's "I got a letter from my brother in Denmark today; He's sitting there eating cake." Or the local lady who ran slap into the side of a police car "Oh, that's all right officer, I live right around here." My baby daughter likewise appeared in her undershirt to state "I always thought that citations were good and now they say they are bad."

A typical case of being honked up by semantics (which most females are expert in) because downstairs we have a marvellous framed Croix de Guerre citation (featuring winged lady and lots of soldiers) earned by my father's outfit in WW I. With visions of poilus dancing in her head, she was probably told at school by some kid that he blew a stop sign on his bike and got a "citation" from the fuzz. For that matter few kids do stop for anything here, giving rise to a race of drivers which will be worse, if possible, than the bunch we already have. However comma there is far too much semantics-bending these days like "peace officer," "compliance supervisor," and "Correctional Facility" which indicate that someone high up has read Orwell's 1984 and thought perhaps well the proles really are proles. The latest kick around here is that the local constabulary have taken to wearing a decal of the American Flag on a front fender of the squad cars. This may just be simple patriotism, or then again may be a dodge to bust anyone touching a squad car for defacing the Flag. More likely some smart laddie thought that it might help change the widespread opinion that the flics are really Martians. Do they have to be so obvious? I remember lots of nice policemen who were just policemen and we respected them for it.

A S ONE HEARS that the Ford Capri may be coming to these shores in the near future, I might as well round things out by commenting on the 2-liter Capri Ford lent us when we were over there recently. In case you are already rushing for the exits, be it known that this Capri has nothing to do with that somewhat unhappy example brought out in 1961 approx but in a new approach, the result of Britain's first feeble corporate steps into the "personal car" market. Now I am treading on semantic thin ice as the English have always regarded their *cartons de savon* in a highly personal fashion anyway (Jeeves, see that the cars are washed before bed) and besides sports cars, chopped-about saloon cars, or even ex-Wermacht Froschkonigs decked out with dayglo sunflowers are personal, aren't they? Apparently not, as officially your personal car, as determined from market research, is a low Mustang-like 2+2 with mag wheels, all kinds of James Bond leather upholstery and 707 switches, the epithet "GT" in chrome showing to all points of the compass, and incidentally enough exhaust pipe muzzle velocity to soot up the garage wall at a distance of three (3) feet measured in meters. An optional extra is seats sited in such a manner that either ingress (L.) or egress (K 429) causes the trademark on the bird's pantyhose to be displayed for a period of time not exceeding 1.062 sec for fear of being awarded an X certificate.

Needless to say the men Dagenham were not satisfied with the package of plans (in plain brown wrapper) plopped on their desk one Monday morning from Detroit but wished to stir in some of their own raisins, as it were, to suit the foibles of the English market. Almost as important an influence, if Ford's PR chief Wally Hayes will mind my saying so, is the thousands of letters in the *Autocar's* correspondence columns since 1947 saying, "For pity's sakes when are we going to have a long-legged car good for those straight Continental roads?" Since most English passenger machinery since 1901 has been built with good top gear performance at 30 mph as a primary design consideration, these were valid questions as there is nothing like the usual cup-sized sump and the long straights down to Bordeaux to get everything perking merrily. It wasn't all that long ago, either, that a Large English Company announced joyfully that their baby now was fitted with bearings (of an improved design) enabling it to be driven flat out down the Autobahn! This was followed by a horrified silence as they realized that Topolinos, Goggomobils, DKWs, and 4CVs (not to mention VWs) had been doing it for years.

Anyway Ford made a pretty good start at it already with the Cortinas of various specs (photographer Geoff Goddard has one) and so we regarded this latest Capri with interest even if all that black leather is a bit lurky for my taste really. The main difference between the 2-liter Capri and the Cortinas, I imagine (not having the specs by me), is the use of the V-4 ex-Ford Koln Taunus ex-stillborn Cardinal ex-dreamcar roadster Mustang. In the Taunus the combination of an unclever fwd and the Heron heads gave rise to more vibration than a cheap helicopter but the Dagenham folk seem to have sorted that little problem out. Funnily enough the 2-liter Capri verges more on being a Continental runner verging on GT than English as not only is the V-4 quite cammy, coming into its own someplace around 3700, but it runs up to its max revs with admirable smooth-

Hey, THAT'S not Our Friend!

ness. We found this out by accident as we were stooging about rather desultorily on a French road trying to get our hand in when we got involved in a mild scramble with a big basking shark (Ed. Note: Citroen ID 19 or 21). For once the gears are high enough (including low, oddly enough) so that you don't think the rockers are going clean around on their shafts during a dustup of this kind but also oddly enough, the Capri showed that it had the power to pull them. Actually if you lived in a place like San Francisco, the bottom gear is a trifle tall, calling for a bit of clutch slipping, but I would trade that for a quiet 70-90 mph on the motorway in any case.

Roadholding, as you would expect, is well above average with the fairly reclining posture aided and abetted with comfortable reclining seats (why don't American cars have these?) and the rather small-diameter steering wheel connected to direct, if somewhat insensitive and casterless, steering. Brakes were no problem on mountain, motorway, or streaming rain— which is the best you can say about them I suppose—the heating-demisting arrangements were the best that I have seen on a British car, and the whole plot was handy, untiring to drive, and didn't get "out of breath" at the end of a long run. About the only real criticism I have is perhaps unjustified, as we certainly had a lot of baggage aboard, but the typically Ford soft rear suspension did cause us to limit our speed severely on those bumpy French Routes Nationales, the more puzzling as on smooth roads the ride was quite crisp. Another leaf in the springs please chaps or perhaps Koni shocks?

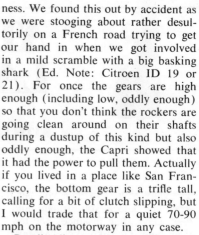

AT LARGE

WITH HENRY MANNEY

SOME OF YOU probably know how it is to feel that you are getting Old; you can't keep pace with the honey any more winding it up out of the honeypot on the spoon, charming young ladies offer you seats on the subway, and the small print is fuzzy close up and invisible way off. I have enjoyed getting old as I always felt pretty old anyway after twenty-one or so as adolescence is a rather painful business, what with boarding school and all. It is better just to pick the age you like best, say ninety-nine, and stick with that. Much more relaxing than holding on like grim death to youth like most of the stylish folks around here. It is nothing uncommon to see grannies with dyed hair, sleeveless tops and stretch pants parading about, their faces pulled so tight from numerous panjacks that their eyebrows are practically vertical. One sneeze and foom! Dorian Gray. The men if anything are worse, especially with the new rage in mod clothing. Used to was that only young people wore that sort of garb but now with Cardin and the usual bunch of designer faggots making it respectable, anyone can do the Mardi Gras bit without being suspected of crocheting antimacassars while watching the late late show. I saw a prize the other day with bell bottoms, Norfolk jacket, beads, hex glasses, boots, sideburns, the lot. It was bad enough that he was easily as old as I am but worse that the lining of the jacket was hanging down, errant threads stuck out from the seams, and the creases and wrinkles showed that the suit was cut of pretty cheap material. Nothing is sadder than an aging swinger who cannot fool anybody, least of all the young crumpet he is after. Much better to grow old gracefully even if you have to start early at it.

I was further reminded of this driving away in the Communal Lifeboat, our old 600 Fiat. Our Mr. Crippen sold it to me over two years ago for $75 and half was promptly snatched away by the celebrated Dr. Boyd, said gent owning four daughters. At least two of them learned to drive on it, another one plus my kids undoubtedly will too, and yet the Fiat rumbles on. She has peculiarities like any old lady, the cooling system being a bit delicate, but no more than ¾ throttle and no speed shifts (we ran out of clutch adjustment in 1968) keep her healthy. That and a constant attention to the water level, as something odd somewhere blows a quart a day out. We have got changing head gaskets down to a fine art but I think the real trouble is that someone has taken too much off the head in the past and c.r. is about fifteen to one. Probably, like Mr. Gurney's rockerarm Fords, she would be happier running on alky but neither Dr. Boyd nor myself wish to keep a drum of methanol in the garage. Performance still exists, as she will still outtorque Volkswagens up a hill, but that sort of thing sends the temp needle banging against its stop.

Still, in spite of the millions of *seicentos* made, our Fiat has grown old gracefully as a car with breeding should. No flowers or psychedelic paint sully her flanks (just a little rust), her bucket seats still support in the right places, everything works well enough to get a safety sticker from the local Tonton Macoute, and she potters along happily in the rain when the family Mustang spits and belches. Fiats of course are built to be driven flat out and this one won't ac-

cept that sort of thing any more (even if a trip up the freeway at 55 mph clears her pipes) but then you didn't see Queen Victoria running the 440 either.

Actually there are a lot of people dotty enough about older cars around these parts to keep us from feeling like poor relations. California has always enjoyed a number of really clean prewar cars owned by kids who obviously had money enough to buy new shiny ones. From time to time these fall into the hands of individuals who deck them out with earthmover mag wheels and the like or even convert them into dragsters of a sort but perhaps care like this is infinitely preferable to appearing on Jalopy Derby or being run into the ground by Low Income Groups, as they are euphemistically called these days. Fortunately most of the uncaring hippie types run to VW buses, a fitting fate as a VW bus is one of the nastiest vehicles to drive that I have ever tried. Anyway the older car thing, as distinct from the vintage or even hop-up thing, has now embraced all sorts of oddities like La Salles, Plymouths, and Packard Clippers that used to be sneered at by the younger set. I suppose that the La Salles and their ilk keep coming on the market in mint state because so many old folks come out here to finish their days in the sunshine. The smog gets them or the DMV says they can't drive anything hotter than a golf cart so the old creampuff goes on the market, usually to be snapped up by some vigilant kid working in a gas station. Long Beach has got many of these; in a half hour recently I saw a couple of Marshall Teague Hudsons like new and a '41 Cad convertible. How nice, even if they look a bit dated and DC-3-ish. I suppose you have noticed that the really classic (as distinct from Classic) cars don't age much, really. A clean TC or Frazer-Nash or Ferrari GTO or prewar Benters looks as good as it ever did whereas most of the current junk, the design based on fashion, will look as funny as those cars in WPA postoffice murals in a few years.

DR. BOYD and I were having a conversation the other day about how factories manage, even with different designers, to turn out cars with a family resemblance. I am not talking about VWs or Porsches as one jellymold is pretty much like another but a factory like Fiat that makes a fairly large and varied range. Ed has a 124 coupe as well, quite a change from the communal *seicento,* and yet if you stepped from one to the other you would know that they were from the same maker. Children have quite different characteristics as any mum can tell you and so do fraternal twin-cars like the regular 124 and 125-engined coupes. Both have twin cams, both have five speeds, they share the same body and yet the 125 version is like a slightly older brother, just that little bit more formal and businesslike. The gap between the 124 and 125 sedans is even more marked as the 124 is a family banger while the 125 is much more posh, an Alfa for those who would prefer a Fiat. The first ones were quite pedestrian but through the courtesy of Alfred Woolf on our last trip we were able to sample a later version brought up to "S" standard with a bit more poke, stiffer shocks, and similar tweaks.

The test coincided with one of those November gales for which England is so famous but nevertheless we found the 125S to be an admirable touring car. As you may remember, the centoventicinque has a 4-cylinder twincam based on the 124 twincam which in turn comes from the pushrod 124 block. The gearbox is also different, being a lot tighter with shorter throw unlike the rather relaxed 124 variety. Anyway, as is common with Fiat sedans the seating is rather high and vintage, an advantage

Our Friend.

MANNEY AT LARGE

to my eyes at least as it helps to know what is going on further up the auto-strada. Seats naturally are reclining and relaxing (why doesn't some American company do that?), all controls fall readily to hand as a great percentage live on a stalk Continental-fashion, and the driving position is excellent with lots of leg and arm room; just as well because the steering, aided and abetted no doubt by huge Cinturatos, was on the heavy side. Annie reported that the back seats were v. satisfactory including legroom and the boot was enormous. Finish was first-class if a bit restrained.

On the move the 125S gives the impression of being a heavy car (which it may be) and a 2-liter (which it isn't) as it whines away smoothly. In any 5-speed box built near mountains there is going to be a super-low designed for getting the familia on the move uphill after lunch; this combined with undercarburetion is no good for the Winternationals but will produce plenty of wheelspin on wet surfaces oddly enough. The other four speeds are very close together with fifth and fourth not showing all that much difference when downshifting but more on the way up without being an old-fashioned overdrive. The action couldn't be better. As on most Italian cars the brakes and handling were both v. good and also like most Italian cars the 125's rather choppy solo ride smoothed out with four aboard without seeming to affect the performance any. Fiats always seem to build their cars to operate with full load, unlike some well-known makes, as practically every Fiat you see in Italy on Sunday has 19 people in it.

Nevertheless no car is perfect and the 125 is no exception. The heater was the poorest I have seen since my old Lancia, warming the rear floor not at all and dealing poorly with demisting, the wipers were not fast enough on "fast" to deal with heavy rain although they did have an interesting intermittent cycle for drizzle, the locks were fiddley and stiff, and the boot leaked. Also the colour, one of those Italian don't-show-the-dirt beiges, was just right to get shunted some dark November twilight. What matters, though, is the manner of the going which was very good indeed. It takes a long run in vile weather to appreciate a fine car; while the 125S was perhaps a bit formal for me in spite of its strong performance, the un-tiredness of the engine after a good caning bodes well for the 125 Sport coupe when it arrives here. Did I write about driving that? Well, next month. ☉

AT LARGE

WITH HENRY MANNEY

ONE OF THE greater benefits accruing to us when we finally came back here was the opportunity of gathering what remained of the family goods (after the employees of the storage company had finished taking what they liked) in one place. Among these were many interesting books collected by my late father; in the days when they were last set up on shelves I read many of them of course including vast stretches of Rider Haggard, G.A. Henty, Kipling, bound copies of Punch, and naturally the Education of H*Y*M*A*N K*A*P*L*A*N* but there were a lot of others that simply seemed to be too dry or were safely put out of reach. Froissart's Chronicles and Pepy's Diary were two that were found recently to be more than just worth the voyage, to quote M. Bibendum, and at present I am sledging my way through Burton's translation of the Arabian Nights. Now this is an earlier Burton than the one featured in the flicks and quite a learned one too. Perhaps some of you remember one of the typically thorough New Yorker reportages on the African explorers . . . steady . . . explorers of Africa . . . Burton and Speke a few years ago in which Burton came out, as I remember, a pretty humorless and hard-hearted type. Consequently the translations were approached with some trepidation, especially since, in

Our Friend's Great Uncle William.

Victorian manner, they seemed to be more footnotes than text at times and the Schoolboy Required Reading version of the Nights was hardly more stimulating than a set of log tables. It turned out, however, that Mr. Burton not only knew his subject thoroughly but was enamored of it as well, a happy circumstance that frequently leads to boredom but in this case to some lively writing about Djinns, Ifrits, and Satan's nine sons. Students of the older cultures will find fresh information on why the inhabitants of the Middle East act like they do and about some of their in-grained social habits, a subject which perhaps some of our diplomats should apply themselves to. Even as television programs today depict Life in the Upper Crust for the edification of those not quite so crusty, many of the tales attributed to Shah-Razad derived from those related by market-place storytellers for the entertainment of open-mouthed rubes and as such deal with fancy dealings in the Sultan's harem. A succession of Hollywood movies invoked the delicious possibilities of being swept up by some sweet-smelling and high-born bint and the Nights do the same, even if they go into a little more detail than the harem oaters starring Turhan Bey; if some young man makes out he makes out in detail without getting tasteless about it and if he gets caught by the guards and suffers you-know-what, well, it tells about that too. The funny thing though is that the Nights are full of business dealings in which a high tone of honesty and morality prevails; of course there is skul-duggery from time to time but if it is major you can be sure that several chapters later (or even more) the miscreant will find himself on his knees before some cat with a sword. I don't think that the Nights are really a collection of morality fables like the Bible is in spots as that wasn't their function. However if you deal with the Algerians in Paris, as well as any other Ayrabs with whom Western culture has made an impression, you begin to wonder if perhaps Mohammed wasn't right.

What brought all this to mind was a spell of tire shop-ping I did recently, a soul-destroying experience if there ever was one. The family Mustang suffered a shrewd blow someplace along the line that caused the Firestone radials in front to chew themselves up and as these tires had other-wise performed good service, I sought to replace them with the same thing. First off for comparison, however, I went over to a neighboring Goodyear store to check comparative prices etc. and I never ran into such a load of old codswallop in all my life. The man came out all nods, becks and wreathèd smiles complimenting me on my choice of auto-mobile as he was just going to buy one (a 1967 dusty, dented Mustang?), telling me what sorts of tickets I was going to get from the cops if I didn't buy a full set instantly (he would give me about three bucks apiece for mine), and baying the virtues of some radials which, on close inspec-tion, proved not to be radials at all. I looked carefully in the rear-view mirror to see if there wasn't hayseed sticking out of my ears and excused myself, never to return. They may make good tires but who needs all that?

I didn't explore Pirellis as they are too good and too ex-pensive for the dumb driving around here and besides it is bad business mixing two patterns, really, let alone carcasses. Or otherwise your Alfa is liable to start handling like a VW, much to your surprise. Pirelli's exclusion left a choice of several discount stores marketing a Bulgarian copy of Palmer Cords, Dunlops (see Pirelli) or the local Firestone store so I went there, curious to see if the blizzard of SALE! SALE! SALE! posters really meant anything. The show-room was littered with tires, most of them with Sale stickers on, but close inspection showed that the merchandise looked as if it had been locked in a cave for twenty years and was intended for the green-Studebaker, Nash-Rambler, Henry-J contingent who are keeping it on the road a.c.a.p. until it won't run any more. A tire that you would contemplate putting on a modern automobile cost just as much as ever if not more, as a chat with the resident manager revealed. Oh I got Oh I got Oh I got Oh everything has gone up Oh the head wagging routine Oh you get from types who Oh think they have found a sucker Oh everything has gone up Oh these tires three times in the last year Oh I can give them to you much scribble and consulting of these are the old prices another catalogue is just due in with higher ones Oh for X dollars and we are only making a couple of bucks each Oh. Well maybe but they make it back on the over-priced and skimpy balancing plus selling you new valve stems ("Use them myself" as if that mattered) at $1.50 each plus a mounting fee if you are unwary enough not to men-tion it plus anything else they can think of. However they were pleasant at least; reflecting mentally that they would have to be selling a tire every two minutes at list to pay the overhead alone.

Next shot was at a much bigger version of the same up in "town" theoretically cheaper. I was greeted in this vast, empty, echoing, customer-free barn by a loan-office calculator whose eyes held all the welcoming warmth of a moray eel. Upon the usual question being posed there was again much scribbling and scurrying about to find any ("getting pretty hard to find") winding up with what looked like a lowish quotation which proved to be for Wide Ovals, a tire I had not asked for and easily the worst one Firestone has ever made. More scribbling this time and finally a shockingly high figure even higher than near here, which fact of course I told them. The moray eel then disappeared into the inner sanctum without a word to talk with his boss, followed by faces peeking furtively out of windows at you and much ostentatious head shaking . . . I suppose this is part of the putting-down process prescribed by the sales psychologist. At any rate after ten minutes or so he reappeared to tell me without much enthusiasm that this was really a good deal and the best he could do was z dollars, a price about $6 above my neighboring shop. I voiced an opinion about this and he said well it would cost me about $6 to drive down there and back; well thought out but then I already live there. As the whole process was getting pretty onerous I almost bit but was put off by the pencil whipping routine he was going through including leaving out one or both of the local taxes, alternately doubling same, insisting on their balancing the tires, *und so weiter*. No wonder there wasn't anybody in the store . . . perhaps the word is getting around.

All this set me to thinking about the notorious business methods in an Arab souk and how much further along the line these characters are. Many people like to do a little bargaining, especially if they are sure that somebody else is getting something off as well, but I am not so sure that the whole routine is not self-defeating and if so, the hand-basket is a lot closer to Hell than we think. When we were in Europe we used to view the moral dishonesty of certain locals on money matters and reflect happily that the Ameri-cans at least were not like that. Since returning we have found that around here anyway the Americans *are* like that and worse, descending to the financial flexibility of a sea-side landlady. The salesmen will tell you, echoing the used-car-dealer's familiar refrain, that the people (1) expect a discount (2) will go where they can get one so that the sales outlets have to protect themselves but it goes deeper than that. Today's mobility means that motorists neglect the garage around the corner and flock to some chromium-plated palace where they have been promised (via advertis-ing) vast savings on what is already an overpriced article; overpriced to pay for full-page ads in the papers mostly although I don't mind paying my mite to support M. An-dretti and friends, rather like a church collection. Said sales outlet has no intention of saving anybody any money but instead resorts to pencil-whipping, bait-and-switch, or simi-lar misrepresentation to scrabble out every last penny, the incentive being some sort of commission system as the tire-sales people aren't interested in cars any more (assuming they know one end from another) but are simply skilled operatives in trick accountancy. Now I suppose that the ads-chasing-sales-chasing-ads, money chasing money, and the ad agency "creating a demand" to sell more tires em-ploys more people etc. and is the American Way of Life but is it very intelligent, viewed in retrospect, as when the crunch comes nobody will trust anyone else, just like the French. And you know what they are like.

What finally happened? A nearby garage fixed me up, one that gives a fair price because they believe in repeat business. "But behold," said Shah-Razad, "the sun brightens the eastern sky and I must cease my tale . . . ." ⌖

Manney's

Helpful Hints for the Travele

BY HENRY N. MANNEY

"I WANT 2500 words by Monday," the Editor said, "on touring Europe by car." The last time this ukase came forth in 1964 it resulted in several articles which wound up in a very fat booklet (which Dottie may still have copies of). This one won't be that long but nevertheless you will recognize that it is a very big subject and difficult to skim over, if for no other reason that a motoring vacation in Europe is an extremely expensive business and may well come once in a lifetime. We traveled about a good deal during our residence over there, even if we tended to follow the same annual migratory flight paths to races while seldom managing the tourist bit, each trip brought forth some new facet which made life more enjoyable. Europe is extremely fascinating because of its variety of cultures jammed close together but on the other hand these cultures are mostly well dug in and difficult to penetrate. A comparable situation would be moving to some small town far from your native heath where everyone knew everyone else's habits, which restaurants were good, what bars were quiet, what nickname (and why) the local garageman went under, and where everyone went on weekends. The natives are pleasant, certainly, but you are always "new." Compound this effect with that of totally foreign languages, food, customs, the lack of a place where you can really get your feet up, and the endless drive to do something with that extra half hour and you can see why some people come back swearing that they will never leave home again. That first day of kindergarten feeling is a really bad trip. If you are pretty well self-contained as far as amusement is concerned and/or have a dear friend along well and good but the human cocker spaniels are going to feel a bit out of it. Nevertheless Europe is marvelous and we hope that you find it so; if we can show you a few short-cuts untainted by guidebook tang or travel agents' grasp, we are happy to do so.

Money

THE BEST thing to do after you have decided your itinerary is to provide yourself with a respectable amount of each local currency so you won't get caught short. For some ob-

scure reason one always seems to cross frontiers at night or on Sundays. The local Change/Wechsel/Cambio may be open or then again may not; it also operates under a good profit ratio and is usually a big time waster. It is nice to be able to buy fuel in a cheaper country, eat dinner straight off without resorting to hotel cooking, or just go to a small hotel. Most hotels will change travelers checks (I find American Express to be the most widely known) and of course it is safer not to carry large wads of currency. Get them in small denominations (abt $20) or inevitably you wind up with a big bag of Dinars the morning you are leaving. A surprising number of stores will take an American personal check, especially if the goods are being mailed home, but get a receipt on a letterhead as sometimes the saleslady just puts the money in her pocket. Credit cards are now quite prevalent; I have an Amexco one which I use for car rentals and airplane tickets only as quite often a restaurant, store, or hotel bill can mysteriously multiply between the time you last see it and it reaches Amexco. Besides that, the places that advertise copiously that they honor credit cards are quite often not only the most expensive in town and on every agent's tour but the worst sort of tourist trap. You will get roundly diddled at least once but keep it to a minimum. A useful safety valve, especially if you are antique-hunting or something like that, is to open an account by mail in an American Express office someplace. Switzerland is central and there are no odd regulations about sending money in and out; for many years I had one in American Express Lausanne (Attn. M. Fernand Domoni) which gave every satisfaction about telexing money here and there with only an hour or so's delay. Summing up, be sure to add up every bill and always count the change. No need to feel awkward . . . all the Europeans do it.

Baggage

TAKE AS little as possible, remembering that you will be humping it around a bit. Even in hotels where there are bellboys, baggage involves you in excessive tipping and is just not worth the delay in the mornings. Women just love to

Europe

fiddle with baggage when you are trying to get an early start, mostly so you will pay attention to them. One suitcase each bod as a maximum plus a smaller one, if possible soft or collapsible. We find this one handy on one-night stands to put shaving gear, underwear, makeup and clean shirt in for the morrow so just that can be taken up, leaving the heavier valises in the car. On going home, purchases and presents can be stuck in the bigger ones while soft goods, dirty laundry, etc., go in the soft one. Have at least one suitcase that locks and use it to keep valuables in when you go down to supper or during the after-dinner walk. This applies to color film, chaps!

DRAWINGS BY JAMES CRAWFORD

Automotive Museums

Austria
Technisches Museum für Industrie und Gewerbe, Mariahilferstrasse 212, Vienna XIV. 27 cars.

Belgium
Automobielmuseum Ghislain Mahy, Watersportbaan (Zuiderlaan 16), Gent. 100 cars.

Czechoslovakia
Národni Technické Museum, Kostelni 42, Prague 7. 50 cars.

Denmark
Aalholm Automobilmuseum, Aalholm Castle, 4880 Nysted. 250 cars.

France
Autorama Musee d'Automobiles, 91 Yerres (Essonne). 150 cars.

Musee Automobile de Bretagne, La Victoire, Gesson-Levigne 35. 60 cars.

Musee Bonnal-Renaulac, 80 Rue Ferdinand Buisson, Begles 33 (Gironde). 80 cars.

Musee d'Automobiles du Forez, Route d'Epeluy, 42 Sury le Comtal (Loire). 50 vehicles.

Musee de l'Automobile, 13 Bd. Rene-Levasseur, Le Mans 72, Sarthe. 150 cars.

Musee de l'Automobile, Esplanade du Paradis 65, Lourdes. 70 cars.

Musee de l'Automobile Henri Malartre, 69 Rochetaillee-sur Saone (Rhone). 150 cars.

Musee National de la Voiture et du Tourisme, Palais de Compaiegne (60). 30 cars.

Germany
BMW Museum, Lerchenauerstrasse 76, 8 Munich 13. 9 cars.

Daimler-Benz Automobile-Museum, Stuttgart-Untertürkheim. 80 cars.

Deutsches Museum von Meisterwerken der Naturwissenschaft und Technik, Museumsinsel 1, 8 München 26. 60 cars.

Great Britain
Vetern and Vintage Car Museum, Caister Castle, Great Yarmouth. More than 100 cars.

Montagu Motor Museum, Palace House, Beaulieu, Brockenhurst, Hants SO4 7ZN. 150 cars.

Museum of Science and Industry, Newhall St., Birmingham 3. 30 cars.

Holland
Het Nationaal Automobielmuseum, Veurse-straatweg 280, Leidschendam. 120 cars.

Veurestraatweg 280, Leidschendam. 90 cars.

Italy
Museo dell'Automobile Carlo Biscaretti di Ruffia, Corso Unita d'Italia N.40, 10126 Torino. 180 cars.

Helpful Hints for the Traveler in Europe

Clothes

DON'T TAKE too many, largely because most of them will get dirty and stay like that. Dry cleaning is expensive, poor and takes longer than you might think. Some hotels, especially in Italy, have fast laundry service but better to do it yourself. This means drip dry wherever possible (as ghastly as it is) as you shouldn't get involved in irons . . . or indeed any electrical appliance . . . with the multitude of voltages and special plugs. Therefore take as well a supply of Woolite in handy packets, one or two of those Japanese lightweight clotheslines mit clothespins and, if you can find them, a few inflatable clothes-hangers. These are nice as they roll up into nothing and do not leave stains like wood or steel ones. For men especially, the woolly nylon socks available are the best as they not only keep your feet warm but cushion the shock of walking. Leave all the sports shirts home barring dual-purpose ones in white or a quiet color; I personally detest white short-sleeved shirts but they do dry fast. For outer wear, if you can find a drip-dry suit like Brooks Brothers makes that doesn't look ghastly, take it for hot weather but it is better to have a light tweed sports coat of good quality and dark color plus dark slacks as it won't be all that warm anyway. Try to pick material good enough so it doesn't wrinkle. Also try to avoid loud colors as no respectable European goes around looking like Mardi Gras. If your outfit above is sombre enough you won't need a dark suit but depending on what expense strata you plan to travel in, a summerweight dark suit might be just as well. Take a warm sweater, or buy a cashmere in England, and at least one pair of comfortable rubber-soled shoes for walking. I like ripple soles. Packing for the girls is easier as most clothing these days is plastic fabric anyway. Avoid the frilly stuff with big sleeves but also avoid the go-anywhere dark dress which makes you look like a schoolteacher (spinster) on holiday. For festive times, there are some nice dresses which either are or look like silk jersey; these pack into nothing and always look well if not in psychedelic colors. Sleeveless dresses are nice if the weather is warm enough but remember that some countries are funny about letting ladies thus clad into churches. That goes for slacks, too. Therefore have a nice sweater handy to cover the epidermis as well as a scarf for the head. For shoes read above with the added proviso that men are almost impossible to fit in European shoe sizes (different shaped feet) but ladies often have better luck. My wife swears by Ferragamo which are expensive but apparently worth it. Both sexes also should have some sort of topcoat/raincoat, a robe for going down the hall in hotels, and if possible a folding umbrella. Don't wear anything too nylony as it not only looks chintzy but is hot in the wrong places.

Weather

IT WILL probably be lousy. Remember that the Riviera is on the latitude of Nova Scotia. Shedding layers to cool off is a lot easier than putting on woolly ones you haven't got. I have been snowed upon in Germany on May 31, experienced 25 days of rain in Paris during August and had coal fires going all day and all night in southern England in July. It can be hot but don't count on it.

Time To Go

DEPENDS ON what you want to do. If you like winter sports, the Alps are great in January and February but forget it (and the rest of the Continent) earlier. Spring and fall are the best for many reasons but the former may be pretty wet and chilly. As far as summer is concerned, June can be very nice and so can July but there are a lot of tourists or vacationists on the road then, especially July. Avoid August and early September at all costs. Millions of working folk take their paid vacations then, the hotels etc are full, and it is all pretty unpleasant with the possible exception of England and Scandinavia, mostly because their seasons lag behind about a month. In early September all the hotels and restaurants are heartily sick of tourists, the cooking is off, everything is off. Of course if you are going for some special reason such as taking in a few GPs you have to make the best of it. The Ile de Levant, for obvious reasons, is at its best during the summer months!

Autoroutes

THIS IS A good time to fit in a small discussion of autoroutes/Autobahns/motorways inasmuch as they are important. Of course you can skip this bit and go look at your own map, but autoroutes are really the quickest, if dullest next to flying, way of getting across Europe. For instance if you are going to Switzerland or Austria from England, most motorists immediately make for the Ostende-Brussels motorway which will, after a short and highly dangerous main-road traverse to Liège, put you on another to Aachen. This of course, pipes into the great German Autobahn system (thank you, Herr Hitler) which will carry you to Salzburg or Basel or Poland or Lubeck with many stops in between, all covered with pine trees. Near Dusseldorf a branch goes north to join up with the comprehensive Dutch system near Arnhem. The Belgians have a reasonably recent bit from Antwerp to Liège (see above) and thank God they have recently completed a massive bypass of sprawling Antwerp. We await eagerly the Antwerp-Brussels (or Antwerp-Ghent) tie in as well as, with the Dutch, a link past Breda towards Rotterdam to get rid of that nasty bit. They also lack an important link from Ghent to Lille to tie in with the rapidly enlarging French system of toll motorways. Toll or not, take them anyway unless you are daft about the country-side and have lots of time. Anyway, the French autoroutes now run from Lille to Paris, leaving you still with the battle to get through, and thence southward to Avallon. The bit from there through the Morvan hills, cutting out one of my favorite GT circuits, will be done late in '70, I think, to tie in with the existing bits which don't start up seriously again until Lyon. You can now bypass that properly and go full tilt, forgetting forever the most dangerous section of the N7, until almost Aix en Provence. The autoroute across the Esterels to Nice is still there and scattered about are a few other pieces, the most important of which is the West branch which runs down the Seine almost to Rouen.

For those going south from Germany or Holland, the Swiss have put in a few chunks to supplant the famous Geneve-Lausanne autoroute which should be extended past Montreux-Vevey before very long. There is a new bit (to me) from Lenzburg (near Zurich) to Bern which should help some and we all await the tie-up with the German autobahn at Basel. Also we await the bit down the Rhone valley to the Great St. Bernard pass!

Big news Italian fans! The autostrada now extends from Aosta, at the other side of the Gt St Bernard, to Turin and of course links up with the Turin-Milan one which links up with the Milan-Venice one or the mighty Autostrada del Sole that goes now well past Salerno. Another slice of slightly over 230 km is now operational a bit further down past Cosenza on the way to Reggio C. and pretty soon you will be able to autostrada all the way to Sicily, opening up some of the starkest and most interesting country in Italy. All these are well-organized, if slightly dear toll roads with occasional medium-quality restaurants but are worth it. Just try the Via Emilia on a rainy evening if you doubt my word.

Medicine

YOU ARE going to get Montezuma's revenge at least once, generally from too much garlic and wine. Forget all that jazz about the water being unhealthy, except in obvious places like Italy south of Rome or where the drains smell. I have found that old-fashioned paregoric does me the most good; in fact it is the only one that does any good at all. The trots are not amusing, especially in a hotel where the jakes may be down the hall. You can avoid them largely by avoiding overloading the stomach, i.e. eating a small Continental breakfast, a →

Race Car Builders

UNLESS YOU *are Somebody, or know Somebody, you probably won't be able to get into the racing shop. If you're in the neighborhood, however, it's worth going past on the off chance that you may see something worthwhile.*

Jack Brabham Conversions Ltd., 33 Centra Rd., Worcester Park, Surrey, England

BRM, Rubery, Owen & Co. Ltd., Bourne, Lincolnshire, England

Ferrari Automobili SpA SEFAC, Viale Trento Trieste 79, Modena, Italy

Lotus Cars Ltd., Norwich, Norfolk (NOR 92), England

March Engineering Ltd., Murdock Rd., Lounton Road Industrial Estate, Bicester, Oxon, England

Matra Sports SA, 49 rue de Lisbonne, Paris 8e, France

Bruce McLaren Motor Racing Ltd., 5 David Rd., Poyle Trading Estate, Colnbrook, Middlesex, England

Surtees TS Research & Development Ltd., Station Rd., Eden Bridge, Kent, England

Tourist Offices

Austrian National Tourist Office, 545 5th Ave., New York, N.Y. 10017 or 195 S. Beverly Dr., Beverly Hills, Calif. 90012

Belgian Tourist Office, 589 5th Ave., New York, N.Y. 10017 or 523 W. 6th, Los Angeles, Calif. 90014

British Information Services, 845 3rd Ave., New York, N.Y. 10022 or British Consulate General, 3324 Wilshire Blvd., Los Angeles, Calif. 90008

Danish Consulate General, 280 Park Ave., New York, N.Y. 10010 or 3440 Wilshire Blvd., Los Angeles, Calif. 90006

Finnish National Travel Office, 505 5th Ave., New York, N.Y. 10017 or Consulate of Finland, 3600 Wilshire, Los Angeles, Calif. 90005

French Government Tourist Office, 610 5th Ave., New York, N.Y. 10020 or 9418 Wilshire Blvd., Beverly Hills, Calif. 90212

German National Tourist Office, 500 5th Ave., New York, N.Y. 10036 or 323 Geary St., San Francisco, Calif. 94102

Italian Government Travel Office, 626 5th Ave., New York, N.Y. 10020 or Italian Consulate, 649 S. Olive, Hollywood, Calif. 90028

Netherlands National Tourist Office, 605 5th Ave., New York, N.Y. 10017 or Netherlands Consulate, 615 S. Flower, Los Angeles, Calif. 90028

Norwegian National Travel Office, 505 5th Ave., New York, N.Y. 10017 or Norwegian Consulate, 805 S. Gaffy, San Pedro, Calif. 90731

Portuguese Government Tourist Information Bureau, 570 5th Ave., New York, N.Y. 10036 or Portuguese Consulate, 1800 Avenue of Stars Los Angeles, Calif. 90067

Scandinavian Travel Bureau, 630 5th Ave., New York, N.Y. 10022 or 612 S. Flower, Rm. 731, Los Angeles, Calif. 90028

Spanish National Tourist Office, 589 5th Ave., New York, N.Y. 10017 or Spanish Consulate, 5525 Wilshire Blvd., Hollywood, Calif. 90006

Swedish National Travel Office, 505 5th Ave., New York, N.Y. 10017 or Swedish Information Service, 1960 Jackson, San Francisco, Calif. 94109

Swiss National Tourist Office, 608 5th Ave., New York, N.Y. 10020 or 661 Market St., San Francisco, Calif. 94105

Automobile Factories

France

SA André Citroen, quai André-Citroen 133, Paris 15e

Matra Sports SA, 49 rue de Lisbonne, Paris 8e

Société anonyme des Automobiles Peugeot, Sochaux

Régie Nationale Renault, Billancourt (Seine)

Simca Automobiles, Poissy (Seine-et-Oise)

Germany

Bayerische Motoren Werke AG, München

Daimler-Benz AG, Stuttgart-Untertürkheim

Adam Opel AG, Russelsheim

Dr. Ing. h.c.F. Porsche KG, Stuttgart-Zuffenhausen

Volkswagenwerke AG, Wolfsburg

Great Britain

Aston Martin Lagonda Ltd., Newport Pagnell Buckinghamshire

British Leyland Motor Corp. Ltd., Longbridge, Birmingham

Bentley Motors (1931) Ltd., Rolls-Royce Ltd., Crewe, Cheshire

Ford Motor Co. Ltd., Dagenham, Essex

Jaguar Cars Ltd., Coventry

Jensen Motors Ltd., Kelvin Way, West Bromich, Staffordshire

Lotus Cars Ltd., Norwich, Norfolk (NOR 92)

Marcos Cars Ltd., Greenland Mills, Bradford-on-Avon, Wiltshire

Morgan Motor Co., Pickersleigh Rd., Malvern Link, Worcestershire

The Rover Car Company Ltd., Solihull, Warwickshire

Standard-Triumph Intl. Ltd., Coventry

Vauxhall Motors Ltd., Kimpton Rd., Luton, Bedfordshire

Italy

Abarth & Co., SpA, Corso Marche 38-72, Torino

Alfa Romeo SpA, Via Gattamelata 45, Milano

Carrozzeria Bertone SAS, Corso Can. Allemano 201, Grugliasco

Bizzarrini SpA, Progettazione Costruzione Automobili, Via Lulli 1, Livorno

Ferrari Automobili SpA SEFAC, Casella Postale 232, Modena

Fiat SA, Corso Giovanni Agnelli 200, Torino

Ghia SpA, Via A. de Montefeltro 5, Torino

Iso SpA Automoveicoli, Via Vittorio Veneto 66, Bresso (Milano)

Automobili Ferruccio Lamborghini SAS, Via Modena 2, Sant'Agata Bolognese, Bologna

Lancia & Co., Via Vincenzo Lancia 27, Torino

Officine Alfieri Maserati, Viale Ciro Menotti 322, Modena

Automobili de Tomaso, Via dei Vitali 55, Modena

Carrozzeria Vignale, Strada del Portone 80, 10095 Grugliasco

Carrozzeria Zagato SpA, 20017 Terrazzano di Rho, Milano

Sweden

Saab Aktiebolag, Linköping

Aktiebolaget Volvo, Göteburg

Switzerland

Automobile Monteverdi, Oberwilerstrasse 14-16, Binningen

Helpful Hints for the Traveler in Europe

wee sandwich for lunch, and then enjoying yourself at dinner. It will be difficult with all those tempting goodies but try to stay fit. Keep the alcohol intake down, especially if the weather is hot, and 85 percent of indigestion there can be avoided by cutting way down on the smoking, especially before and after meals. Trust me. Otherwise, most of the normal medicines like aspirin, etc., are readily available and if not the pharmacist/chemist, not quite so commercially oriented as he is here, can suggest something. If you have special medicines which works as for athlete's foot, the Itch, migraines, or the dreaded lurgy bring them along. That also goes for hay fever pills, as Europe is packed with pollen, or cold pills. If the gals need a special sort of Pill bring that as well as that rectangular package she is always rushing out to the drugstore for in great surprise. I am informed that the European sorts are really nowhere.

Roads

GENERALLY SURFACES are good but can be exceptionally vile in most of rural Belgium, France, and Germany. There is no speed limit except as marked in most countries (England, Sweden, if not all the Scandinavian countries, have limits, I think) but don't plan on packing 500 miles into the day. Read kilometers (0.6 mile approx) as miles in terms of time elapsed and even then 500 km in a day approaches Mille Miglia standards, even on autoroutes. Don't worry about the Fuzz except in marked speed limit zones but do not, for any reason, cross a solid yellow line (in France) or a double white. Keep your eyes open and watch for drunks, especially on Sunday after lunch.

Guides

YOU MAY well laugh at this heading which brings up visions of little Arab boys shepherding Victorian ladies, Baedeker in hand. I don't stir without my Michelin Guides, not M. Bibendum in person but the tire company's little books. The red ones, for France, Benelux, Germany, Italy, and I think Spain-Portugal (the covers of the Benelux and Spain may be yellow) give lists of recommended hotels and restaurants for every town with representative prices, grades them, gives town maps, lists garages, notes telephone numbers and does a host of other things beside telling you what pressure to blow your tires up to. The Green ones, mostly for the various districts of France plus Paris but also including Germany, Switzerland, Austria, Italy, and New York City (!) are comprehensive, well-written touring guides giving places to see, their history, and so forth. They are meant to be used as a complement to the Red guides where applicable. About half of the Green ones are obtainable in English but the Red ones are mostly in symbols with four-language translation panels including English. They are all pretty scarce here but you could telephone Brentano's in NYC to see if they have them; if not, write Michelin direct at 97 Blvd Periere, Paris 17e, France, or failing that try the French Brentano's on Avenue de l'Opera, Paris 1e.

The French Red Guide started everything off with its system of rating hotels by size and posh-ness but it is in its ratings of restaurants by quality of cooking and posh-ness that it has become famous. A five knife-and-forker is a pretty fancy place with prices to match while a 3-star plus the above puts you into the highest ranking of Paris restaurants. Five forks with no stars is apt to be lots of show with very little go, a simple goblet is just a recommended eating joint, while one or two stars with perhaps one or two forks is what we always look for. There is a map to match, so you can plan your trip from one gustatory pleasure to the other, as well as a map for quiet hotels, wine vintages, I think, winter sports, mountain passes, etc. You cannot afford to be without it; the town maps alone will save you many hectic moments.

There are lots of other guides, most of them of the all inclusive or buckshot variety. The greater number are hustled out to grab the tourist dollar, are useless except as a source of background information which is usually out of date, and in this day and age of flying visits are redundant. The Fodor ones are pretty good if dull and a lot better than those which either give all the most expensive places, in exchange for advertising money under the table, or try to fit you in a series of fleabags under the guise of saving a buck. You are not going to save much as Europe has ceased to be cheap so why not be comfortable?

Some others we used for guides or just for reading were the ill-tempered Mr. Fielding's book, the *Auto-Journal* restaurant guide for France (cheap eats but in French), Postgate's *Good Food Guide* in England, the list of Trust Houses in England, Guide Renault *Marine des Ports de France*, Hallwag *Europa Touring* (a big book of maps; the hotel listings are paid adverts), the *Susse Camping Guide* (French, but covers some other countries, I think), Sam Chamberlain's massive tomes like the *Bouquet de France*, Italy, etc. Lichine's book on French wines, Simon's *Great Wines and Noble Grapes of France*, *Varta Battery Guide* (Germany) plus another on country eating houses the name of which I forget, the *Shell Guide to Ireland*, the early *Julliard Guides to Paris* and London if you can find them, *London Perceived* by V. S. Pritchett, old copies of Punch, etc., etc.. There are many more worthwhile ones and also a lot of pure passionate-echo-flung rubbish. What used to be pretty reliable, *Holiday* Magazine, went off on the wrong track several years ago.

Duty Free Airport Shops

FORGET IT. The only thing you save much on is booze and weeds, all of brands that are "popular" but not necessarily good. As an example on other things, I once priced a light meter in Frankfurt *zollfrei* shop which was $5 more expensive than downtown Frankfurt. Likewise a stopwatch in Geneva ditto was cheaper downtown. Beware things not made in the relating country!

La Douane/Dogana/Zoll/Customs

THEY DON'T want to know about you and you won't have trouble with them providing that you obviously don't have too much of anything sticking out and your papers are in order. This means a current passport but most importantly, that the European Third Party section of your insurance (known as the Green Card) is in force. If you are planning to smuggle pot or watch movements, remember that 90 percent of arrests are made from tipoffs from the guy who sold it to you. Concierges of hotels are automatically police spies, as is the porter who takes the bag up. They get a bit of the action.

Tax Free Prices

A FEW countries, France and England among them, have/had this sort of arrangement to get foreign currency, even if the shops don't tell you about it (especially in England) to save the inevitable paperwork. One big store in London would give us the discount but wanted to charge more than that for "sending the merchandise in a taxi, three days hence" out to the airport. France has a better deal which really amounts to knocking off the luxury tax. You can have the store mail it, (get a receipt) in which case you get the discount toot sweet, or else you take it along, paying full price, bearing a blue slip that you give to the *douanier* at the border when you go out. He may or may not want to look at the merchandise but eventually a refund equal (approx) to the tax arrives via a local bank. One friend had a helluva time as everybody leaving on one of these big jets tried to crowd into the *douanier's* booth at once to get their blue slips stamped. He didn't feel like hurrying so most of them lost out. I don't think that it is French Gov't policy to do this go-slow; it is just that the *douanier* isn't getting paid any extra for it. The refunds do seem to arrive, by the way.

Tax Free Car Licenses

PRACTICALLY EVERY manufacturer, a couple of airports (notably Amsterdam) and a few specialist companies are in the business of selling you a car delivered in Europe, reportedly at some gigantic saving. If you are going to buy the car anyway it will make visiting Europe easier but otherwise I do not think there is much difference. If anybody asks me how to work this I almost always say go to the manufacturer unless that, usually via the dealer, doesn't seem to work out. My sister-in-law Janie works for Auto Europe and swears by them, naturally; she has been in a couple of binds but then so have people who worked direct with Mercedes in Stuttgart. Anyway it would not hurt to research where you want to go in relation to the car you want; for instance it works out, if a bit dear, to pick up a VW in Bari but unlikely for a Saab. Another aspect often ignored is the tax-free license plate, hereinafter referred to as the fiddle plate. These show that you are a tourist, are driving a car that local taxes have not been paid on and are intending to export it inside the calendar year. The year proviso only applies in the country of its registration; i.e. you can drive an "EE" plate car for years in Europe as long as you don't go near Italy or they will stick you for road tax, etc. The French are the most relaxed about the "TT" plates and will hardly bother you at all; the Swedes, Danes, Germans, Dutch and Belgians commence to ask for a few bucks in road tax (I am told) after six months if you pass by, the Italians are relaxed enough up to the end of the year but getting the license in the first place is a complicated business (thus it might be wise to order your Fiat delivered in Paris on TT), while the Swiss used to be easy but are now getting delusions of grandeur. Also they insist on your having a Swiss insurance company; these treat the Swiss pretty well but can be very offhand with foreigners. Insurance companies are offhand enough anyway without compounding it. By the way, ask your friendly insurance agent at home to write your Green Card for you as otherwise (1) the dealer/auto club/factory on the other side has been known to write it at 900-percent profit with some sly French outfit, (2) ask friendly insurance agent to cover it via somebody else except American International Underwriters. I had need of them once and I never met a more *unfriendly*,

➡➡

Buying a Car in Europe

BECAUSE OF *the current restrictions on all cars sold in the U.S., it is better to make your plans and place your order for your car before you leave the U.S. It has to conform to the smog and safety regulations before you will be allowed to bring it in, of course, and the cars sold in Europe to Europeans do not necessarily meet the U.S. requirements.*

The U.S. distributors all have European delivery plans and on all of them you can save money by taking delivery in Europe and then having it shipped back. They also have machinery set up to handle delivery in all major cities and shipment back to the U.S.

Your warranty is still good and you get the same service after a European delivery as you would if you bought it in the U.S. Your warranty booklet assures this.

If you're planning to buy a pre-safety/smog model (1968 or earlier), you may have to make your own shipping arrangements but most dealers who participate in this kind of business can help you in this respect. We would add that you should be very careful when making such a purchase, however, as what looked like a bargain in Turin may not turn out to be much of a bargain if you have a lot of grief getting it home.

There are also U.S. companies that specialize in arranging the purchase of European cars (Auto Europe, Pamosa, etc.) and these companies also make shipping arrangements to suit your schedule. The warranty, via the booklet, is also honored after your return.

If you are thinking of buying a European specification car simply to use while you're in Europe and then selling again when you're ready to come back, we'd say good luck to you. That can't be a very good idea unless you're a far better used car salesman than we are. In some countries there are also restrictions on your re-selling the car—so be careful that you understand all the local ground rules before acquiring a car and then finding out you can't sell it.

You should also be aware that the federal government wants 7% excise tax on any car you import and that you'll be receiving a letter and a form to fill out after you bring the car home.

Renting a Car

IN GENERAL, *a rental car is a good way to cover the local area in Europe. There are rental agencies everywhere—Hertz and Avis are familiar names to most Americans—which offer a variety of local machines. The procedures are as simple and easy as in the U.S. and a credit card is far easier to use than money as you don't have to worry about cash deposits. (You can get a Hertz or Avis credit card application by calling their local office.)*

You'll need a valid U.S. drivers license, just as you do at home. You can also make "get it here, leave it there" arrangements for rental cars although you will probably have to pay a pick-up charge when doing this.

An additional benefit in renting cars in Europe, to our way of thinking, is that you can sample a wide variety of different machines—makes and models you'll probably never get a chance to drive any other way—Vauxhalls in England, for instance, a Citroen 2CV in France, a Taunus in Germany, one of the bigger Fiats in Italy.

For the average car, rentals are slightly cheaper in Europe than in the U.S.

Travel Documents

FOR YOUR *trip to Western Europe you'll need a passport and that's all as none of these countries now require visas for tourists. You'll also need a smallpox vaccination certificate for your return to the U.S.*

There is a document called an International Driving Permit which is issued by U.S. national auto clubs (AAA, etc.) but this is not required in Western Europe. Your valid U.S. drivers license is all that's required—but be sure and have one of those since it is not ordinarily either simple, easy or quick to obtain a local license.

Border Formalities

AS AN *American, you'll be amazed at the lack of fuss and trouble at national frontiers. If you're driving, you simply roll up to the gate, hand over your passport and car documents (including your insurance forms) and, in all but one time in a thousand, you'll be sent on your way without so much as a glance into the trunk of your car. That other time in a thousand, you may have your luggage looked at but in an accumulated total of more than a hundred border crossings in the past three years by R&T staff members, none of us has had even so much as a cursory glance made at our luggage.*

So don't worry about it. It's far simpler than crossing from Canada to the U.S. And in some countries—like between the Scandinavian borders between Sweden, Norway and Denmark —there are no border formalities at all. You don't even have to stop at the frontier to show your passport.

Other Inspections

BECAUSE OF *the recent rash of aircraft hijackings, you may also find an inspection going on as you board your aircraft bound for the U.S. This takes place at the gate getting onto the plane where a couple airline employees go through your hand luggage looking for weapons and explosives. In our experience this is a much more thorough search than most customs inspections —which could be embarrassing if you were planning to hide your pornography later. They're very polite and full of unctuous explanations about it all being for your own good but these are strictly token searches, of course, since any airplane hijacker worth his salt would carry his weapon hidden on his person, not in his camera bag.*

Helpful Hints for the Traveler in Europe

uncaring lot. Be sure to get all sorts of collision coverage, including your own car, as I don't ever remember hearing of a European company (the other chap's) paying off to a foreign driver. It just isn't on. And the English companies are worse, if anything.

One of the trickiest bits about buying your own car over there is getting it home as most of the shipping lines seem out to screw you, the stevedores seem to have contests bashing the car about, and the shipping agents handling the paperwork have got their hand in your pocket most of the time. I have only found one reasonably honest one and they charge too much money for insignificant paperwork but at least they don't telephone collect (when they telephone at all) on a 50¢ call from Los Angeles. Your factory will have its own shipping program like as not and so does Auto Europe; it doesn't hurt to call them as well as other makers' representatives to compare prices. Some ports are pure death to ship from (especially London and the Mediterranean ones) and some lines, euphemistically called "conference" lines and offered enthusiastically by the big travel agencies, cost almost twice as much as the others. It is worth shopping around and even leaving your car at Antwerp, one of the Dutch ports, or even Hamburg, for a cheap shot. Shop around. Ask questions of people who have just shipped a car back. And at the other end if you will go down and clear the car off the boat and through customs yourself I guarantee that you will save at least a quarter of the price you would pay if you let the agents handle that. And insure it down to the last scratch. Dockland is traditionally rotten to the core with wholesale crookery and they really like to stick it to car owners.

Car Ferries

THESE WILL not bother you too much unless you are in England, which I will treat in a moment. If you are going to Scandinavia (which includes Finland), there are nice clean ones that run from various points on the Danish Jutland peninsula, Kobenhavn, Nyborg, the island of Fehmarn (unless the Little Belt bridge is finished), plus longer ones to Trelleborg and Finland from Grossenbrode in Germany near Kiel. Check at Thomas Cook & Sons or Amexco for schedules and book ahead in summer as they get full up. For Greece there is frequent service from several Italian ports; the one we tried, which was very nice, was the Brindisi-Patras one which also can start at Venice. A friend did the Naples-Haifa run on the Somerfin Line "Bilu," I think, and found it good value even if Israel isn't really Europe. There are so-so car ferries to Corsica and Sardinia, I think, but don't waste your money; fly. If you are going to Sicily, take the Kanguru Blu line from Naples and not the other one, state run, which is really a bad value. Seems to me there is a car-carrying boat to Majorca but I can't seem to find out about it.

From England, as you would expect, ferries run to practically everywhere from Sweden to Spain—and they are all booked solid in late July-August when school holidays are on. For straight cross-channel work I prefer BUA's ancient Bristol air freighters (Lydd or Southend to Le Touquet, Ostend, or Calais; longer ones go to Amsterdam and Geneva) if a bit more expensive as you don't ponce around all day getting on, getting off, queuing for passports, tea, and so forth besides being inundated with small children. We tried the Southampton-Le Havre run on one of the Thoreson ferries; nice clean Swedish boat and not filthy dirty, rusty, and scaly like the British ones. British Rail now has a cross-Channel hovercraft but just take it as a lark as it doesn't run when the waves get high. And we know about English Channel weather, don't we? You can also take ferries to Ireland but they are pretty grim. I recommend writing to *Car* magazine (21 Ebury St, London SW 1, England) for a back copy that had their car ferry rundown. And don't forget to book well ahead.

Mountain Passes

THE WORST ones like the St Bernard have a road tunnel through or, at the very worst, a train with flatcars for automobiles. Don't ask at the station if the pass is open; naturally they want your money. There will be a notice down below. Actually they are great fun (if you remember to come down in the gear you went up in) and provide a nice cool place to take a picnic. The dates of usual opening and closing are in the Michelins. Watch out for Germans who stop in the middle of the road with all doors open to take photos. *Ah, ist schon der Blick!* Not to worry, keep charging in a low enough gear and if you hit snow, keep on the sides where the grip is and keep moving. Mind the postbuses in Switzerland; they have right of way.

AT LARGE

WITH HENRY MANNEY

O NE OF THE greater benefits of our breaking loose from the thralldom of the Victorian age is a more relaxed relationship with the opposite sex. As recently as in Mary Roberts Rinehart's novels it just wasn't the done thing to address a young lady by her first name unless you were her fiance, even if the two of you were bound to a railroad track waiting for the 12:05 R.F. and P. express. This attitude wasn't entirely due to the influence of the nutty religious sects that pioneered our country as they were pretty square in England too; it isn't generally known that Wm. Penn of Pennsylvania fame was very much an early hippie much to the disgust of his father, a full Admiral and boss of the King's Navee, and came to this country after a visit to Holland largely to avoid a sojourn in the Tower. Nowadays of course the young ladies are wearing the sort of costume on the street that we used to see Wilma sporting in science fiction movies, one often doesn't know if they have a family name, and a trip down the beach will show you bikinis brief enough to have provoked a raid at the Gayety theater of sainted memory. In a way this is very nice even for younger folk as instead of a thrilling glimpse of an ankle as a guess at what sort of chassis your intended had, you can actually count the dimples. I suppose that bikinis would be bad from the girls' viewpoint as the acres of fat backsides and tires round the middle might scare somebody off but then love is blind, they say. I was once very sweet on a girl who was as straight as a hop-pole but then I ain't any prize either.

All this came up after a conversation with a good grey friend while we were discussing the ads in one of the local underground newspapers. Those happy souls having some odd kink can place an advert couched in suitable language like young swinging couple wishes to meet couple having similar views, young man wishes to meet older gent for

Our friend.

tutoring in French and Greek, strapping young girl with high boots wishes to leave mark on suitable man, or even docile young chap with full wardrobe wishes to act as French maid to severe dominant lady. All very well but as friend observed, half of the ads would probably be answered by members of the LAPD or at worst, you really would get some earnest Central European pedagogue with pebble glasses and frayed cuffs ready to teach you Greek. As for the last one, it might be one way out of the servant problem even if it did involve getting into full drag yourself and putting up with some fruit in high heels and frill cap mincing about the house. These ads are a bit tragic, really, as most of them (not counting the ones inserted by the Editor for amusement value) are probably handed in by married men who have found that True Love as exemplified by Hollywood flicks and steamy romances simply hasn't worked out. After several years of the Great American Grizzly Bear treatment from their wives ("If I lie very still maybe he'll go away") they figure that they're not getting any younger and why not take a chance.

At any rate it was in a conversation with another friend (yes, Virginia, I have two friends) that I thought of taking an ad to read "Presentable if somewhat hairy gent wishes someone skillful to fix Mustang. Somewhere there must be a man who will do it right the first time." Friend was going on about all the foreign cars he had tried including Mercedes, MGs, Porsches, and so forth, saying that he had definitely had it with them and now owned two Fords and a Chevy Nova or something similar. This guy is of an old moneyed family, wears really good shirts of conventional cut and color because he doesn't have to be flashy, and has fric enough to fly Momo in from New York if he wants . . . in fact I think he said that he bought a foreign car agency at one point just so he could have some hope of keeping his bolide running. Apparently it didn't work out as not only was the service manager a bigger villain than Edward Teach and incompetent besides but the West Coast distributor made Sven Forkbeard look like a Salvation Army major. Monkey business like this has cut the sales of several good makes down to a fraction of what they could be and whether you like Volkswagens or not as a car, you have got to applaud the business sense of Wolfsburg in seeing that they had to play the game properly. After all the VW had several glaring defects (and still does, come to that) besides being manufactured by a country that was recently shooting at us; lots of money had to be spent getting the parts over and policing dealerships to give the customer a fair shake and as a result, a VW dealership is a license to print money. I have told all this to the bosses of various other European manufacturers from time to time and all I get is polite noises. Of course some of them are still laying eggs, too. As Afferbeck Lauder says, aorta be a crime to take the public's wages for sutthin's not right.

Neglecting to explore for the moment the sort of abnormal psychology that possesses men to buy a certain marque when they know the dealer is bent, what got my dander up was my friend's bland assumption that simply buying a domestic car meant that your motoring days henceforth would be trouble-free. Of course after listening (1) to the oddities and derangements his cars had suffered, (2) to his avowal that his present bangers had "never been near a garage," I am inclined to think that he is one of those mechanically insensitive types who never can tell how a car is running until something actually breaks. Just owning nice equipment doesn't mean that one can feel the moods of an automobile any more than owning a Strad qualifies you to play any better than B. Kubelsky. There are Grand Prix drivers like that. Anyway, his difference in repair records can be attributed not only to the fact that a 300 SL asks to be driven hard but also that it makes an expensive noise if overrevved; I seriously doubt whether you could do much damage to an automatic Nova by holding it flat out in second, assuming that anyone would

CONTINUED ON PAGE 71

69

THOSE OF YOU possessing more than one means of transportation (not counting the trolley of course) are undoubtedly familiar with the sub-heading of Murphy's Law providing that sheer numbers of vehicles owned is no guarantee against being stranded. A friend of mine who owned four motorbikes and five cars found himself one day with none of them running and the predicament was made more poignant when he fell off his daughter's fairy-cycle while shagging parts and skinned his knee. And all his machines weren't old junk either; most were in a state of disassembly because he was one of these chaps who always wants to restore an old MG TD to original running shape, not that they were anything special at that time anyway, and thus has entrails spread all over the garage. I often wonder if Briggs Cunningham ever finds himself with no wheels to go home from the museum in and has to cadge a ride from one of the mechanics.

Things were almost that bad *chez nous* as the battery gave up on the boat, the boys fiended the gearbox on the Yamaha, and the trusty Fiat 600 about whom we spoke several months ago finally was struck seriously ill as a result of carrying several overweight teenagers with not enough water in it. Trying to start it the next morning resulted in a sort of iffy-plut, iffy-plut noise and removal of No. 1 plug revealed a nicely rusted electrode. We had had a few indications as it was running rather like most of the field at 3:00 p.m. at Le Mans and coming down the hill the other day, there had been a horrid noise like a half gallon milk carton breaking the sonic barrier followed by a smell like a Turkish bath as the bottom water hose blew. So out came the tools and the head came off, not an onerous process as the whole affair can be carried out sitting on an empty Bordeaux case, revealing a neat passage carved in the head between the first and second combustion chambers.

Now in the prehistoric past this Fiat must have had a very checkered career, including, I am sure, at least one thorough hop-up somewhere over the limit followed inevitably by a succession of cooling problems. With every blown head gasket something must have been planed off, in fact we did it twice ourselves, and another skimming would have resulted in the first Heron-headed 600 on record. In fact, if the bottom end would have stood it we probably could have taken out the plugs and run it on Diesel fuel as close measurement with a new head that a friend had put by showed a difference in combustion-chamber depth of something like 5 mm. Accordingly we decided to go back to Square One to do the job properly and, collecting a new set of odd bits like valves from friend, set to work. Now I am not really a mechanic and progress was complicated by the fact that the old head, from which we were to get sundry other items, had been modified from time to time as various studs pulled out due to helicoils ceasing to hold and were replaced with bigger American ones. Also numerous new parts found necessary often turned out to be tipo 850 Fiat requiring a small bit of adjustment here and there. Fortunately I didn't break anything off flush but there were a few cases where I got a stud of the wrong thread in the wrong hole and had to leave it there, making up to space with an odd nut. The biggest battle was with the rocker shaft which apparently is fractionally different and made the rockers bind a bit; the rocker-stand hold down studs also leaked water a tad when we took the rockers off for retorquing but Permatex took care of that. A last minute drama came when the Fiat 600 distributor turned out to be too big to fit in the head but descending to Coarse Bodging, I filed it down to fit. The rest of the engine must be pretty tired as well but peculiarly enough it doesn't use any oil, not near as much as the transaxle unit anyway. Our Mr. Wakefield suggested that perhaps the transaxle unit was keeping the sump topped up (our own little office sunbeam) so that will be the next to get done, especially since it is getting almost as loud as that on a Milan Multipla minicab. Following the instructions of both the Fiat head office

and Commonwealth Imports agents nearby, I will fill it with antifreeze as soon as we have stopped all the leaks but partially due to the new head and partially due to having 4 lb of boiler scale removed from the radiator, the 600 now runs cool and goes like a bomb. There *is* joy in Mudville.

You may well ask why we bother with an underpowered old banger which only cost me $75 in the first place when there are those marvellous new cars to be had. The main reason is that it is fun to drive, offering a palliative to the dumb series of stop lights and right-angle bends around here, and besides that is part of the family. Additionally we know what is still wrong with it, an assurance lacking in a new car in these days of nonexistent quality control. You can put up with a lot of little bothers with a $75 car which would be unbearable in a $3200 lemon, especially one which dropped a quarter of its value the moment you drove out of the showroom.

In another part of the forest an insurance gentleman has written complaining about a bit of plain speaking. Insurance is very much on my mind on the moment as in spite of our dealing with the only company who has ever acted to us in a really correct fashion, the premiums have gotten to the state where one hesitates to buy a certain car or motorbike simply because the insurance will cost too much money. This is in spite of a clean record and no shunts since a drunken Frenchman backed into us five or six years ago. However the concern is for a lady friend of ours who moved out here a couple of years ago and bought a small white sports car. As she is Norwegian and the cops in Norway are old-fashioned, she didn't realize that a good-looking blonde

Our friend.

MANNEY AT LARGE

CONTINUED FROM PAGE 70

driving a small sports car is fair bait for every cruising squad car in Southern California. And as she is not interested in chatting up the fuzz, she soon had a ticket or two for speeding and suchlike. Disregarding the other ramifications of these matters for the moment, she has been thundered by her insurance company by a premium hike which may mean that she will have to sell the car . . . a sad business as she drives a considerable distance to work *chez* her doctor. The insurance officials cry real tears across their new teak desks and tell us that they are losing money. Piffle! Many of these companies are making money hand over fist by cancelling anyone out who has the misfortune to be in an accident, thus reducing their policyholders to those who pay in lots of money and never take any out. Not only that, they are taking the function of the judiciary upon themselves by adding their penalty to that imposed by the cash-register police departments when a ticket is handed out. The answer to that, they say, is not to get tickets but tickets are big business to the State of California as well as many others. There was a story in the paper recently about how the San Diego coppers went on strike and gave out only some 35 tickets a day; needless to say this caused great panic in the city government as the normal income from tickets there is $7000 to $10,000 a *day*. And you wonder why you get busted?

Getting back to insurance for the moment, of course they run a risk on losses like the Titanic as well as drunken drivers, compulsive red-light shooters, and the ever-loving teenager showing off his 440-cu-in. dragster on the street; obviously police matters which should be sorted out by license suspension. The vast body of motorists would be better off under a nationalized insurance company run by the government, a suggestion which pops up now and again in England where the abuses are even greater than here. Drivers would be assessed a certain minimum figure according to the way they drove, not what age they were, what town they lived in, or whether they happened to cross Ludowici, Georgia on the way to work. Accidents and/or tickets are a police matter, not a case of double jeopardy, and rates couldn't help but be lower without the vast sums spent via television to persuade (or frighten) you that friendly smiling man is really going to make things right when something nasty happens. Accidents after all are accidents; nobody in his right mind goes looking for them. ◉

MANNEY AT LARGE

CONTINUED FROM PAGE 54

tury methods. I am sorry to see them go as they made *nice* automobiles; it isn't profitable to do that any more for a reasonable price but at least it stays Italian.

Showwise the show was the same as when I last left too with the same warty old bat guarding the toilets and the bodywork exhibits stuffed down in the cave. Probably I am getting old but it seemed like a bad year to me with trickery reigning for trickery's sake. Ghia was bleagh except for a Lancia with Rover nose, Vignale more so with one car even sporting Buick portholes, Zagato with one of the many dune buggies (including a Volga personnel carrier!) bleagh, and usually tasteful Bertone went up the wall with a vile green BMW and odd metalescent 128. Pininfarina hasn't really recovered from the sad loss of Ing. Colombo and looks it. Actually the semi-production or pure production stuff was the best for a change; the new little Zagato 1300 Giulietta coupe was as pretty as anything I have seen in a while. Of course I am contradicting myself as things like that chez Alfa have a habit of not appearing. Immediate customers with money in the hand had better plump for the Fiat 124 coupe which now may be had with 125 engine and gearbox or maybe the latest Dino, more about which will appear in due course.

Ummmmm trendishly speaking everybody seems to be going full blat on the small level with fwd Mini copies and a little bigger up station wagon copies including the latest Renault 12. This year also brought forth many more applicants in the ugly stakes such as Skoda and the DAF 55 but the new champion for my money is the VW-Porsche roadster. Of all the slab-sided motorized ashtrays!! But then a lot of people will find, like the original Beetle (no beauty contest winner either) that it looks better in the tin.

Naturally I could go on for days but that is Cyril's bag. In any case Watch This Space for more news about Travel, Food, Wine, A Hoft of Pekuliare Carriagef, Gossip (how the Rover works fire engine stopped on its own hose), and more Opinionated comment. Win! Call me a twit in four words or less (Citroen employees not included) and win a used Paris metro ticket. But watch this space. ◉

CONTINUED FROM PAGE 69

be daft enough to stand all the noise.

After asking around a good deal to supplement my own experience, the impression is that it isn't any easier to get a domestic car fixed than a foreign one and may well be harder. This is especially true if you have something fancy like one of the big hairy Camaros as not only is the agency liable to make a bodge of working on it, but it is liable to have its valves bounced while being trundled around the back lot by the parts boy. The owner of one I knew got tired of being b****d about and bought a BMW. Similar reports come in from various acquaintances and coupled with the automobile sections of *Consumer Reports,* it paints a pretty black picture. I must admit that I thought the foreign car picture would be a bit dodgy over here when I returned but if you ask practically any owner of a domestic car whether he is satisfied with his dealer or not and you get a slow shaking of the head, at very least. A case in point is our family Mustang which is a shopping-wagen, a going-to-school-wagen, and occasionally a trip-to-L.A.-wagen since the Fiat 600 doesn't like to go that far. It isn't a lemon, we haven't been stranded anyplace, but the blasted machine has never been right. The original 2-throat carb was replaced by a Holley of similar format so that it wouldn't blow out the fire on every corner, the transmission has always made numbing noises loud enough to warrant turning up the radio, the plug wires were replaced early on in an effort to get it to run on something more than 7½, the original wide ovals fouled the fender and cut themselves, and the differential grinds away like a coffee mill. I won't go into my adventures with a local Ford dealer as they might be libellous but suffice it to say that there have been perhaps two kind words said about his service department, which apparently works on commission, and very many bad ones. Accordingly I went to another Ford dealership in a neighboring town who seems honest and cheerful enough but the work all needs doing over! A fancy scope tuning job produced some of the oddest symptoms I have ever seen, a rusty wheel bearing was replaced still leaving the rust in the spindle housing, and while back axle carrier bearings were done on guarantee happily enough, the growl remains. Wottermeantersay is, the 1967 Mustang Milquetoast 289 V-8 is a pretty simple piece of machinery really. If the Ford agencies either can't or won't bother to keep something like that right, making a nonsense out of the easy-to-fix ad routine, what hope is there for more complicated domestic cars? Anybody know where I can get a clean 1954 Plymouth six wagon? ◉

AT LARGE

WITH HENRY MANNEY

WHEN WE WERE young and beset with the Scylla and Charybdis of Parents and School the only thing that kept us resilient, really, was the happy pursuit of daydreams in which we became Frank Merriwell/King Kong/Babe Ruth/Sulyaman the Magnificent or perhaps even the lucky chap who had a date with Pagey Carrington in her satin evening gown for the dance. It seems as time goes on these turn over into proper or nighttime dreams and just to digress a moment, I find that the more interesting ones, as distinct from another-five-minutes-in-the-rack fits, appear in full color. There seems to be some subdivision relating to profession as many old ballet dancers, for example, dream uneasily of losing their toe shoes or makeup or costumes at a critical moment when they are due to be On. Although I am not really a theatrical person, I had a pip the other night in which I was clearly due to be On but couldn't find a straw skimmer which was an essential part of the props. The dressing room was deserted, the overture was almost through playing, and that blasted hat was no place to be seen. As I grabbed a replica of an old hat which my wife used to have many years ago in Switzerland and shot towards the wings, I remember realizing that I was supposed to be doing the lead and was late already. Casually strolling onto the stage and enduring a venomous glance from the female lead who was delivering her lines from upstage right, I propped myself up against the piano in what I hoped to be the right attitude and was struck by the thoughts that (1) my fly was possibly open (2) I had on the wrong hat of course (3) I didn't know the songs, much less all the stage business in between, and was sure to make a huge mess of it. Muttering aw rats, I turned my back on the hopefully scanty audience and was immediately exposed to the view of a row of startled ladies in full Sylphides rig. What the audience thought of a gent in straw hat and striped blazer in the first scene of Sylphides I will never know for at the thought of doing the Mazurka Champ in that outfit I woke up.

Actually this sort of thing does happen, y'know. A friend of mine from upstate New York once auditioned for a touring opera company there and as he has a fine bass voice, was hired on the spot. Put on your makeup, the manager said, and you will go on in an hour as the King in Aida. All very well as my friend knew the part but having learned it from the libretto, and never actually having seen Aida, he was in the dark as to what really went on. So the music was playing and people were singing and nothing sounded awfully familiar and here he was standing in the wings like a berk covered with No. 3 pancake, ill-fitting garments, and crêpe hair. The manager suddenly appeared during a quiet bit and intimated that he was supposed to appear from the other side (where a dim group was forming) whereupon the painful confession was made. Sundry words like *Cretino* were bandied back and forth and then the resourceful manager picked out a likely and experienced slave girl, attached her to him with a chain, and deputized her to lead him about and hiss instructions at the proper moments. Actually the event came off all right as the slave girl knew the opera better than Verdi himself but he said that he kept pinching himself hoping to wake up and never did.

All this was probably jogged into life by too many years of rushing off to races while hoping to remember press passes, cameras, film, umbrella and so forth but listening to the steam radio broadcast of Indianapolis helps. There always seems to be some unfortunate figure whose car craps out on the pace lap, has some important suspension bit come off, or slides on a hitherto unsuspected dribble of oil and smacks the wall. It passeth all understanding how professionals, with a whole perishing year to prepare for the one race, can't make the blasted thing run for five minutes but I suppose that the whole thing can either be laid down to Last Minute Demon Tweaks (to which some of our better known drivers are regrettably addicted) or too much division of labor. Having known many mechanics I would say that they were all equally dedicated but when the areas of operation are not clearly defined or there is a last minute flap, such as a brand new engine showing no oil pressure at midnight before the race, details sometimes do get left out. It has always been a mystery to me how any of the cars run as long as they do but that proposition taken, there is no reason really (if you discount a driver to whom instruments are only decoration) why all the cars shouldn't at least carry on for 20 laps or so.

A nightmare almost as horrible is the last moment aberration that loses the race; "almost" as at least the driver has

CONTINUED ON PAGE 74

Our friend.

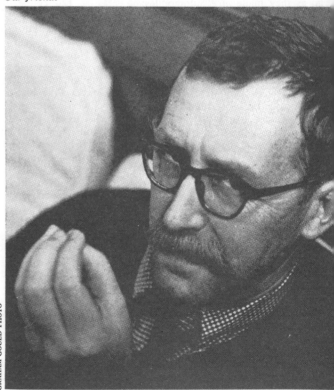

GRAHAM GOULD PHOTO

72

AT LARGE

WITH HENRY MANNEY

I HAVE RECENTLY been reading a most illuminating book entitled *Kitsch: The World of Bad Taste* by one Gillo Dorfles. There are those among you who will say that I have no need to read about bad taste as I invented it but it appears that Kitsch has been going on much longer than that. Without going into involved definitions, it appears that kitsch can be translated by Schmaltz (in the non-culinary sense), Cornball, or even Ingenuous. A rough guide is to look for something regarded as really arty by the generation or generations immediately preceding your own, thus providing you with that delicious feeling of instant superiority. The well known human being Ursula Bagel brought this truth to light some years ago by stating that her mother had a Kitsch Collection, pointing as proof to a framed color litho of the famed scenic Rhine S-bend complete with castles, etc., and tastefully decorated with silver sequins. Souvenir shops abound in this sort of rubbish although such a pure example is getting hard to find, due to the high labor costs involved in applying sequins. I have a few examples of this genre including a bottled statue of Jeanne d'Arc with water and imitation snowflakes, Dave Fairchild almost bought mama (the shop was shut) a Dutch wooden shoe tricked out with sails, little men, and wired as a lamp, while one of the best was a naked shrub complete with two koala bears and "Souvenir of Villars, Switzerland" on the base.

The writer Ludwig Giesz states that the epithet "kitsch-mensch" or kitsch-man should be applied to those who have an attraction for this sort of thing but I think he is referring to those who really think it is the cat's pajamas, to use a kitsch expression. They really adore Kitschschloss Disney-land, any Doris Day movie, and satin pillowcases with "Mother" stencilled thereon in multicolored flocking. Southern California is a paradise for Kitschmenschen as a look at our harbor on Sunday will show; long-suffering Monterey shrimpers are decked out with wet bars and striped awnings, five bods in a 14-ft outboard skiff will all be wearing yachting caps, and the names of the boats themselves like Fish Killer 2, Chug-a-Lug, Fight On, or Yakydak illustrate the kitschness of the owners. They are serious. On the other hand you could also call the owners of the small sailboats named Chicken of the Sea, Queen Mary, or Titanic as Kitschmenschen but with a difference. They, and we of course (of course!) are on the outside looking in. We are the ones who buy a ghastly Victorian lamp to give to a modern friend, we are the ones who covet an elk-antler hatrack for the front hall, we are the ones who buy some lurid King Kong poster to put in the terlet. But do we subconsciously crave the stuff for its Kitschness or because sometime in our deep dark past we saw one like that and always wanted it; before we became fraffly cultured I mean?

In this house we draw the line at satin pillowcases but why be ashamed of the rest of it. Bach and Mozart become pretty twiddly at times while Bellini or Donizetti (or come to that most operas) are as kitschy as you can get. A series of soprano trills echoed by a flute, resoundingly bellowed by a solid lady with 54-in. bust and not much less than that waist. Come now. The august *Road & Track* itself is not innocent as the spectacle of a bunch of grown men occupying themselves with grown-up toys (with the utmost seriousness) is pretty hard to take, even if the ones out zizzing around on the track with them are worse. I am sure that all of you know some fine examples of kitsch (examples gratefully received) and I am also sure that the world of automobiles has provided an inexhaustible mine of material, especially in the advertising sections. The sight of a regal couple in evening dress mooning over some dumb, cheapo, Detroit iron has without fail caused me to roll on the floor in convulsions. And the copy! Advertising as a whole is almost completely Kitsch and it is a sobering thought that either (1) the originators are really true Kitschmenschen or (2) they are smart enough to realize that most of the buying public lean in that direction. My wife growls at me because I sit in bed, reading a magazine like *Holiday* or *The New Yorker,* and snort about the ads so it may be that I am in the minor-

Our friend.

PHOTOS BY P. NO. 2 SON MANNEY

ity. Besides, she doesn't like my wearing my Napoleon hat to sleep in.

Body design is another fertile source of material. Cars that look like salmon, cars that look like rocket ships, cars sporting mags and spoilers and racing stripes and high-overlap cams that never stir off the boulevard. All pure kitsch. The champion Kitschwagen is of course the late lamented Edsel, all the way from its vast pubrel campaign to choose a name already chosen, through the careful styling, a careful mixture of subconscious libido-ticklers with a leavening of something-for-everybody. The rejection of this tin orgasm by the American public rates (with the Boston Tea Party and the repeal of the Volstead Act) as a high-water mark of the innate good sense of American civilization. I only hope that that innate good sense has not been overwhelmed by the barrage of trash hurled at us via television but there are signs that it still lives. A case in point is all the kitsch commercials put forward by gasoline refineries including hula girls on tropic islands (what in Tophet has some Chinese bint to do with gasoline?) or more recently, celebrated astronauts backed by suitable scientific noises. Yet another company comes on with aviaries of twittering birds, working the clean-air bit for all it is worth, while yet another spends millions to show you that not only can your little girl use the john for free, but that you actually are doing the atmosphere a disservice by not using their gas. They don't say buying, they say using. They also don't say that they are not only polluting God's blue sea with their leaky oil wells but that they are pulling strings in Washington as strongly as possible to get leave to drill many more. Where the good sense of the Peepul comes in is apparently that sales of the new lead-free gasolines produced (under some pressure) by all these fine ecology-minded gentry is quite a bit below expectations. Whether this is because their specious arguments are rejected as the worst sort of kitsch (in this case, plain bad taste) or because these special mixes seem to be more expensive than the "old" regular is not yet clear. At any rate, if the refining companies were really interested in cleaner air instead of a fast buck they would not only clean up the premium (after all, how many modern cars use regular?) but make it economically desirable for the customer as well . . . in other words, put the price below that of leaded gasoline. For myself, I avoid these guys like the plague, pocketing the difference. Flatly refusing to buy their product is the only way to bring these types around.

I got a letter the other day which should answer part of my heartfelt query on where to go to get things done properly. Perhaps some of you remember our jolly test of a Lotus 23 at Brands back in those happy days, the process being presided over by an anxious Peter Arundell. The chief mechanic on that caper (the car went on to win quite a few races in spite of my attentions) was Steele Therkleson, a gent who also went on to bigger things with practically every racing team you could mention. He eventually wound up with Shelby-Ford and watched over the fortunes of the successful Cobra Coupes as well as the J-cars at Le Mans. Space does not permit a recital of his qualifications but he has recently opened a machine shop at 338 A Carson St., Carson, California (part of the Los Angeles agglomerate sprawl), called Racing Services West. After doing first-quality work with hand-file and chisel in an inky-black Reims garage he should be able to do wonders with a proper lathe. Needless to say he is also keen on proper racing tuning so if you are suffering a series of mysterious Big Bangs, why not drop over to see him? Maybe yours will be the first dollar in that frame on the wall.

On another subject, perhaps some reader can answer a question. The family 600 Fiat has bit the dust again, this time because the water pump commenced suffering Garibaldi's Revenge from both ends, exhausting my high-priced anti-freeze into the street. An autopsy revealed that the seals were foutu but also that the impeller (apparently cast iron) and the shaft (steel) were pretty well eaten away, not to mention parts of the alloy housing. Now I am aware of the problems concomitant with using dissimilar metals in sea water but to my knowledge the Fiat has never been cooled with sea water; the damage, however, looks very much like that produced by electrolytic action. Now Fiats run all over Europe and to my knowledge they don't have much of this sort of trouble. Is the water out here really that poisonous through State-added chemicals or is this some problem stirred up by non-standard components, such as wiring changes, for the American market? In the meantime my old GTO has been taken to H'wood Sports Cars' Ferrari department where Gene Curtis has promised to see that it gets its first good tune since 1965 or thereabouts. It says a lot for the inbuilt sturdiness of these machines that the Marchal plugs had been in situ since that time and yet it started and ran without too much fuss. Furthermore, a 3-year-old battery would suffer layoffs as long as a month at a time and still spin it. Every automobile designer should drive a Ferrari GTO; not for the suspension which is Early Brick Lorry at low speeds but for the lovely gearbox. It is really nice to have the lever directly connected to the gear-bone in these days of macaroni linkage padded out with plastic sponge to protect Moddom's pinkies from pernicious vibration. That's why we keep it, I suppose. Real class.

74

MANNEY AT LARGE
CONTINUED FROM PAGE 72

looked good for a while. We all watched the Monaco GP on television with more than usual interest as Monaco is one of our favorite races and we photographers have recently been be-deviled with a full-dress appearance of numerous TV cameramen, helicopters, and the like. In short, we wanted to see if the bother they caused was worth the trouble and the answer is, of course, that it ain't. If the amateur commentating had let Phil Hill get on with the job and call the race we might have had more idea of what the backmarkers were doing, what cars they were driving and perhaps even seen some of the scraps going on. Especially thorough, however, was the coverage at the end of the Brabham-Rindt scrap and we all agreed with Phil that Rindt's getting by Black Jack, even with the Brabham's obviously being ill, was as unlikely as the Pope marrying Sophia Loren. Jack is a kind fellow and makes a good cup of tea but his car has infinitely extensible wheels as some of the finest drivers of our time have learned. Consequently we were completely flabbergasted when Blackie went straight on at the Gasworks, letting the young and talented Austrian (who learnt a good deal from Jack, you can be sure) through to win. This set up a good deal of discussion before we learned that his brakes were dodgy and one side had locked on; I thought that Jack saw Rindt going round the outside and was going to use him for brakes (and missed), my wife thought that the cars being lapped put him off his line and thus onto the marbles which abound off-line, Dave thought that he had gotten extremely tired and blacked out for a moment, while my daughter thought that Jack was just being noble. At any rate I am sure that poor Jack, who deserves to win any time he goes out, gave himself a good hard pinch in between Antipodean remarks to make sure that it wasn't a bad dream. And what a gracious second place man! A real gent.

A difficult paragraph at the end about Bruce McLaren and Piers Courage. We try to be rather matter of fact in our reports about drivers being killed to disguise our real feelings about them. We know them, we work with and sometimes against them, we say things that they would rather not have had said but underneath it all they are part of our family. Every one that goes while doing what he likes best leaves a gap unfilled by recollections of their smiles, their jokes, images of them intent over a recalcitrant car. If it is God's will that they go, then go they must but we will surely miss such fine, brave men.

AT LARGE

WITH HENRY MANNEY

WE WERE LISTENING to the baseball game on the steam radio tonight when the name of Roland Fingers, an Oakland pitcher, came up in the box scores. The English language is a funny creature and names, derived as they are from various sources, are even funnier. I have always wondered just where "Fingers" as a surname came from, what was its Old World equivalent, and how much better it would sound, even if a little George-Raft-movieish, if it were the other way around. Fingers Roland really says something, joining the ranks of figures of our time like Little Farfel, Paul the Waiter, Willie the Actor, and so forth. This is not to say that the estimable Mr. Fingers should be lumped with the above gentlemen, oh no, even if he does wear white kangaroo shoes to work, but it shows how combinations of syllables do form an impression.

Racing used to be better provided with colorful names than it is now even though the dirt-track lads (viz Porky Rachwitz) give what help they can. Today's drivers are a pretty sober bunch and practically nobody calls Jack Brabham "Blackie" to his face or Colin Chapman "Chunky," unless he wants a punch in the hooter. Intimates use "Tatty Atty," "Chrissie" or "Porridge" but you don't see these emblazoned all over racing posters more's the pity. Think how much more colorful it would be if you were promised Fearless Foyt, Burrito Rodriguez, Crasher Ickx, Slider Surtees, Lover-Boy Ireland, Racer Regazzoni, Jack the Black Brabham, Hunter Hulme, Cannon Cannon, Ripper Rindt, and Garibaldi Andretti, the Idol of the Banks. Stories would be written by Admiral Garnier, Bomber Smith, Collision-Mat Jenkinson, and Jimbo Crow while photos are snapped by Cards Biro, Mini-Bike Brady, Tortellini Tronolone, and Flasher Long. The oft-ignored Press could even be announced beforehand (if it could be winkled out of the bar) to cheers and tipping of hats even as other exalted folk. After all they go through quite as much mental strain as the drivers. You try covering Le Mans sometime.

The car manufacturers, fortunately, have fairly well scraped the barrel in an attempt to personalize what is really a mass-produced lump of iron little different from an icebox. There are Maverick Grabbers (kitsch!), Vegas, Mustangs, Stags, Lynxes, Hornets, Road Runners, Rockets, and Wyverns, all through the animal, celestial, and mythological kingdom. I really don't know if the chap driving a Wyvern, say, feels any more like one of King Arthur's Court while pootling down the A 20 to Dover than he would if the car was called, say, Herman. After all, there must have been a knight named Herman. And come to that, Vauxhall would have made more sales to people named Herman than they would to people named Wyvern. Consequently it wouldn't be a bad idea at all for General Motors, say, to name each one of its numerous options after some person rather in the fashion of hurricanes. This would have certain complications in the shape of angry letters from young ladies wanting to know why, in the name of Women's Lib, the Chevrolet Ronald had just a little more chrome trim than the Chevrolet Dorothy but this could be worked out by having all the ladies-named models flossier while the gents-named models

were replete with carbs, disc brakes, and limited slip diffs. You would have to be careful, naturally, to avoid the tendency of naming a rather fine example after some public figure lest the figure, and thus the car, should lay a large egg just after introduction. The Lincoln Spiro, for example, might share the fate of the Edsel, the Denny McLain Oldsmobile's sales would rise and fall with his E.R.A., while the Cadillac called after some father-figure of the entertainment world might suffer when the news broke that he was keeping a stable of fifteen-year-old girls in his garden shed. Or then again it might not. Color, as well, would be a source of awkward moments as a certain southern governor (who certainly deserves a car named after him) might object to some of the proposed shades. Then there would be the horrible prospect of election year! Can you imagine a manufacturer, promised all sorts of lucrative contracts by a hopeful party, naming all its range after local politicians? Perhaps we had better stick to food. What about a ride in my Fiat Fettucine?

There has been a lot of hoo ha in the papers around here recently about the California Republic wishing to run a freeway slap through the middle of Newport Beach and the citizens thereof not necessarily wishing it to be there. Large numbers of names were signed to a petition and a local representative presented this as support for a Bill to delete said freeway. As one might guess, the State legislature deleted the Bill instead which is par for the California Republic. As a sign of the times, I suppose, the projected freeway really doesn't go anywhere (as most of the arterial traffic is carried by the San Diego Freeway) but is designed, apparently, to enable fresh Legions of the Great Unwashed to come down to the area on weekends. It goes without saying that the area is extremely full of residents, already a fair number of whom are going to be evicted, have their view spoiled, or otherwise b***d about by said freeway. Since a large percentage of the L.G.U. already go to the beaches north and south of this town, one asks if the freeway is really necessary.

Nevertheless the State governments move in peculiar ways. Sort of like the Army; once they have decided that all the coal will be whitewashed for General Soandso's visit, you will go on whitewashing even though it is well known that Gen. Soandso has decided to go fish/ on an important conference instead.

Our Friend.

We first started to get an odd feeling about this when we saw men with their transits where men with transits shouldn't be and then later, when the freeway recall measure was being bruited about, bands of little official men in their little floppy short-sleeved shirts standing around our traffic lights with stopwatches and clipboards. Now clipboards, of course, have replaced the top hat as the badge of Gov't. Anyway, there was a fresh burst of publicity about the freeway recall

SCULPTURED FROM LIFE BY LHO BESTGEN

CONTINUED ON PAGE 77

AT LARGE

WITH HENRY MANNEY

THOSE FEW READERS who have been with us longer than a year may remember our adventures in behalf of Kawasaki on the good ship "Marqueda." Recently we got a simpering note from Kawasaki's Mr. Collins relating that they had been giving the captain of that retired blackbirder flying lessons and he was now ready to take us off on a mystery tour. The instructions had progressed swimmingly, Mr. Collins went on, and it only remained to perfect his landings.

Being fatalists at heart (it couldn't possibly be as dodgy as last time!) we thereupon appeared in due course at the strangely named Hollywood-Burbank airport which is, of course, on the side of Burbank *away* from Hollywood. Our promised Great Silver Bird elicited mutters about whitey speaking with forked tongue when we saw it as there were big enough puddles on the tarmac under the engines to give my Fiat an oil change, the props bore scars from taking off through yucca bushes, and there was enough topsoil affixed to the gleaming aluminum body to preserve footprints as far back as Orville & Wilbur. Inside a new patch betrayed the spot where a potbellied stove (and its flue) had been removed, the terlet featured a pre-plastic cedar bucket (thank *you*, Nat Herreshoff) and tasteful notices enjoined the passengers not to shoot Indians from the windows. We were clearly part of a Vintage Happening.

After a takeoff run timed at 14 Our Fathers and 6 Hail Marys, this device lifted itself shudderingly into the upper levels of smog and commenced to flap its way toward Arizona. There was no need for inflight movies (even Pearl White) as window-seat occupants were fully engaged in timing the progress of a trail of oil at so many rivets/minute when they were not wondering if the statute of limitations of metal fatigue had been exceeded. In fact, this flying machine was so ancient that a depiction of the constellations on the ceiling showed the preceding Pole Star to the one we use now. However the somewhat matronly chief stewardess was equal to the occasion, freely passing out nerve medicine to those who required it with the aid of her charming if slightly beamy assistant.

Someplace over the Colorado River we finally got shed of Los Angeles poisonous effluvium and saw that we were back in the U.S.A. again. I disremember exactly whether our target airstrip was near Prescott or Flagstaff, Arizona but it was the sort of location which sells real estate in the twinkling of an eye. The somewhat hilly ground looked like a location in any cowboy movie you ever saw, the trees were real and not plastic disposable ones, and the whole schmeer was presided over by the bluest of blue skies dotted by white fluffy clouds.

Eventually we were decanted at a dude ranch situated in a grove of proper oak trees where we were invited to try the new Kawasaki range and/or avail ourselves of refreshment inside. As I was then left pretty much alone by the Gadarene rush, I thereupon inspected the 2-wheeled offerings which turned out to be mostly dirt-cum-street bikes in the fashion nowadays. Kawasaki was feeling the pinch a bit from Yamaha and others as their small real trailbike (as distinct from minibike) was 90 cc approx and the next up, the Bushmaster 175, was really a dressed up and rather heavy roadster. This has been rectified with the introduction of new rotary-valve singles of 125 and 175 cc approx, both being fitted with Hatta forks which permit alteration of trail, damping, and even channel I suppose. The 250 has been also spruced up to be more of a companion to the 350 Big Horn; one of the factory engineers thought of calling it the Little Big Horn until somebody clued him in on Custer. Detail mods have been carried out on the rest of the range, mostly for the better, and there is a minibike added as well to siphon off some of the Honda market.

Anyway I got off around the marked course which wound up hill and down dale, discovering soon enough that I am not much of a dirt rider especially (1) on a strange 250 with lots of poke (2) on hard dirt mit marbles gefüllt (3) on trials tires. In fact it wasn't till I was tipped on to the 100 cc Trail Boss, which not only has a quick-change lever to switch its five ratios from dirt to street (or back) but in this case knobbies as well, that I began enjoying myself. Frankly I was the most comfortable on this one as the ride seemed softer and it could be slung about with impunity, even if it naturally suffered a certain lack of torque at low revs, but could you ever wind it!

As the day progressed I put in more time on all of them and even got so I could go reasonably quickly on the 125 and 175 instead of grinding about in low cog. These share the same frame etc, the only difference really being in stroke I think, and were great fun even if the front end seemed a bit "loose" to me as if it could use a steering damper. A knowledgeable friend stated that was because they needed knobby tires (on this surface), a 21-in. front wheel, and a fork brace in that order for serious work. In fact, he said, I wasn't going quickly enough to make the bike handle. That was certainly true on the 250 and 350 which seemed hard-mouthed but then if you don't get out of second!! I went around a few times on those however and they do require a different technique; you can "plonk" your way through places in second or third where on the 100 you were beset by wheelspin in low cog. All the bikes—at least the ones I rode—have five speeds now even if there is more than one shift pattern.

By that time the refreshed hordes had reappeared and the fun began. The usual racers started racing (while Mr. Collins tried to smile), the usual *in'a tu vu's* started showing off, and the less skillful among us wobbled off into the forest. One gent, who apparently had never driven a motorbike before, was placed on the hot 100 cc TT Green Streak and

Our friend (r.) and friend (l.).

MANNEY AT LARGE

shot straight ahead into a fence, a respected elder member of our profession mistook a fast left for a slow left and damaged his veritable gourd, and there were the usual near misses resulting in no more than a broken taillight and much grass trailing from footpegs. Reliability record was way up this year with no engines erked (perhaps the extra power is the answer) and nothing busted except the taillight. Summing up, I would say that depending on your age and seriousness the new 125 or 175 would be my best bets for fun work in the tules. If you are light, the dual-purpose 100 would be nice even if it handles so well as to be forgiving! I can't really speak for the quick ones yet as I am a slow learner and slower knitter but the fast boys seemed happy.

The other extreme, really, was the 350 road-going Avenger twin that Kawasaki lent me to do the Ontario caper. After my light 100 cc Yamaha twin the Kawasaki felt as big as a police Harley and I really had a time getting used to it, especially since a plain van delivered it with no tools, no handbrake, no registration, and (as I found out down the road) no gas. Just like stealing a strange motorcycle, in fact. Anyway, my headlong progress was tempered a bit as the bike only had 12 miles on it and a note on the speedo said "Only 6000 rpm for the first 300 miles." The 6000 rpm turned out to be plenty as the twin was quite "cammy" and came on with a rush above 3000 or so while six, on 5th gear, worked out to be just under 70 mph.

Frankly the 350 felt as big as a house to start with, in spite of being largely light-alloy, but it soon got to be very comfortable on the move. Starting was quite simple using the handlebar-mounted choke lever but it did require a good jump on the kickstarter. One carburetor must have been richer than all getout as the bike would blubber on anything except full acceleration; somewhat embarrassing as those rotary-valve twins rattle like a hay-baler anyway and that bass popping was too much. Nevertheless it never sooted a plug although one would load up a bit after a bout of slow traffic.

As far as other bits were concerned, the transmission was perfection with up-for-up (neutral at the bottom) and down-for-down; this must be natural as I have been trying to shift the Yamaha like that ever since. The brakes were another matter, the front one especially taking an awful lot of pressure, and I never really had much confidence in it. Suspension was stiff initially but got softer as it wore in; perhaps it was designed for 2-up which suited my daughter to a T anyway. Handling was always good with the proviso that the steering damper needed tightening above 30 mph or so to avoid head-wagging. I put over 500 miles on the 350, including going home from Ontario by way of Oceanside (a hundred mile trip) and really it was a great experience. Electrifying acceleration and 80 mph up hills plus good handling makes you wonder why people are satisfied with closed cars. The only thing I never got used to was the riding position at speed. A fat crankcase and narrow tank means that you must be double-jointed to get a good knee grip. The high-set bars do nothing to offset a 70 mph air blast at speed and the rider is simply hanging on for dear life. For freeway commuting a fairing would be mandatory and come to that, a bigger tank. Three gallons is not enough at 33 mpg.

My daughter and #2 son rode on the back and loved it. My #1 son, after some soul-searching (he weighs about half as much as the bike) rode it and came in beaming. When can we get one daddy? The eternal roadtester's dilemma.

If all this makes less sense than usual, it is because I am sitting in a hotel room in New York doing it by hand. New York hotels tend to be non-hotels featuring non-service and non-comfort such as the Metro running under the bed, Pélé and his pals playing Puerto Rico F.C. in the hall at 3 a.m., and a thriving surly school for employees. The rest of America tends to forget how self-seeking and downright odd New York is and yet, via advertising, it swings an influence out of proportion to its weight mostly because (like the hotel) the patrons let them get away with it.

The other evening I was eating in one of those "little" French restaurants that has grown up into a larger French restaurant overnight by pushing Martinis and replacing Momma (who used to cook) with a Wog of some sort. Anyway, two guys from some ad agency and two from some paint company were at the next table. One of the adsters was going on with all the clichés for these cats (from Pittsburgh, I think,) and doing the economy a great deal of harm just by hustling. For instance in one breath, referring to the well known lasting quality of that paint, he said that if each customer decided to keep his Cadillac three more years that GM would be out of business while in another breath he said he had noticed the price of the paint had been "static" for at least three months. That's what he said, "static." People like him cheapening the product and then hiking the price just because it has been "static" is what has put us in the present situation of 15¢ worth of goods costing $1.15.

MANNEY AT LARGE

CONTINUED FROM PAGE 75

bill and then practically at the same moment, all the periods of the lights changed. It had been pretty difficult to make two lights in a row without one slamming red in your face but now it is so obvious that whenever we roll through a green one without stopping precipitately, my son remarks sotto voce "Somebody's head will roll in Sacramento for that."

Not content with screwing up all the lights on the main highway, they screwed up all the lights on feeder or bypass roads. Why? Obviously if there are monumental jam-ups all day long through Newport Beach they badly need a freeway, don't they?

Don't think that it is just our baby as it is going to happen to you as well, even if you live out in the boonies. Politicians love to play with Budgeted money and if the Budgeted money isn't spent every year, the Governor won't give them more next year. They also like to be Doing things, preferably something expensive that gets their names down in the records. I am not going to bring up all the fiddle money to be made from freeways as all our politicians are as clean as a whistle.

There is no denying the fact that freeways in Los Angeles (just to take one example) have made life a lot easier but they have also made Los Angeles a lot like East Berlin. It is by no means certain that it is a Good Thing for people to rush around that much to and from work, stinking up the atmosphere as they do, and quite frankly I don't see why Los Angeles needs to be something dreamed up by Dr. Huer when it used to be pretty nice as it was.

It seems to me that they could have had their freeways without so much dislocation by siting them in the air over railroad tracks, river beds, and other crude bits of real estate. Right now they are about as popular as airports because of the sneaky way they go about things. People buy houses and then one day, plunk, there are men in hard hats and bulldozers in the ranunculi. Sorry, lady, progress. Playing their radios and chewing gum with the mouth open. A case in point is around here where they plan to lay a freeway (another Great Unwashed branch) over, more or less, a perfectly good four-lane road. A three-to-four year old tract of moderately expensive houses is on one side. A brand new golf course is on the other. Guess which side the engineers with transits have been seen on?

And they wonder why nobody seems to trust the Government any more!

AT LARGE

WITH HENRY MANNEY

Yes, Virginia, there is a Fittipaldi. I couldn't bear to leave that line to Rob in his Watkins story so have pinched it. As you probably know by now Emerson Fittipaldi won the U.S. GP via the usual combination of circumstances that involves a GP win but after all he had to be there to do it. Colin Chapman should be proud of the latest of his crop of young men but I was even prouder of the resolve shown by his faithful Team Lotus racing mechanics, soldiering on amidst a considerable blizzard of bad publicity caused by Rindt's death. There are a lot of people who think that any crash is caused by driver error and a lot more people who, looking at the history of Lotus over the years, think that any crash is caused by the car falling to bits. I would be lying if I didn't say that the latest Lotus F1, although a truly marvelous device, is really not my cup of tea to go racing in but then if you are interested in winning, Lotus has a very good record indeed. But the point I am trying to make is that Dick Scammell and the lads make it as safe as they possibly can. Probably a contributory factor is that the Lotuses can be driven really hard by the most skillful drivers so naturally there are going to be breakages; approximately 75 percent of the cars are not driven really hard in any one race so you can see how the percentage of probability works. Then there are all the dramas about the poor quality of bits supplied by outside firms, late delivery, design faults, and the like; due to the hurried nature of the F1 schedule there is no time to do much development work and sometimes sins are perpetuated long past their allotted time. We, the journalists, don't know about most of all that and by extension you don't either. Sort of like baseball in a way as we cannot see why McCovey went 0 for 4 or why an apparently good player gets traded off to Tacoma. I have just been reading Mr. Jim Bouton's book *Ball Four* about the trials and tribulations of a pitcher and recommend it highly to anyone wanting to know what the real face, as distinct from the party face, of a sport is like. Perhaps Mr. Bouton hoked it up a bit but I doubt it; the ins and outs of baseball management sound suspiciously like the ins and outs of fuel contracts, second drivers vs team managers, and just plain dirty pool. You just wouldn't believe some of the things that go on and some of the personalities involved. When you sit there Monday morning reading that X dropped out again and Y blew up and Z dropped a valve, you may not know (for instance) that Cosworths have something over 60 racing engines "out," a certain number of which are delivered back to them after each race in various stages of disrepair. Without being unkind to Cosworth, they have bitten off a bit more than they can chew as the works, which must rebuild these engines and ship them back toot sweet, is still small and also there are certain modifications for extra horses which don't seem to have worked out too well. This rebuilding costs about $2500 a time I gather and

Our Friend.

CYCLE WORLD PHOTO

MANNEY AT LARGE

on top of that some team managers feel that their engines aren't getting the attention other team managers' are etc. Then there are the drivers who say that they cannot do well because Goodstone doesn't want to know about giving them the right tires etc. This unsatisfactory situation of having the race decided before it is actually run, as it were, has made Jack Brabham retire at the end of this season, finally fed up. And he is good enough, all other things being equal, to have taken the lot. It isn't all just jumping in the car and blowing everyone off. Perhaps someday one of the drivers will do a really literate version of what it is all like; of course by that time he had better be living in Argentina with all the Nazis as the slander writs would be coming thick and fast.

It was pretty strange being at a GP race after all this time and I had to wander about with program in hand to identify both machines and men (thought I was going to say Car and Driver, Elaine?). However there were lots of old friends, ranging from the Hackfleisch Queen to the Plaster Casters of Chicago, who all told me that they had heard I was coming "back" next year; my only reply was to ask if they had heard who was going to pay for it. Frankly things have moved so fast since I left that part of a season back there been every year is really necessary to stay "au courant" and not feel that one has been away since the introduction of front-wheel brakes. Anyway, many of the old guard were still holding forth like Stewart, Surtees, G. Hill, et al but kids like Ickx were already seasoned veterans. There was very definitely a new wave of recruits from F2 like Fittipaldi, Weisell, Peterson, Schenken or sports car specialists like Stommelen. To find out what really goes (besides expediency or fuel contract) with some of these lads you have to consult one of the older racing mechanics who will say (about Stommelen), " 'E'll be all right, likes the really fast stuff. 'E can pick up the Monaco nadgery later." Or Fittipaldi, "Mad as a b***y hatter. Gets it sideways. Sideways!!" And to a request for information about one of his own drivers, "Same stupid b****y nit he always was. If we didn't shorten up the throttle cable he wd never finish a race." Ha. Walking around eavesdropping is better than drinking in an Irish pub for conversation: "How're things going? Like a waltz; slow slow quick quick."

Funnily enough in the ranks there doesn't seem to be much consciousness of the drivers' nationalities, although Franco Lini took care to inform us that Fittipaldi's parents were "Calabrese." Of course with a mishmash of English, Scottish, Belgian, French, Italian, Swedish, German, Spanish, Australian, Schwyzerdeutsch, Brazilian, and Midlands floating around the pits nobody has time to be chauvinistic. Yacht racing apparently is different as the celebrated Ursula Bagel writes from Paris that while Baron Bich was doing well with the 12-Meters he was wrapped in the tricolour but when he lost, *Paris Match* turned him into half-Italian with Swiss trimmings, thereupon dropping him in favor of the bicycle races. She notes that one of the etoiles de velo is named Helmut Chan, "a good old German name" and that there was a bullfighter in Lisbon named Gustavo Zinkel. While they lack the sheer poetry of Emerson Fittipaldi, it is nice to know that sports is getting away from the Jacks and Joes.

I was pleased to find out that apparently many folk back there read R&T and quite a few sociable questions were put about the health of the famous Fiat 600. One gentleman even asked solicitously if I were going to have it bronzed like a pair of baby shoes; now that is something that never occurred to any of us but would give it a snappy weatherproof finish.

On a more somber note, I must report that I have decided to sell my Ferrari GTO simply because it isn't being driven enough. We went out to practice at Ontario in it but with Spa gearing and an eye out for the fuzz it simply wasn't much fun. After an expensive tuneup chez Gene Curtis it now runs very well (the old Marchal plugs had been in for five years) and is quite tractable although of course pretty noisy. Ferrari experts tell me that it is one of the last of the proper GTOs before the flattops and was a works cars owned by Jean Guichet, who won the Tour de France among other things. No Le Mans, no Targa as he went on to driving works roadsters, and consequently is one of the very few that hasn't been through three sets of owners and thus through every stone wall in Europe. If there is anything wrong with it, I don't know it, as I can't stand unreliable high-speed automobiles. Frankly I would prefer to sell it out of Southern California as this is a dumb place for a good car. Yes it is licensed and has a few spares incl. two different ring and pinion sets, spare tires, and even a set of mag wheels which may work if you want more understeer than it has already, as they (originally for my 330 GT) are offset an inch or so. Offers to this address please in plain wrapper; no silly offers as I am not going to give it away. Cash deal although I might just take something like a nice Flavia coupe in part trade. I hate to let it go (and in fact may chicken out yet) as owning a car like that makes you feel like the Plastic Master State hasn't got you yet . . . and besides the Ferrari mechanics always ask about it. But, as the man said who blew his brains out while dressing, too many buttons. Too many stop signs. Bleagh.

MOOSTANG!

CONTINUED FROM PAGE 47

effortless poop, especially in the 70-90 mph passing range, where the Mustang would inflexibly barge ahead.

Driving it in Sicily was a bit of a problem and the guy who wrote, in *Car Life* I think, that the Mustang was the American car for European roads has never been there. The acceleration was doubly valuable as there is lots of traffic, mostly 500 Fiats, mixed up with even more heavy trucks. This leads to long creeping strings and, as the straights are short, one must get a wiggle on or meet a *shinqueshento* or monstrous Lancia transporter face to face. The clutch took some getting used to as it tended to hang up at high revs and thus impede the natural progress from one gear to another. This was at its worst from low to second, but we developed a technique of shifting at about 2500 rpm and then floorboarding it. The next problem was steering while accelerating furiously, as steering wheel control was approximate on these bumpy and heavily cambered roads. A trip or two around the Targa course showed that the Mustang would never win in stock form, as the front end tended to lift like a speedboat on the sharper corners, cutting the already limited vision and making the load on the front wheels even less. As if that wasn't enough, the shocks were getting weaker (total mileage at that time about 5000 mi) and the slightest irregularity would cause the car to pogo toward the edge of the road. We were reasonably brave but we had the utmost difficulty in shaking off 850 Fiats and the like; even on the faster parts of the course, admittedly rather bumpy, we felt as if we were going like the wind at 60 mph. And it is *too big*.

In spite of the above criticisms, I enjoyed the car very much indeed and hated to give it back. Most of all I liked the effortless horsepower and torque—there aren't many cars that can do a lap of the Madonie circuit in high without slipping the clutch. The faults in braking and roadholding are soluble without resorting to Mr. Shelby's full race treatment, the looks are good and attracted much favorable attention, the mechanical components seem reliable and should be so for some time, and it offers performance beyond most Europeans' wildest dreams. At least over here, you have to buy a very expensive sports car to get that sort of dig, and expensive sports cars are neither reliable nor cheap to fix.

You may see me in one yet.

AT LARGE

WITH HENRY MANNEY

A WEEK OR SO ago we trundled out to watch the so-called "Times GP" at Riverside; naturally this is not really a GP at all in the definitive sense of the word (although I suppose any race where they gave a Big Prize could be one) but the final in the Can-Am series. Now it is no secret that I think Can-Am cars are a little less than riveting but there are a few facets of the exercise which made it all worthwhile. One is, of course, to see a really professional team like McLaren's in operation and the other to inspect the Chaparral. Technical details are fully covered in another part of the forest but speaking from my experience, it was really remarkable to see how that thing whizzed around corners as if they weren't there. It would be beautiful to see it at Spa in the long-distance sports car event as that fast, winding, bumpy circuit is even more demanding than the Nürburgring I think. The mind boggles at the thought of the Chaparral in a typical Spa rainstorm, though; the roadholding shouldn't be affected much but the amount of pulverized water shot out the back would make following cars act like dinghies in a Force 8 gale. Do you suppose they could fit deflectors?

Not the least interesting question is how fast the Chaparral could go if really pressed. And what would happen if someone really lost it! Jackie Stewart drove it when it was still pretty new and Vic Elford has been doing a good job since then even if he wasn't, not to take anything away from him, most likely picked for his professional qualities of adaptability rather than blinding talent. I have watched Vic since his rally days with Ford GB and he has always given 100 percent and, more important, never stopped trying to improve. At one point he tried out for the saloon car racing team of Fords successfully and has gone on from there. Most rally drivers do not make good racing drivers as they are too untidy; the essence of rally driving is going fast on any old kind of surface and if you happen to knock down a few trees *tant pis*. Vic, along with a few others, was always very neat which helps explain his adaptability to sports car racing. He is also very ambitious which explains why he pays attention to what the team manager says. Too many drivers, as Black Dick O'Hagan says, are solid bone from crotch to crown and throw away their best chances. Nevertheless even Vic would agree that Mr. Stewart, for example, is a bit faster and it also would be interesting to see what Denny Hulme would do if he had a chance to drive both cars in the same day. Denny, y'know, doesn't just go fast because the McLaren is fast; he could drive my USAC car any day.

Racing is really a loony business and perhaps that is why it is so fascinating. Suppose you had a big bag of gold and I burst in one day saying that I had a wonderful idea for a Can-Am car that operated like a hovercraft in reverse, sucking the air out to hold the wheels on the road. You would undoubtedly roll on the ground and get all black in the face with laughter. Not that the idea is a new one either as a mechanic I talked to the other day actually built a go-cart affair like that (powered by an Olds V-8) several years ago but ran out of money before he could develop it properly. But then it isn't any more *auslandisch* than the device powered by four snowmobile engines that appeared at Laguna Seca. Reminds me of some of the oddities perpetrated by the Cannon Bros. or even the late great Ernie McAfee. You just never know. More's the pity that the snowmobile engine powering the fans on the Chaparral crapped out before it could show its potential, thus disappointing at least 150 of the 200 people in the stands.

A rather unpleasant part of the scene was the amount of uproar over the Chaparral put out by people who should know better, really. Their point was that the fans were a moving device contributing to roadholding and if you put a fine legal point on it, they are. The wheels are too. A lot of talk was bruited about on the subject of protests and withdrawing from the series next year if it wasn't banned, etc which strikes me as just poor sportsmanship. As far as I can see there is nothing to stop anyone from copying the fans as wings were copied but as McLaren, Chapman, and others have demonstrated, there is always a fresh idea coming up just a little bit better. In the final analysis, the race will be won by the best-prepared and best-driven car which is as it should be. Come to think of it the Chaparral people weren't all that fat on sportsmanship either as when it was seen that the fans were not going to operate, the car was withdrawn. Most of the scant

crowd came to see the Texas car and many a driver soldiered around with his Can-Am machinery in something less than optimum operating condition. In the last race of the year with an otherwise healthy automobile, it wouldn't have hurt to pick up the odd place like everyone else. You just don't take your football and go home. But of course Can-Am racing is no longer a sport. It hasn't got much style either, as epitomized by the awards dinner where Economaki made a long and tasteless speech about Bruce McLaren while his widow and the team were sitting there. On behalf of American racing fans I apologize to her.

Almost as bad was the TV presentation that evening of the race, a presentation which I assume was carried earlier to other parts of the country. If they wanted to kill the Can-Am they couldn't have done any better as the programming followed the leading car round and round, bringing in the same fatuous comments from the poor commentators at every corner. We were shown very little of the duels between other runners, we never found out what happened to the Chaparral, and Stirling Moss in the pits was completely wasted. For the next time, if there is a next time, it would be nice to have Stirling give the main commentary, another experienced person in the pits (and use him!), still another driver in charge of the monitors, and take the cameraman to at least one other race before coming to Riverside. Camera positioning was very good and many of the shots were scenic in the extreme but the whole effect was ruined by just showing Denny, and occasionally the Autocoast car, circulating around alone. Not having commercials every five minutes would help too. Pity that they can't hire Stirling, P. Hill, and Pete Biro (for sound effects) and give them their heads. Consider the improvement in the pro football game telecasts that have ex-quarterback Meredith assisting. No matter how clever the Normal announcer is, he still hasn't done it.

Incidentally, none of my remarks about the Mustang's being impossible to get fixed produced the slightest response from readers in a constructive sense; those who did write said wasn't it true! One indignant chap added that he was up a gum tree with his Cortina as since the introduction of the Capri and Pinto, no Ford agency near him wanted to know about stocking Cortina parts and indeed, he had been told that none were being ordered. If true, this makes Ford and their Better Idea a co-winner of the *Prix Bête et Mechant* along with Attila the Hun and the Captain of the Torrey Canyon. And they wonder why people buy other makes?

AT LARGE

WITH HENRY MANNEY

QUITE FRANKLY, I think that all this business about automobiles has gone too far. What I mean to say is, there are far too many different marques and types for any rational person to keep track of and furthermore, roughly 85% of the owners have got the wrong sort. Disregarding the little old ladies ("I still drive, you know") with vast Cadillacs for a moment, most of the citizens promenading around have either picked the wrong sort of automobile for their particular conditions or else have been conned into buying something they really didn't want by salesmen, wives, friends, or television commercials. For instance at the moment we own three cars and none of them are really suited to this particular district; the 600 Fiat comes closest but it isn't really up to freeway mileage. Perhaps all the VW owners around here are nearest to the truth but then for that matter, VWs are much more appropriate here than in their homeland where a high degree of acceleration and good wet-weather roadholding are at a premium.

Just to digress for a moment, I recently drove a Mercedes 280 SE for a couple of weeks and barring rather heavy fuel consumption, it was well-nigh the perfect car for Fall motoring back East, covering ground from Tidewater, Virginia to Massachusetts. The capacious boot swallowed all my luggage (including a "sahd" of bacon) without trace, everything worked so well you didn't notice it, the comfort and performance were beyond question, and the road manners, thanks to Mr. Uhlenhaut and friends, were so far in advance of any conditions I came upon that one could spend time in the long-forgotten art of driving for amusement. Icing on the cake was the sunshine roof, from which one could view the ever-changing cloud formations and let in a bit of fresh air. Around here the car would be wasted, I think, as Southern California seems to have degenerated into a series of 35 mph grunts from one stoplight to the next.

All this came to mind because we got another in the series of letters asking what sort of car to buy. One chap in darkest Nevada asked me to choose between a De Tomaso Vallelunga and a Lotus Elan, another fellow in Manitoba wanted to know what we thought of a Marcos, while gents living in plein Manhattan would like to know our preference between Lamborghinis and Ferraris. Mercy me. If I lived out midway between Elko and Hangman's Tree I would have a nice long-legged Citroen DS, in Manitoba a Volvo with a really good heater, while the only decent wear really for Manhattan is the scroungiest 2 CV corrugated van imaginable. The knicker-elastic suspension soaks up shocks from the vile streets, nothing short of an armored car can hurt it, the performance is more than adequate in NY traffic, and Joe's TV Repair painted on the side would insure against being towed away from unauthorized parking slots. Several people of my acquaintance, including the comely Mrs. Karl Ludvigsen, have owned these little devils in the USA and while like Gentiane they are an acquired taste, also like Gentiane there is nothing to replace it.

Different circumstances of course require different cars. Most of the motorists buzzing about in big towns would be better off aping the Londoners and opting for a good 1275 Mini, really and truly one of the world's greatest sports cars. And think how much more room there would be! On the other hand, if you ever have taken a middlish long trip jammed into a Mini (Minor, not skirt) especially with kids, it is easy to appreciate the feelings of those who buy Checker aerobuses. Perhaps some sort of governmental control has to be imposed to avoid the one-man-in-a-vast-four-door syndrome and allot the space to those who need it.

When I am King I will set up a far-reaching scheme through my Minister of Transport which will make a lot of people mad, make no mistake about that, but also ensure that the roads are a lot safer for those who like to drive. First off, there will be a much more comprehensive written exam for drivers' permits than is normal now, exams that will not only include the usual dumb questions about giving a yak the right of way in a pedestrian crossing but also dig into what actually makes a car operate. The actual driving test will be in two parts; one half around town with the usual manual skills (but with a rather higher standard needed to pass than now) and the other half at a convenient road-racing track specially built for the purpose. Required lap speeds would not have to be especially high but a knowledge of the proper line, braking, and positioning would be essential. Those passing this test would be put into Grade 3 and given a special identifying red license plate. Holders of Grade 3 would only be permitted to drive cars or motorbikes of a certain modest specification and would be required to follow certain rules such as staying in the two right-hand lanes of freeways. After one calendar year Grade 3 license holders would be permitted to take exams to advance themselves to Grade 2, rather as in the Merchant Marine, and put their money where their mouth was by posting a stiffish deposit to be refunded if they passed. Again the successful ones would get a blue plate and the right to drive a little more interesting equipment. After another two years the Grade One exam could be approached in the same manner but in this case the aspirant would have to complete several races, rallies, or similar sporting events (in case of financial hardship, cars would be provided by the State) as well as a really searching long road run under the eye of observers. Once over that hurdle, the Grade One driver

The Fiat, mechanic and Our Friend.

PHOTO BY PATRICK MANNEY

MANNEY AT LARGE

could wear his white plate with pride and succeed to a variety of privileges including immunity from meter maids, freedom of choice of car, and so forth.

Naturally the various grades of automobiles would be tied into the grades of drivers, the proviso being made that only cars which passed certain stringent tests (ibid) would be permitted sale in the Kingdom. On the one hand there is no point in having tiny Subarus that can't move out of their own tracks while alternatively no one needs huge Cadillacs holding no more people than a Fiat 125. It would be a point worth considering that Grade 3 drivers should be restricted to front-drive vehicles as in my experience they are twice as surefooted in evil weather; students of racing, though, will have noticed that really quick Mini drivers hardly ever were successful in rear-drive machinery.

There would be all sorts of details to be worked out but what else are Ministers of Transport for? Speed limits would be graduated according to class with Grade One scot-free but to keep everybody honest and engine sizes down, gasoline would be one dollar a gallon. As small engines seem to combust more cleanly, smog levels should be reduced ad lib with a further proviso that carburetors be designed without accelerator pumps, even if this meant the return of the dreaded SU. Anyone who has smelled the blast of dirty air when one of those big V-8s accelerates will agree. Insurance would have to be run by the State instead of the present robbers' roost; the driver's premium is only determined by grade as a spotty record means that he is "busted" or eventually cast into outer darkness. Accident claims are viewed in a rational manner with damage claims paid; a driver would be obliged to protect his grade however by appearing before an expert to explain exactly why he was involved in a shunt. Certain aspects of rear-enders, for example, are manifestly unfair under the law as it stands. Drunken driving would be treated in the Scandinavian manner as it is a Bad Scene. One little beer on the breath in Finland and you build airfields for six months. Car licensing would be supervised as well from a safety standpoint. In Switzerland, for example, new purchases or every car changing hands has to pass by the county inspection station where it is checked out for proper operation of all its components, bald tires, excessive smoke, tired shocks, or anything else likely to cause an accident. Elect me King!

AT LARGE
WITH HENRY MANNEY

DOWN HERE IN Buenos Aires, a week after Giunti's death in the 1000-km race, the town is still buzzing with discussion on how it happened and what to do about it. The Argentines are intensely concerned as not only were they trying to make a good impression (as this was their first Championship SP race in some time and they hope for their GP to attain Championship status next year) but they had literally left no stone unturned in an effort to make it really go. In our travels, of which more later, we are repeatedly asked if there is any way the accident could have been avoided, if the organization is deficient in any way, and where we consider the fault lay. Unlike similar occurrences in the past (vide Monza) this is just not an attempt to lay the whole thing on the nearest foreigner; I get the feeling that they really care.

The correct answer is, of course, that however much Nomex, Armco barriers, and haybales are produced at race tracks, you are still going to have the occasional accident, not only because everyone is hustling along at a great rate but because you cannot legislate out driver error. The long-suffering mechanics do their best to rule out mechanical failure but drivers are a different matter. By the nature of the sport, drivers are often psychologically unstable individuals who simultaneously release and restrain varied impulses by practicing their art. In short, they are all a little fada (to a greater or lesser degree) but might be really odd if they didn't drive. Anyone who doubts the above statement should see the lads circulating around Spa in the wet at 150 mph +. No rational person would even think of it.

The background of the accident, therefore, was that Beltoise's Matra commenced running out of fuel while still a kilometer or so from the pits. He made two-thirds of the distance, just barely around the last hairpin and right in front of the timing stand. The road here curves broadly to the left, past the old pits and tower, to the new pits. The old pits were abandoned, incidentally, as being too dangerous.

Now we ask the question: why did he run dry? Most SP cars these days have a warning light, a small reserve tank with tap, or sometimes both as it is futile to spend thousands getting the car in the race and then go en panne. Most serious teams run careful consumption tests to see how far apart they can space their pit stops as pit stops with their attendant flap use up a lot of time. The Matra perhaps circulated on Friday with Pescarolo and certainly on Saturday with Beltoise, enough to get an idea of the consumption. Matra won here last year, by the way, but naturally changes would have been made in the car. There only remains the possibility that the Matra suffered a fuel leak or perhaps a fuel blockage; several cars also had fuel pump bothers but then several cars always do. The Matra was coming up to a pit stop, as was the Ferrari of Giunti, and possibly Beltoise let it go on too long. He powered through the back hairpin by us well enough and then went blip blip as if he had trouble getting into gear, before charging off in pursuit of Parkes who had just passed him. Frankly, I don't remember whether he came around again.

I had an interesting conversation with Maestro Ugolini about relative fuel consumption, pit stops, and race strategy thereby. Now on the face of it, the big Porsches are quite a bit faster—say 35 sec in 30 laps—than the latest Ferrari, not unexpected as there is two liters difference in capacity in the two cars. However the Porsches were coming in for refuelling in the 30 lap range (Sif 34, Rod 36, Fitt 33, Elford 32), a fairly accurate indication as to what was going on as Elford and Siffert were traveling the fastest. In fact, Siffert had to make an extra pit stop later on. These refuelings, incidentally, were taking about 3 min 25 sec each, or a bit under two laps' running time. The Alfas were pursuing a different path, being 3-liter V-8s, and were coming in at 40 (Stom) and 42 (De Adamich) laps although both made an extra stop at 42 and 46 respectively. Whether the extra ones were for punctures, mechanical ennuis, or news of ex-Alfaiste Giunti I do not know; these stops were all over the four minute mark and Pescarolo also made a short one to have the bodywork taped up after hitting a corner marker. At any rate, their strategy was to go through with only three scheduled stops as opposed to the Porsches' four (Rodriguez) or five (Siffert and undoubtedly Elford had he kept running). As it turned out, the extra stops plus a long stretch of two minute plus lap times toward the end as they were running a bit rat kept them in third and fourth slots. A good finish, extra stops or not.

The Ferraris remain a question mark as the private ones were too slow to count, really, and the Parkes/Bonnier car had been bashed about a lot even if Parkes said it handled better after the practice shunt! They were all coming in around 29 laps and Parkes made no less than seven stops although Gosselin's Belgian car, probably a better indication, made five. Giunti's Ferrari was much lighter as the latest model and, of course, a 3-liter quasi-GP. At 39 laps when the accident actually occurred Giunti was still going strong and although Merzario was waiting in the pits ready, was not planning to come in for a few laps yet. Beltoise, of course, had run dry on the 36th tour, also with a 3-liter. What brought all this to mind was the fierceness of the fire that consumed Giunti's Ferrari; I asked the Maestro therefore how much fuel he thought the Ferrari still carried when it planned to refuel. His reply was that some 40 liters probably still remained and that being lighter, the Ferrari possibly would go on till 45 laps or even longer. This would have given it three fuel stops with the last, at about the 140 mark, a quick one with only 25 left to do. Given a trouble-free run, the Giunti/Merzario Ferrari might have been able to pip the Porsches. Actually the Ferrari was chucking out a fair amount of oil and water but that may just have been over-filling, viewing its steadily lowering lap times.

At any rate, all this strategy was for naught as Beltoise, ignoring the passage in the FIA regs stating that a stopped car may be pushed *only* if in the approach lane to the pits (otherwise removed off to the side), hopped out and commenced to push the Matra uphill at least 200 yards to the pits. While he was doing this, all the cars passed at least once. Unfortunately, in the process the Matra steered itself, although he tried to correct it and was alongside doing that when the Ferrari hit, across the chord of the curve into "line." A group of cars rounded the corner, Giunti behind them, another Ferrari suddenly darted out of the way, and Giunti's Ferrari struck.

Now the timers are alongside the pits at that point and the lone flagman is in his tower at the apex of the preceding hairpin. All have orders, especially the flagman, not to leave their posts. Graham White of the BARC, also down here, has suggested that some extra personnel on corners to deal with situations like this are needed (as in English or American races) and I concur; the flagman, however, was agitating his yellow violently (as he had the previous lap). Short of installing spring-up net barriers at 50-foot intervals in the track and hovering helicopters with hooks, I don't see how one can guard against everything.

Speaking of guarding against everything, it is not generally known that some 24 Indy cars are coming down here the end of next month for a race in Rafaela, I think, up in Santa Fe province. Apparently Rafaela is the closest place to have a suitable track, even though it is about 500 km from B.A. Four of the machines are destined for Argentine pilots and to avoid any recriminations, USAC drivers will set them up, making competitive lap times, before handing them over. Mr. Cagle of the USAC has already been down here and racked the lads up with his insistence on suitable safety measures as in the provinces at any rate the racing tends to be a little casual. I have been regaling the local lads with horror stories about big, hairy, alky-burning Indy cars and their unsettling habit of refueling with fire coming out of more places than a cheap samovar. Too bad that the USAC cars can't run on the road course at the autodromo as I have said before and will again, the racing fan deserves the rortiest cars possible, not a piddly gasoline-burning 3-liter. Bring back the Auto Union.

We have been traveling around a good deal and have been pleasantly surprised by the widespread interest in motor racing. Places way out in the boonies have perfectly good asphalt road circuits laid out, invariably dignified with the name of Autodromo even if the furnishings remind one of early SCCA days. This sort of effort is all the more remarkable when one considers that Argentina some years ago had to slap on drastic import controls to rectify an awkward economic situation; all automobiles and parts thereof are now made here under license for example. This has led to a reasonable body of new cars like Argentine-built Fiats, Peugeots, 2-CV Citroens ("*cucarachas*"), Falcons, Chevy IIs plus a Willys-Kaiser-Renault hybrid called a Torino mixed up with fleets of BMC Farinamobiles (mostly taxis) and pre-war American cars. Up in Paraná the other day I saw a really cherry '34 Ford, a '39 Plymouth, and what looked like a gigantic Lincoln 2-seater roadster although Philip Turner swears it was a Stutz, all inside five minutes. Outside B.A. it is like pre-1940 Middle West with acres and acres of rolling land and little population.

It has really been a First-Cabin operation and most gratifying, really. A select number of us furriners have been toted up to San Carlos de Bariloche, way in the bloody Andes no less in what used to be all Patagonia (Lat 41°S Long 71°W approx) and now is Rio Negro province, to see the "Swiss Argentine" and naturally a new road course. Bariloche is on one of a series of big lakes, over which, at this time of year, a 25-knot breeze blows off the Cordillera. You could run a beautiful catamaran or dinghy championship there as the wind comes up about ten and fans all day from the NW. Also it is lovely motorcycle country as in the Argentine fences are mighty far apart. The weather wasn't cold, just cool, as this is summer but winter is the big skiing season. If you like fishing there are monster trout and, reportedly, Other Beasts as well. A band of Swiss settled here in the late 1800s and the town still looks like that.

The funniest part of the whole trip is that we are carted about in Argentine Air Force planes and treated like visiting royalty, what with bands and dignitaries, etc. At odd times we are whisked off to press conferences complete with newsreel cameramen and have even been shoved cold in front of TV cameras to tell what we think of various aspects of racing. As I have just barely enough Spanish to order a meal, we have been given a charming young lady interpreter, Mlle Sestre, but I understand enough Spanish to realize that she is making her own version of our comments. So far I have made something like ten speeches, an ordeal worse than going to the dentist, but fortunately they let me get away with short ones. Sooner or later there is a banquet with scrolls and little flags and things being presented, and usually we all sit down to eat about 11:30 p.m. or even later. In the morning, of course, we all get hauled out of the sack early and are escorted by a horde of smiling enthusiasts ("*tuercos*") to some local site like a mountain, new river tunnel, ceramic works, trout hatchery, or what not. We have been practicing waving our hands in salute like the Queen Mother but it doesn't come off as well.

Sundays we were popped into Cessnas and flown up to Entre Rios province to inspect a new tunnel between Paraná and Santa Fe. After all the tunnels and radio interviews and TV slots (being driven between all these at 90 mph by the local hotshoes) we went out to an *estancia* owned by the Mayor, an old bicycle racer no less. There are a lot of people of German extraction around here as in most of Argentina and we were tormenting a German member of our party by saying that we had seen Hitler twice and actually met Bormann.

Looming before us is the prospect of going back to work Sunday for the GP. Ferrari has pulled out his cars and Beltoise has had his Matra entry turned down but I think Chris Amon is going to have another one. The March team will come as will Lotus and Brabham and at least one Surtees but some others like BRM are unlikely. I gather, the pack will be filled out with Formula 5000s and F2s, it seems. You will hear all about it next month!

AT LARGE

WITH HENRY MANNEY

ONE OF THE features of our magazine is that apparently everyone has a hand in cutting copy to fit the ads from the mail boy on up. Consequently, in spite of my remarks that enny fool can cook lean pork, it is the cracklin' that is difficult, certain bits get cast into limbo that have a considerable bearing on the event. For instance in the late 1000 km BA the celebrated and articulate Sam Posey came in for a good deal of bad-mouthing from the Argentine sporting Press because he didn't go any faster. Now Sam isn't any particular danger to Jackie Stewart at the moment but what nobody took into account was that the NART Ferrari wasn't the world's fastest anyway and besides, in one of those typical NART deals, was largely there as a glory object for the locals Garcia-Veiga and Di Palma. In fact, a large bag of gold had reportedly been set aside if either lad should shunt it, an event which might have been construed as a blessing in disguise. Sam was there as a Ferrari setter-upper and under contract, as one not likely to panic in the first lap sprints, to deliver it safe and sound after the first hour. This he did admirably and in a respectable position too as Sam may do odd things sometimes but he likes Ferraris. In his words, he would rather drive a mezzo-stanco Ferrari than a first-rate example of some other makes as he knows the Ferrari won't do anything awful like break in half. Besides, it sounds nice. Those big V-12s are very nearly indestructible as was the GTO in its day, a point proven by the California one seen in the Can-Ams recently where they only changed the oil once in a while. A wagon like that is actually cheaper to run than a Lola or Mc-Laren, say, that uses up a pair of Chevvies every race. At any rate in the 1000 km Garcia-Veiga treated the 512 pretty kindly but Di Palma absolutely used it up, handing it back to Sam near the end with the needles all against the stops, balky shifting, and the diff growling like mother bear with cubs. There is more to driving than just going fast.

Another humorous bit was the performance of Trevor Taylor in the V-8 Cosworth-McLaren. As you may remember, Trevor used to be No. 2 Lotus driver and a very good one he was too, a lot better than his record would indicate. In fact, if he had not been plagued with a series of shunts (mostly not his fault) he could have gone a long way and in fact I have often wished that he drove something else. Anyway after that mixup with Mairesse at Spa he was never quite the same and effectually retired, to appear only intermittently. It was good to see him again in pretty good form even though the McLaren, being built

for a big V-8 and housing a somewhat clapped Cosworth 3-liter, was scarcely calculated to raise the hackles on your neck. He and Chris Craft were making up time by late braking and during one of these excursions Trevor had a front tire deflate on the approach to a hairpin. No fool, he buzzed straight down the escape road which by coincidence led straight into the course again so naturally he carried on to the pits. Naturally again the scorers saw him and docked the car several laps but the IBM computer credited him with the fastest lap of the race, understandable as Trev left out about a kilometer of track and three turns. However it has been reported that one of the team duly showed up to collect the loot for fastest lap! Ain't racing funny.

When I was still a spectator and reading motoring magazines for my news and dreaming of going to Le Mans, we all used to think that the better reports were Gospel and were only mildly disturbed by differences between them. It was only later when I got well into the racket that I realized that nobody can get the whole story, partially because you can't be everywhere and partially because by accident or design you rarely get to know the whole truth from involved parties. Drivers are notoriously inaccurate, usually from automatic compensation, and team managers or mechanics dole out half truths as they simply don't figure it is any-

Our Friend

BILL MOTTA PHOTO

MANNEY AT LARGE

body's business but theirs. It is only by haunting the garages night after night that you learn the case histories of a marque and persuade the mechanics that you aren't out to make them look bad. And all that is the subject of another much longer story, not written yet, entitled I Love Practice But You Can Keep The Race. Anyway you see the mass of motoring journalists swirling around, all trying to learn enough to ask the right question, while the daily boys or wire service stringers (who may have done a bicycle race last week and will do roller derby next) just head for the bar. I remember just after a particularly horrid shunt we were all teeming around in the Press room when one of the English daily lads, his eyes wide with panic, came barging through shouting, "How old was he? How old was he?" Actually none of us knew.

What this leads up to was that by accident, from an Argentine sporting magazine, that I learned the 1000 km was stopped several minutes under the red flag following Giunti's crash. Never noticed a thing as we were over the other side of the course and a few cars kept coming through, fairly normal as it was refuelling time when the whole order is jumbled up anyway. Not only that, nobody said anything about it afterward and the race bulletins that would normally take note of this said nothing either. The peculiar side of it, however, is that the whole field usually stops when the red is hung out, right? and yet quite a few cars kept going including the eventual winner. No wonder that the scoring was so screwed up. I suppose that I would have to say that the organizers really dropped the ball in the grass here as they should have done a few rapid disqualifications. On the other hand, they felt in a cleft stick as the European cracks had come all this distance for a Championship race, there

was already an unfortunate fatality not to mention a sticky situation with Beltoise, and they didn't want to make waves. Decisions decisions. At any rate I didn't notice anything amiss, in fact I just thought it was the usual Sports-Prototype pit fire, so you see how even experienced reporters can louse up history. Think how it was at Waterloo with no race bulletins.

The GTO is sold to a nice gent who will give it a good home so interested parties may quit writing in. Actually I had some charming letters, a large part of them wanting photos which I didn't have by some oversight. I also had some interesting callers, one or two of whom I wouldn't have sold it to at any price. I am sorry to see it go, largely because it represents days that never will come again, but at least I had a taste of the real thing. Just after it was turned over to me in Modena I was en route to Paris over the Great St. Bernard pass that leads from Italy to Switzerland. It was after dark and I was grinding upward through the millions of hairpins after Aosta and before the road tunnel, the driving lights projecting their jiggling beams alternately on rock face and out into space below the brooding peaks. Low and second on that marvellous gearbox were mostly in use, the healthy V-12 winding away in those long long gears between hairpins before bubbling pock-splat-pock-splat in typical fashion in the corners themselves, the carburetors still being fitted with the short-pipe jets although the long pipes themselves were still on. Nothing got hot, nothing got breathless, the driving position was perfect, and although in the stripped body you could check on every tappet, the clicks clacks and whines all merged into a harmonious whole. Florini had checked it out well. Eventually I learned to deal with the typical Ferrari understeer by horsing the back around, listening for the chippa chippa out of hairpins, and wondering about the artistry of a man who

could design such a device. All I could think of was my old friend Ernie McAfee, a dry-lakes boy who started tuning sports cars with great skill and eventually drove them with no less skill. All he wanted to do, he said one day, was get a job sweeping in the Ferrari factory and sweep a part out every day until he had a whole car. Eventually he was killed in one, that pig of a 6 cyl. Monza, but if resurrection was possible he would have popped up to be with me that evening.

He also would have enjoyed the scene at the frontier where all the Italian customs guards shot out of their little house as soon as the whine and rumble echoed down the tunnel. They all stood in a row, very respectfully, and looked it over. Poor boys mostly from Calabria and aspiring at best to a Vespa scooter. My heart is not stone and I invited them all to sit in it. *Ahhh . . . che bella macchina.* Very carefully, one by one, they removed their hats and lowered themselves gently into the driver's seat, being careful not to lean on the flimsy door, to wiggle gently and lay delicate fingers on the wood and aluminum steering wheel, Ferrari's black horse leaping out from the center. Heavy breathing, thoughtful staring ahead with soft smiles. They all waved goodbye when I left. The lone Swiss border guard? "Have you any merchandise to declare?"

In a GTO??

At Large

WITH HENRY MANNEY

EVERY NOW AND then somebody asks if I have been to Willow Springs or Riverside recently and I say no; from that they assume that after Spa and Luh Mans nothing else is interesting any more. Actually I like any sort of racing but have reached the stage where it is tiresome to drive x miles there and back in Sunday traffic to a race at which I don't know anybody. Another deterrent is the prospect of writing about a race when there may not be anything to write about, really, or on the other hand (like Luh Mans) far too much. Then there are Can-Ams which just don't prove anything. However there was a big stock car go called the Miller High Life 500 (absolutely the last plug) at Ontario recently and even though Jim didn't want an all-singing, all-dancing report a couple of us went out to check the action. After all, some day we might want to do a George Plimpton.

Stock cars are great fun even if it is a mystery why they are called stock cars. The celebrated A.J. Foyt's Mercury was an example with the inside full of roll cage, the remainder smoothed all out with fiberglass moldings, a net over the driver's window, the doors presumably welded shut, a shaker screen over the grille, alloy discs over the headlights, hold-down tabs or straps over the remaining windows, aluminum fillets between the body and rear bumper, a small spoiler, and a gynormous drainpipe for the exhaust. A quick look underneath showed sundry beefed-up components and the tires, just to take one exception, were certainly not stock equipment. This is a stock car? Of course no rational person, especially A.J. Foyt, would be daft enough to try to lap Ontario at 150 approx in a truly stock Mercury even supposing that the Mercury would do anywhere near that without flying to bits. I remember seeing photos somewhere of a 2-CV Citroen race that preceded a minor GP in France; it was good fun for all with cornering on the rims, bellypans showing, and spinnakers set. I would imagine that a showroom-stock race for American cars would look much the same. At one of the early Santa Barbara sports car races there was a misguided individual competing on one of the first 2-seater Ford Thunderbirds. The thing went well enough and even stopped for a few laps but his hectic progress was mostly hampered by having to shut the doors all the time after they sprung open on corners. All the more credit therefore to my rednecked colleagues from the South for making a current passenger car go, stop, and handle. Instead of Mr. Nader's wasting his time railing at the manufacturers (who only want to make money anyway) he would be quids ahead by consulting the Wood Bros and their

ilk. The only way to make a car safe is to improve the stopping and handling, not by frigging about with foam-rubber interior trim and Orwellish spy devices that blow the horn at anything over the legal speed limit.

One of the fascinating things about racing is that the local scene changes so radically with the different types of racing, rather as touring in Europe offers you fast changes in culture as you cross different borders. The "good ol' boys" look quite different from other sorts and it isn't just Flying Tiger Pilot boots coupled with sideburns and Nomex, although you would have to look rather far in GP to find a driver named Elmo sporting a Roscoe Turner moustache. Perhaps it is because everyone seems to be so relaxed; the gentlemen wait calmly in line to qualify without much jangling about and when called, are just as apt to shove a cigar butt into the mouth and motor off as if going to the station. The engines are equally relaxed, idling away amiably while some point is discussed with the officials. Most of the drivers look as if they enjoy the whole process which after all is the point, really, for the majority who never finish in the first five.

Perhaps the lads were a bit bemused with the magnificence of Ontario's plant compared with a few of the Southern tracks in use. All that fancy equipment like dudey fire trucks and there wasn't a peanut stand anywhere, let alone the old school bus with bars on the windows to lock the drunks up in. Just to make them feel at home, though, there was a suitable race queen with massive hairdo and mini mini borrowed from some C and W tv show; she duly piped out her message of welcome over the p.a. to the 150 souls present

PHOTO BY GEOFFREY GODDARD

for qualifying in the right sort of accent but later spoiled the home-grown pitch by appearing in kinky fancy dress, escorted by a typical PR type in even fancier. Lil' Euphalia ain't the same since she took on city ways. It is all very typical thank God for that. Tradition carries on nicely in some parts of the country without the usual opprompling, protest marches (except about the concessionaire's weenies) and so forth. Some day I would like to cover the whole Grand National circuit start to finish as there must be an awful lot of interesting stories in there that we should all know about.

Mr. Foyt won as most people expected him to do. There was a lot of swapping places with MM Lorenzen, Isaacs, Petty, Baker, Allison etc but the ebullient A.J. seemed to have the right combination of speed and chassis tuning, thus enabling him to keep on top of things generally. A friend remarked that it was nice to see close racing; close racing was an accurate description as there was lots of 2-abreast drafting stuff in spite of the relative low angle of the banks. Nobody seemed to worry much about the groove and in fact the apron came into use from time to time. Perhaps the high volume of traffic kept the surface swept of marbles. The professionalism of the drivers was quite impressive as early on the track was quite slick and there were not a few spins and bobbles at our corner. You would see the car start to go and the driver look around a bit to ascertain just where everyone was while still winding busily on the wheel. The thick traffic would part without any panic, those in a position to shut someone off would lift a bit, and everyone would motor calmly by. The only actual jalopy derby work I saw was between Pedro Rodriguez and Benny Parsons which figures as Pedro may know the words but he doesn't know the music, in that company at least. Some of the drivers commented that they actually prefer the flatter bank as drafting was easier and it wasn't so hard on the car. It seems to me that a really good driver, like Mr. Allison perhaps who started far back and pulled himself up until the engine blew, would be at less of a disadvantage here with a slower car than at Daytona for instance. As I understand it, keeping up at Daytona is a matter of horsepower (with all other things like webbelos being equal) while on the flatter banks perhaps more driving skill is involved. This is not taking anything away from the professional Mr. Foyt who managed to get in front when he really wanted to. The quote I liked was from Dick Guldstrand who complained that he didn't realise until practicing that the oval was so small.

They had a pretty good crowd for it but not enough, considering jillions of big stockers are probably better entertainment value than the Indy cars. There were a few little grandstands at the ends completely packed, the cheap bleachers, while the posher grandstands nearby offering almost the same view were practically empty. Of course it depends on what you want to see but a fellow photographer was observing that racing as a family entertainment (along with baseball) was on the way out simply because it cost way too much to take everybody to the event. These big operators get money-mad and build big plants; because they have big plants they feel they have to charge sky-high prices. Average people cannot cough up $30 to $50 for an afternoon's entertainment and so the kids, who might grow up to be supporters of the sport, stay at home watching Speed Racer on the tube. Being so far away from the action that you don't get dirt flung on you doesn't help either. I would never in a thousand years pay a big wad to sit that far away from the smells and faces and noises. Maybe that is why motorcycle racing is getting so popular and why Riverside survives.

At Large

WITH HENRY MANNEY

IN ANOTHER PART of the forest you will probably find our Mr. Girdler's reportage on the recent Questor GP (absolutely the last plug); a reportage which needless to say I haven't seen as does Bloomingdale's tell Macy's? At any rate, some time prior to the event there was a fair old barrage of bumf in the publick print depicting this GP as the first time that the nasty devious slit-eyed foreigners in their tricky little rule-bending Formula One cars would meet the upstanding Alger-like American true-blue heroes in their American Formula A (or 5000) cars. Discounting for the moment that this sort of approach is easily 50 years out of date, the respective classes met recently in Argentina to name just one place. Furthermore, it would be nitpicking to point out that most if not all of the Formula As were built in Merrie Old England. In fact, the joint was awash with nice shiny new Lolas which Eric Broadley, a chap as far from American as you can get, must ship over in wire baskets stacked like milk bottles. More's the pity that the truest bluest American of them all, Dan Gurney of Presidential campaign fame, was seen wandering lonely as a cloud around the pit area in civvies, Nomexless and carless. Also more's the pity that his representative Swede Savage was driving an Eagle charitably described by one of the pit crew as "a real log."

Seeing somebody like Gurney on foot is always sad as he has still got more talent than 95% of the field and furthermore knows it. Perhaps the presence of the charming Mme Gurney in an advanced state of pregnancy had something to do with his retirement. If so he must be very fond of her as that sort of thing never stopped him before. The no less celebrated and talented Black Jack Brabham was also to be seen mooching about, ostensibly keeping an eye on the care and feeding of Graham Hill's Brabham and feeling about as useful as a teddy bear on a honeymoon. Since Jack's forte was painstakingly sorting out a car himself (and nobody else ever made a Brabham go so well) he felt rather ill at ease watching Graham starting in his famous chassis-tuning performance which drags on like one of those supposedly consumptive sopranos in Grand Opera. I love Graham like a brother but at times he does drive people straight up the wall. The trouble is that Graham really isn't interested in going fast in practice, especially that soon in practice, as the butterflies commence their formation flying way too early. He would undoubtedly be just as happy if they drew lots for the start and somebody else, preferably Ron Tauranac, trundled around to scuff in tires. In spite of the stone-face act old Grime probably gets more worked up than any driver in the business; the only way really he can deal with practice is to save it all up and have one mad dash just before the end of qualifying. The race itself is probably easier as you have all the other chaps around to keep you company. It is easier to gauge progress by grid-mates who are undoubtedly scratching just as hard, not just whizzing around taking impossible chances to grab 1/10 of a second all by yourself. And there are lots of other facets too. At any rate Blackie was standing around trying to look casual, wishing that Graham would get on with the job and also wishing that Betty Brabham hadn't finally prevailed on him to hang it up. As it turned out he wouldn't have had much luck as Graham's practice engine never did run properly and the race one went up with a bang. Cosworths weren't as reliable in 1970 as formerly but for 1971 things are supposed to be different. I was told that Jackie Stewart had the only one of the new supertweeked ones the first day of practice but as it had probably done either practice or the race at Brands recently he pulled it out for the second day. Apparently the newer one wasn't as satisfactory and he was making up time by driving harder. Wonder if he could have held off the Ferraris with a new super one?

Just watching Mr. Stewart at work gave one the same sort of thrill that watching Mossy or Fangio used to give. When Stewart first broke into GP racing he showed his class instantly and unlike some others I could mention he has improved consistently. Part of this of course must be due to his mentor Ken Tyrrell as it must be nice to have a boss one can trust; in most of the other teams half the time is spent in worrying about palace politics or else what is going to break next. If Jackie would give over the Moss syndrome, quit trying to see how much money he could make, and concentrate on F1 racing there is no telling how good he could be. Any aspiring drivers watching Jackie dodge around that mickey-mouse infield course got an object lesson on how to make the best of a bad thing. The cornering alone was worth the price of admission in the off-camber hooks. A case in point was his short trip in the Formula A to be driven by our A.J. Foyt who of course has won a few races too. The best Mr. Foyt could do was in the region of 1 min 52 sec or thereabouts whereas Jackie in a few laps got down into the 1:45s within a second or so of the best A time in what was by no means a cherry car. Even allowing for the fact that Foyt was there for window-dressing, having his mind mostly on the Phoenix USAC race on Saturday, you would think that he would try a little for the fans who paid to see him. I gather that there was very little wrong with the car when Foyt retired it on Sunday; he looked very pleased with himself and didn't put on one of the spirited Thespian performances we have seen elsewhere. Fortunately Andretti had style enough to attend Phoenix and try at Ontario too.

At that Foyt may have been turned off by the road course, one which will never be spoken of in reverent terms like the Nürburgring or Monaco. It reminded me of the artificial GP circuit at Le Mans, one which has fortunately bit the dust, in its steppes-of-central-Asia atmosphere and impossibility of seeing anything worthwhile from ground level anyway due to the hundred thousand fences. From the stands I gather it is Slotcarsville. They had better stick to the oval. Incidentally I am unhappy to report that the usual amiable atmosphere present backstage went belly-up as some of their little blue-clad marshals got a touch of the Hitlers. We even got henhoused about trying to work the race in the pits until Pressgauleiter Monty Roberts went to bat for us. Allegedly this atmosphere was by orders of the sanctioning body which was the SCCA of course; the guano flew thicker than French races even and you know what they are like. I realize that some of these lads are borrowed from the police academy and they must get their practice in but we have our job to do and are responsible people. The race needs the Press and not vice versa.

It was interesting seeing the revamped BRM team in action. Apparently the V-12 engine was one of those turned down (the other was the Eagle, I think) when BRMs went to the ill-fated flatiron a few years ago. No less interesting was the driver complement of Mm Rodriguez, Siffert, and Howden Ganley as there has always been gossip about certain BRM drivers paying their own way and then some. Now you *know* Siffert isn't paying his own way, opinion is equally divided on how much Rodriguez is paying (although he may be out of that stage by now), so poor Ganley must be coughing up a goodly wad. This sort of thing does crop up from time to time; Mimo Dei of Scuderia Centro-Sud was famous for it as is Chinetti. Still, it is very difficult to break into top-class racing and many people don't have the talent or the time to work up through the ranks. Even Fangio never would have made it without help from the Argentine club as I doubt he ever had money enough to pay for a good ride.

The Ferrari lads, plus some local talent, did an astounding job patching up Andretti's Ferrari after he crunched it early in practice. The mechanics were quite at home in the haze and stony ground as Emilia is like that in the spring. What a marvelous bunch of characters; they would prick up their ears every time the howling Matra would go by at speed as that is how Ferraris used to sound. Head mechanic Borsari was given the Tinkertoy award for the patch job which included a big box of tools I think, probably not metric sizes. Borsari is a proud man and whereas the thought is nice, I hope he never finds out what a Tinkertoy is.

Actually it was not a very clever time to run a GP as none of the proper cars used to be ready for the Goodwood Easter Monday meeting, let alone a month earlier. What there was ready, i.e. the better-engined Ferraris etc were run at Brands Hatch a week or so earlier but those races are really used for sorting out. Pescarolo's March for example had had inboard front brakes the week before but as it had only done some 30 miles was not really ready for a race. Frank Williams was complaining that the rear suspension was not working properly because of a batch of bad springs and in fact it broke. Surprisingly on what is by no means a rough circuit there were many suspension breakages although it is uncertain, drivers being what they are, how many came from running over immovable objects. The BRMs had trouble with rear wishbones letting go and Lotuses were not too happy about the front. I think that it is about time that racing cars were built capable of going the distance chassiswise. For that matter it has always been a matter of wonder (1) why any of the cars make five laps, the complexity being what it is (2) why they can't make them finish after all the loving care; even allowing for the usual dodgem routine that put out Ickx, Siffert, et al. Who would want to be a team manager? Especially, like Ken Tyrrell, when you come five thousand miles to a race and then get rousted about by a veal-faced pit steward. Stone the bloody crows. ⊕

At Large

WITH HENRY MANNEY

EVERY NOW AND then all the big wheels are out of the office and I get a panic-stricken call from Dottie who is holding down the fort; usually asking me to go cover something. Panic-stricken because I don't always react the same way as the Editors and then there are anguished calls from PRs using "Deano, Baby" (at one extreme) and rather stiff little notes from attorneys on the other. Anyway when the squeaking died down enough so that words could be distinguished, it turned out that some men frm the Gummint were having a conference on the morrow about safety cars they had commanded to have built and a live bod from the office really should go in case a great truth should reveal itself, rather like Godzilla rising from the swamp. Our Mr. Wakefield, the Mario Lanza of the Laguna Hills, has been doing a giant screed on safety cars as that is one of the fashionable subjects for all technical magazines these days, just as Ecology and Pot are for the public print. And you never know when something good might appear. But Mr. Wakefield was in Detroit along with everyone else who had ever held a slide rule; that left me, the mail boy, and two other chaps who didn't have enough seniority to get free trips but promised to take photos as BPB's representatives to the Department of Transportation. And a fine figure we cut too, even if none of us knew Sweet Fanny Adams re this safety car business up to now.

However we were nicely filled in at a Press conference the next day out at olde worlde Orange County International Raceway, up in the top floor of the tower no less which affords one an unmatched view of USMC jets playing touch and go at El Toro. Now I apologize if I am reiterating material already known to you but it seems that the Dept of Transportation, presumably agitated indirectly by all the Nader business, gave a contract to Fairchild-Hiller and AMF to produce, modify, or otherwise cough up a pair of safety vehicles apiece incorporating a list of requirements which the Dept would like to see incorporated. The primary goal appears to be that said cars will withstand a 50 mph shunt against a stationary object without scrambling the occupants. Naturally there are many others including a resistance to the Dreaded Sideslip, undue shedding of doors, etc etc but surprisingly enough not much attention is paid to the problem of braking, presumably because Detroit already knows how to get cars stopped even if they don't always do it. There has been a lot of testing going on for the last couple of years to the tune of some 7 million plus but we were cautioned that the vehicles present for us to drive were not necessarily those chosen or even terribly sanitary. These two firms would be asked to deliver their finished products in December but what we were seeing today was in the nature of a progress report. Don't ask me what suddenly triggered this display off as I don't read the political pages.

GM also was awarded a contract and is producing 9 cars, of which 3 are "fully configured" as the spokesman put it; these will eventually be stacked up against fresh cars produced by Fairchild and AMF to see which is the best. That doesn't mean that the losers will be cast into outer darkness with gnashing of gearteeth as they will continue to develop on a smaller scale to provide what is referred to as engineering feedback. In spite of the fact that all this was described as a "limited engineering and dollar program," you are probably agreeing with me that it sounds like a typical Government project and a very pleasant deal for all those involved. However the engaging Mr. Doug Toms, head of this particular branch of the Dept of Transportation, appeared about this time to observe that they had hopes of cutting down the traffic death rate by a third; if so, money doesn't count for very much does it?

He also observed that the Department was not in the business of producing prototype production vehicles; a relief really as one could see ahead the prospect of utilitarian safety cars rather like a Polish Syrena being turned out by one or two big companies with nothing else allowed on the road. I am sure that the temptation is there, though, if for no other reason that politicians fall heir to the Do-Goods when they take office. Anyway, the Dept has signed concordats with firms in four foreign countries, i.e. Toyota, Datsun, VW, Fiat, Alfa Romeo, and British Leyland to pursue research along the same common lines. You may well ask what possibly British Leyland (for instance) might pass on that GM didn't

CONTINUED ON PAGE 93

MANNEY MEXICANA
At Large at Auto Expo Mexico

STORY & PHOTOS BY HENRY N. MANNEY

No DOUBT IT is owing to the mysterious machinery of destiny known to us as Murphy's Law that I have been recently packed off to Spanish-speaking countries speaking little more Spanish than, *"Mas cerveza, por favor."* Still, as Barry McKenzie says, it's better than a poke in the eye with a burnt stick. So what would be more natural, when the news came through by Yaqui runner that Mexico City was about to enjoy its first auto show, that somebody really fluent would be sent down. *"¿Eh? Mas cerveza, por favor."*

Automobile shows are pretty dodgy apparitions at best, depending as they do on carpenters, painters, decor folk, electricians, tickettakers, cops, sweepers (and all the relevant unions) plus of course the automobile people and their charges all coming together at the same time. Of course they never really manage for the same reason that all the cars at Indianapolis aren't 100 percent ready; no one starts in enough time to take care of the million and two details burgeoning at the last minute. Hammering, sawing, and moving of potted plants fell upon the ears of Pres. De Gaulle as he toured the Grand Palais and unseemly over-alled forms flit among the topless birds on Earl's Court Press day. And three days into Geneva a tardy Farfellini prototype is hustled in, much to the fury of the magazines that printed the night before. No show is ever ready, even on the day it closes.

Actually the Auto Expo was not a brand new show as the bare bones of it, as it were, had been presented a month or so before in Los Angeles. Photographer Rick McBride has a lot to do with the Los Angeles one (as he is vigorously engaged in advertising) and had a lot to do with the Mexican one, in this case operating with John Bannon, a Kansas City businessman and longtime resident in Mexico City. Off-hand the show looked like a very good idea even considering the limited purchasing power of the average citizen down there as the recent Homemaking exhibition drew countless millions to look at dumb mixers and iceboxes, especially since the Mexicans are notoriously nutty about cars. The Tourist Board was happy to have something else to advertise, the Government was happy to get some use out of the Palacio de Deportes with its copper dome (having stood idle since the Olympics), and the taxi drivers were happy at the thought of ferrying lots of people way out in the boonies near the airport.

Unfortunately there were a few problems. For example the powers that be specified that the salon be limited to products *hecho en Mèxico* (with the exception of a few prototypes) as there was no use stirring up the masses with goodies they couldn't buy, barring a massive fiddle of some sort or else a thunderous import duty. There are quite a few cars made/assembled in Mexico but at least one large Detroit-based manufacturer, taking the negative attitude that he had already sold much more than the year's production anyway, declined to spend one centavo for a show appear-

ance. Needless to say every bit of the business of the salon had to be cleared from the President down, keeping all the channels clear with good relations so that if some minor officials kicked up a fuss, pressure could be immediately applied from above. Old Mexico hands are probably rolling their eyes and muttering about the *mordida* or "bite;" really I don't think that situation was any worse than elsewhere as politicians, especially poorly paid ones in a seething bureaucracy, are all cast from the same mold. Generous gifts of free tickets, according to Mr. Bannon, solved the problem as politicians love nothing better than being important, handing out free tickets to all their friends. Favors are the currency of politics. Then there was the never-ending battle of Doing Things The Mexican Way which almost put poor Bannon into the loony bin before he was through; for example all the tickets had to be printed in a specified office and then counted and stamped by hand (for tax, I suppose) before being handed over to the sales outlets. Naturally all of this ran late along with everything else but it looked like being a pretty good show . . . The organizers were actually making an

effort with an antique car parade scheduled, exotic prototypes (even if one was still on a ship drydocked in Tampa), a fashion display, scads of pretty girls in checkerdy miniskirts to show off the prototypes, racing movies in the balcony, and a super folklorique decor by J.L. Vergara who deserves mentioning.

As the opening day leaped forward, the usual sort of emmerdements commenced viz: the Mexicana 727, arriving with important Press folk on board, being greeted by the gaudiest sheet lightning storm since Weiland Wagner produced Gotterdammerung.

Then there were slight frictions such as the antique car club suddenly going all reluctant about their parade because nobody loved them. This was tracked down to the organizers' rep having been talking to the wrong bloke in the club organization and was soon smoothed over.

With all these commotions going on the publicity end of things perhaps wasn't getting all the attention it deserved as very little was appearing in the papers in advance. Also there seemed to be some delay in both printing and distributing the advertising posters, further complicated by the fact that as fast as what posters they

had were put up, somebody walked off with them as souvenirs. However some things were done; for instance the Porsche Tapiro was driven up in front of the Presidente hotel whereupon a very toothsome model girl, clad only in Paco Rabanne chain-and-plastic top plus miniscule bikini bottom, strode out of the hotel entrance and entered the car. This was filmed several times to an ever increasing crowd including the inevitable Indian woman with baby, all admiring the car but chiefly curious as to whether one of Pam's features would escape from behind a strategically placed placque of plastic.

Mixed in with all this was the famous antique car parade which turned out to be quite pleasant even if most of the cars weren't appreciably older than some of those running about the streets but usually in a better state of preservation. Naturally the parade got away late to the accompaniment of an enormous traffic jam but nobody, especially the cops on point duty, seemed to mind very much.

Prominent among the attractions was the Principal Model, a statuesque young lady indeed. Those gathered around the gangway fell back making Bert Lahr noises as she presented herself Ta Ra in full Frederick's of Hollywood regalia of bright red tights, black satin hotpants, Baroness Steel boots, and a full-sleeved pink chiffon blouse open down to her navel. To give her credit, that's what she gets paid for and she carries it off very well but you could have hung your hat on the eyeballs of the baggage porters. Anyway what with one thing and another the parade finally got under way to a good-humored if slightly bemused crowd who really hadn't heard there was to be a parade ("but where is El Presidente?") let alone an auto show.

Meanwhile back at the ranch, there was still a lot of hammering and sawing going on not to mention little men painting intricate designs on the floor to go with the Tree of Life and enormous Roi Soleil faces, whatever they may be in Mexico. The whole production seemed to be getting together even if everything was clearly going to be late for the opening reception and fashion show at seven. I was favorably impressed by the quality and rapidity of the work compared to Earls Court, for example, as there was very little standing around in groups gossiping and no going for Tea every fifteen minutes let alone a new strike every ten. The setup was circular with a sort of dumbbell-shaped runway down the middle featuring the Porsche Tapiro on one blob and a special Lancia Fulvia on the other (both at Turin, I

MANNEY AT LARGE

think) with room for the fashion folk to rush about.

Eventually 7 p.m. came and with it the opening ceremony with ribbon-cutting in the glare of TV lights by the Minister of Thingummy and MM Bannon and McBride, an event largely unnoticed by the cheerful workers who went on shifting things about and painting spots or curlicues on the floor. A small crowd gradually flowed in, not paying customers but members of the diplomatic community, Big Wheels, high Government figures, social lights, and similar gratin, I suppose on the principle that the Show might as well be on the social pages as anywhere else. In the middle of the babble of Spanish I heard paterfamilias of an Indian (turban) family proclaim in pure Peter Sellers, "Oh my goodness!" and here came the ubiquitous dog, trotting happily along leaving one set of red and one set of green pawprints. However at that point a burst of deafening music heralded the fashion parade and the mannequins (plus a couple of checkerdy girls moonlighting) shot onto the scene to give us the most fast and furious rendition ever seen, rather as if they were counting on making the 9:30 plane home no matter what.

Oh yes, the Show. Limited to Mexican manufacture, there was not too much there that would interest you after the refined glories of Turin and Geneva but the Detroit contingent showed what cars they do like Darts and Chevelles etc; Mustangs are extremely popular but were not on show except for a superboss on the Shelby stand. Hopups got a lot of space with Shelby, Kelsey wheels, and a firm called Impre that produced a highly professional-looking "Super Bee" with fiberglass bodywork for saloon car racing along with lots of accessory bits. Renault had a big stand with a 65-hp

1300 "Dinalpin" coupe that looked like one of the earlier Alpines plus, of course, several of the R9, L4, R8 ilk. VW of all people also followed the performance line with three Formula Vees of all things (but no dune buggies) plus a beetle with sunglasses and another with blue-and-white fretwork all over to kick the utilitarian image; not too successfully as lots of attention was going to the Safaris. The prototypes have been mentioned but not McBride's GTB filling in for the absent Modulo, still languishing in Tampa. Surprisingly enough the enthusiast market is booming enough to support thinking about local GT coupes. There was a rather sad FTL, sort of equal parts GT 40 and early Alpine, a more interesting angular Sotter by a young Mexican designer carrying the Matra and/or Sting Ray ideas out and incorporating such ideas as fiberglass wheel covers, and a very handsome Neretti available in either racing or street trim. All of these were heavily based on VW components and the finish on the last two was really very good, as was practically all the Mexican work we saw. Filling out the chinks were such oddments as a Mexican-made Hobie Cat, trucks, buses, a strange trailer that pivoted up on the roof of the towing car, limo rentals, a giant lottery by *El Sol* newspaper, old cars, not to mention miniature Can-Am racers in GRP to be used as kids' beds or bathtubs.

Altogether the show seemed to have gone down very well, Bannon and McBride are still speaking, and was even held over a week as the word spread around the city that there was really something going on. What kind of business they could have done with a little publicity, a bus shuttle running from some central point, and perhaps the fashion parade every day is unknown but at least they didn't lose their shirts. The thought of Next Year is enough to make everyone concerned roll his eyes wildly, but for an enterprise of this sort, the first year is always the worst. ◼

MANNEY AT LARGE

CONTINUED FROM PAGE 89

know or else pretend it knew but apparently different parameters are envisaged for 2000 and 4000 lb cars. I was a bit confused at "pounds" at first as I kept reading it as pounds sterling; there will now be a short pause while all of you go umm hmm and tap your heads meaningfully. Said weight categories are approximate at best and will be even more approximate when they build in all the safety gubbins. This very point opened up a lively discussion between some of the Press and a BuTrans apparatchik in mod spectacles who displayed all the modern flexibility with the English language as to using nouns and adverbs as adjectives. As to a question about how all this jass would be added on and how much it would cost, Mr. Toms replied that it should all be designed in from the start and thus, with luck, would neither cost appreciably more nor make the car much heavier. Whereupon another Bureau type observed that "the genius of Detroit would rise to the occasion" (ho ho ho in my notes) and that there was an analogy with the automatic transmission, really. When they started out automatics were fiendishly heavy and expensive but now practically every make of car had one. Anyway, he said with mod spectacles glinting, nobody put up much of a squawk about paying extra money for vinyl roof and eight-track stereo. And you can draw your own conclusions from *that*.

Another Pressman then asked how these safety gubbins would affect collisions between little cars and big ones; in reply he got a fine burst of officialese about "agressivity" (the big car squashing the little one) and "forgiving front ends" (ones that fold up and cost $845.62 to fix) besides a strong intimation that he, the apparatchik, thought all those funny little cars didn't belong on any safety-conscious road anyhow. Which naturally brought another question about the growing trend of American motorists toward the 2000 lb car; what if Detroit came out with a really cheap, light car in this class? Mr. Toms fielded it neatly by saying that he had heard "vibrations" about one but of course he didn't say that Detroit, after educating the people for years to think that a heavy car was better, wasn't about to build something really light even if it were sound.

We then set forth to try the Fairchild-Hiller and AMF at the bottom of the garden on a little slalom track. The first of these *testwagen* was a much-modded Plymouth presided over by none other than ex-*Car Life* staffer Jon McKibben who was limping slightly from having bailed off his Honda in a m/c race the previous weekend. Nice to have somebody around a project who actually knows what a racetrack looks like. The AMF I never did really identify but it had a trunk full of electronic gear, protuberant bumpers, and was reminiscent of a customized Chrysler Airflow. Neither one had much in the way of interior padding etc and were absolutely full of dials; the Plymouth was also "pretty tired" and had dodgy brakes as a rear axle seal was leaking.

Naturally we all charged off in these things and found that the handling was a lot better than that of a normal American car. I hope that I won't do any disservice to the engineers involved by pointing out that big flat NASCAR racing tires and wheels will do wonders for even a flexible flyer but of course there had been a lot more work done than that as body lean was kept within reasonable limits, violent understeer or oversteer was absent (at least at our speeds) and yet unlike the normal NASCAR stocker both had quite a reasonable ride. The Plymouth was perhaps a little more pendulum-ey but then much needed bracing had jacked the weight up approximately 1000 lb. As another engineer observed, perhaps unkindly, it is difficult to make a silk purse out of you-know-what. Quality was to be built in from the beginning, something Ing. Uhlenhaut of Mercedes has known all the time. At any rate, we didn't try to prove out Mr. Toms' requirements for a 50 mph crash but both in general solidity and stiffness, the safety cars showed that much profitable work had been done.

We enjoyed talking to all the lads, especially to the pleasant and un-stuffy Mr. Toms who was seen riding happily around on a road-going MV 4 motorcycle afterwards. It has always been my feeling that box-stock American cars are diabolically unsafe and that the manufacturers were not going to do anything about it as long as the same product sold so well as is. Anything the Government can do constructively for a change is welcome, especially if they save a few lives in the process. However I can't help feeling as well that the problem is being approached from the wrong end; surely it is more important to design cars that feature swerveability (to quote Issigonis) and good handling first so that the driver can steer himself out of trouble instead of proceeding willy-nilly in a straight line with brakes locked. Another important but unmentionable fact, at least politically, is that of tightening license requirements so that people holding drivers' licenses really could drive. Lead on, Mr. Toms!

PLENTY OF ROOM

Manney discovers Baja in a Land Rover

BY HENRY N. MANNEY
LEO BESTGEN ILLUSTRATION

For a number of years now I have been subjected to a barrage of propaganda about how nice Baja California was and we all said uh huh thinking of one gas station in 800 miles, crummy border towns, prickly pucker-

bushes, distinctly colonial roads, and manyleggeds (not to mention nolaggeds) anxious to creep in bed with you at night. Also the last time I went camping was during WW2 in the Engineers which tends to put one off camping

for life. So it came to pass that after a lot of jolly conversation about the Baja 1000, we found ourselves throwing enough junk into a borrowed Land Rover to keep Boney on the road to Moscow, committed to taking photos of said race. We were not really setting out cold as besides bringing a variety of maps and guides (auto club, Jim Crow's Baja book, Gulick's ditto, Cross' ditto) we were accompanied by the Ed Boyds and their GMC camper device. Actually, after doing the Monte Carlo Rallye the thought of warmish weather and no snow seemed to make it almost a picnic.

Land Rovers are always a comfort to have around at a time like this as they have been in production long enough to get all bugs ironed out and have a well-deserved reputation for going practically anywhere the driver is willing to take them. Ours was the short wheelbase 4-cyl model of song and story, improved since the last time I drove one to the extent of much better seats and disimproved with the addition of smog gear, much beloved by the State of California but no perishing use whatever in the Mexican desert. Of all the places you don't want an engine running excessively lean, the Mexican desert probably ranks with the Great Karroo as not every adobe garage carries Rover parts. Anyway, the Rover had all the usual equipment like rather small Goodyear knobbies, 4wd, etc and actually took some prying out of British Leyland as a previous tester had allegedly fiended a piston, equally allegedly from running flat out on the freeway. The real blame probably lies with the smog gear as every Rover I have ever seen has been driven as fast as it would go, the usual feeble English valve springs acting as a built-in governor before piston speed totted up to dangerous heights. Also like every British car I've ever tested, it had something wrong with it when delivered, to wit inoperative dash lights, loose ignition leads that caused a sooted plug at an inopportune moment, and a locking front hub that refused to unlock, causing us to whir the front differential around all the way down and back. The door locks were also real buggers and one eventually came out in my hand complete with key.

God only knows what we would have done if the Boyds hadn't been bringing a lot of their stuff as the Rover seemed awfully full; of course we didn't need to carry a couple of umbrellas, a reclining beach chair, and an extra camera but we did have Dr Clarke's Thermos popup tent, a Coleman lantern with fuel, a couple of sleeping pads, many gallons of spare water, more clean clothes than we ever used, two quarts of oil, a USPS star finder, tons of food, a Coleman cooler and besides all the other gubbins eight or nine chunks of nice eucalyptus firewood plus USMC issue machete.

Looking back, the long wheelbase Rover might have been nicer but Annie would have managed to fill it up anyway. At any rate, the race started on Wednesday so we lurched out into the dawn on Sunday, planning to have plenty of time to enjoy the scenery and recon a good photo site without being driven by that gnawing devil of "you are too late already." Whining down the freeway at our requested 55 mph, we eventually found the Boyds at our agreed rendezvous and then whined some more to the border at Tijuana. We had provided ourselves with a notarized letter from Leylands and also Mexican tourist cards but nobody wanted to know at the border, even the cheerful girl who wrote up our Mexican insurance (Oscar Padilla), something you must have in case of a shunt. We took ours out for a full week Just In Case and it cost $20 approx.

Tijuana is a mad mess, making the Parisian "bidonvilles" look like a luxury suburb, and the Boyds took us on a bypass route that eventually landed us on the toll road to Ensenada. The coast along there is lovely, a bit built up with Mexican ideas of California motel architecture, but it isn't everywhere you get to see a Mexican destroyer decaying in the surf alongside the road. Somebody turned left too early for Ensenada. We didn't and even stopped for lunch at a nice clean, but not cheap, restaurant next to Hussong's motel. I get the tummy rumbles just thinking of Mexico but my chicken tacos and Annie's chile rellenos produced no symptoms besides being really very good. Ensenada was soon reached, a bit of a disappointment after all the glowing stories, as most of it is pretty ratty and infested with importunate small boys looking for something to pinch. The ladies went off to the supermercado to buy bread and eight kilos of limes while I did my homework on the maps. After that, we went by the fish pier where the ladies came up with lobsters ($3 each) and a nice slab of yellowtail before whirring off once more.

Navigation is a bit of a problem going out of those towns as there are no signs and somebody takes the road away at intervals, leaving the sort of goat track that usually winds up in Pedro's farmyard. Actually the main highway is being rebuilt or whatever they do there; the best method is to follow the sun and the mainstream of traffic. Barring the bombed portions, Mexico 1 is paved now down to St Quintin and even if you have to lumber alongside like an elephant taking a dust bath, the causeway is always visible. At any rate, it wasn't too long before we were motoring through soft bare mountains to Santo Tomas, birthplace of some quite pleasant wines originally planted by the missionary padres, where we found a monster camping park right before the entrance to the town. The wall-eyed gent in charge (there is also a store and gas station) took $2 from each couple and let us in to camp under the olive trees in practical isolation if you discount the inevitable local dog and cat.

I don't think I had realized up to now that we were actually going to camp but there we were. First night out there is always a lot of fumbling and fruitless searching but eventually a fire was built in a sunken washtub, Patty's Coleman stove set up, tent erected, drinks provided (choice of tequila or rum with grapefruit soda), wine set out, and everything chucked out of the Rover to get our boots in the darkest corner. There was plenty of firewood available, mostly old dug up vines, but these didn't seem to be providing proper coals so we threw in eucalyptus which really does the job. Ed cut a pair of still-wiggling Ensenada lobsters up, hung a handy bit of expanded metal over the fire, and dinner was on the stove. Fresh lobster with melted butter, cold white wine, and canned asparagus may be really roughing it but the wall-to-wall stars and gentle breeze, not to mention the lack of assorted jets and copper chopper, made up for it.

Next morning took a bit of doing but eventually everything was back in and we whirred on some more. The paved road is rather twisting for a while and also steep in places (that's where we pushed the ignition leads back in place) but generally well within any decent driver's scope. We stopped for gas at Colnett, I think, at a Pemex station (rest room at Bradley's v clean) and as the Rover has a giant filter in the filler pipe plus another in the line, we didn't think it worthwhile to go through the chamois-straining exercise recommended by most of the guide books. We never had any trouble, nor did Ed, but if you were going to La Paz it might be worthwhile installing one of those big Fram filters found on diesels, the sort that drains at the bottom. Certainly the car should be kept topped up as these country stations do run out; we had a spare 5-gal. can just in case and also an Okie Credit Card as Ed carries about 55 gallons in the camper. Another necessity is a living breathing operating air cleaner as dust is everywhere.

After a picnic lunch by the bay of San Quintin we carried on, soon running into a lot of dirt road around construction or sometimes running on the dirt roadbed of the new one itself. In a way the bypasses are more restful as the new bits are up on a causeway and not too wide at that. Furthermore it necks down from time to time at a bridge or you may find a tasteful selection of rocks and bits of cactus in the way. Do not continue as the bridge isn't there yet. Tightrope walking on the causeways, anywhere up to ten feet above the surrounding countryside, requires constant attention as not only is the steering of the numerous Mexican-registered cars a bit suspect (judging from the amount of wheel winding) but the Rover has little or no caster action. It steers but you have to steer it.

All this construction continued, or rather the construction area as nobody seemed to be working, down past an occasional fishing camp to El Rosario. Pat had been filling us with horror stories about the ravine down into El Rosario but this too had been scarfed out and in any case wasn't at all bad compared to parts of Saddleback Park where I have been falling off my Bultaco with regularity. Some experience on a dirt bike does powers of good when negotiating dirt with four wheels, teaching that the least slide doesn't mean disaster and firming up braking distances. Anyway, El Rosario was a bit of a shock as it is in big letters on the map and all but turns out to be about ten houses plus a couple of cafes-cum-gas stations, one of these being the celebrated Mme Espinoza's where we topped up once again to the tune of 23 liters. Our 23 liters cost about $5 or just about the same as 33 liters we got on the way back, Incidentally we went to some trouble to get Mexican pesos before leaving but needn't have bothered as everyone seems to use American currency, even if it isn't wise to come out with a $50 bill as it may bankrupt the town. Oh yes, south of Ensenada at Maneadero we had our tourist cards checked at an immigration post as theoretically you aren't supposed to go any farther down without one. I gather that you can do the whole business there if needed but it is just as well to have all the papers in shape when going foreign.

El Rosario is the end of civilization, more or less, as the phone line stops there. The road also reverts to, or rather remains, the one-lane potholed mess used by all the trucks, buses, ancient Chevrolets, and probably the padres themselves on the mission tour. It starts out with a neat detour around the local junkyard and then bounces alongside the "river" for a while before crossing over. This used to be a fairly decent crossing but recent heavy rains which caused a change of route in the race also deposited a full load of nice new marbles. We put 4-wheel drive in play here for the first time (and practically the last) as the banks were a bit abrupt; Ed had had his 4wd in since we first hit dirt as he paid $700 extra for it and was going to amortize it. Nobody had much trouble, even the ancient Chevrolets, and I really think you could manage without provided you didn't go charging off up a sandwash. On the Rover 4wd is quite fun as it is also in the granny box; in low gear you can run along and push if necessary while flat out in top gives you a rousing 35 mph or thereabouts.

Actually the short normal gears and good torque make 3rd and 4th useful most of the time.

After wandering about in Rosario Wash we turned southward again in a subsidiary one near a giant butte resembling a castle. There is, as often happens, a choice of roads but the one with the most recent tire tracks does well as all go to the same place eventually. The high ones are in use for rainy weather but the lower streambed ones are more direct. Actually ours wasn't all that bad in the wash even if a trifle high-crowned but one soon develops a technique of leaving two wheels on the center and two on the edge, avoiding thus the worst of the corrugations. Thoughts of really roughing it were dispelled by sights of passenger cars lumbering along, obviously having come from La Paz. Some of these machines are pretty decrepit and at night you can tell what sort of vehicle it is by the squeaks as grease jobs seem to be unknown. The great Baja occupation, by the way, seems to be sitting on the rad with feet inside the engine working on something. It is still the Great Frontier and everyone who passes one of these stopped cars pauses to see if he can be of any use. After all, the next one may be you.

So to bed in a godforsaken place with north wind blowing and support vehicles rumbling by all night en route to one check point or another. We were just down the road from the Aguajito ranch which serves as a rest stop (as does any inhabited locality) and it was interesting watching trucks weave up the renowned grade. And what a grade, as we found next day . . . steep, rocky, narrow, and a worthy trials section for motorbikes. One lane on the side of a mountain and no guard rail. However we bumped over without difficulty, stopping at intervals to let trucks through, and wound down past one of the Big Cacti to another valley. The road along here for quite a spell can only be charitably described as vile with potholes, rock ledges whenever it crosses the edge of a stratus, transverse ridges, and just bumps. The Rover had a lot of difficulty thereabouts because of the short wheelbase that just seemed to fit into pairs of transverse ruts/potholes; it would get to hobby-horsing after the front end dropped into the first one and everything in the back would lift up vertically then crash down in a different arrangement. Recurrent sets of these were *penible* to say the least, making a lot of 2nd-gear work, and many dark thoughts were formulated on unsprung weight and full independent suspension. Better shocks would help but barring that fatter tires and a longer wheelbase. More joy arrived with one of the flat bits that turn into mud in the rainy season. About a hundred tracks fan off in the general direction of travel and you just chose the least villainous, gen-erally picking far left or far right (or just out in the desert) to avoid giant truck-sized potholes. Clapping on the brakes before a crater invited disaster as besides the cargo's shifting, your attendant genie-like dustcloud of fine talcum-powdered silt would overtake with a whoosh. The Rover is reasonably well sealed but even so everything inside got pretty well coated. Ed Boyd had air conditioning and just kept his windows shut but we found fresh clean air such a novelty that we had to develop a trick of slamming the sliding windows shut while decelerating. Along here we found one of the infrequent road signs (shot full of holes naturally) put up in a bygone age by the Auto Club but there was another saying simply "Guyaquil" pointing south. You couldn't ask for more than that. Nearby was the reasonably neat Tres Enriques ranch at which we topped up out of jerrycans provided by a cheerful Enrique, petted a large black dog (enrique?), waved at a small child riding a broomstick-horse with goat's skull for a head, and picnicked down the road in a most African-grassland setting. All we missed were wildebeest.

Eventually we arrived near the Virgin Shrine which lives in a large boulder, appropriate enough in a country which is sandy, covered with large boulders, and populated with many sorts of cacti including the engaging Boojum. One doesn't know what to think about these things really as they start out bottle shaped at the bottom and then rise precariously to a long inquiring finger or fingers which may point any direction that takes its fancy. The hide is a sort of greenish-yellow leather and in this season at least the whole gemilla is trimmed with a green spikey fringe (with leaves) featuring yellowish flowers at the very top. After prolonged study we decided that Bjørn Winblad must have designed them in concert with the Martians or that they really *are* Martians; I don't know how they escaped being starred in the junky SciFi movies Hollywood used to make as Boojums look much more convincing than rubber lizards. That's because Boojums are real, see? Wolfman meets the giant Boojum.

Backtracking a bit, we dived up a sand wash that promised several good angles for pix on the morrow, space between us and the road, shelter from the now chilly wind (a cold front was coming through) and not least a veritable jardin exotique of cacti big and small including of course boulders and Boojums. We stayed there two nights and could have managed more as when cars didn't come or darkness fell we always had plenty to investigate. Cars didn't come till about three on race day, actually, so we had plenty of time to police the area of beer cans, bottles, broken leaf springs, and other artifacts besides inspecting spikey plants at close range. As Annie said, anything not spikey in the desert gets eaten. We had plenty of false alarms as something like 20 planes flew over before the competitors arrived and when the first appeared it was PJ and Stroppe, naturally, obligingly putting it sideways for us, the Bronco jumping and bobbing about. How they went quickly over that revolting road above us I cannot think but they were something like an hour on corrected time ahead of the next bod, a Husqvarna. The bikes seemed to be having an easier time of it but then they weren't going as fast. Dune buggies of various sorts looked very comfortable but didn't have the raw power while a lone Volvo was quite neat and didn't even rattle. All night they went on, late starters or those detained by mechanical ills trundling past, and we basked by our fire of ocotillo and ate our steaks unknowing that just over the ridge poor Ak Miller and Jim Hunter were spending the night in a windowless pickup. It got below freezing, especially around 3 a.m. when the wind picked up, and while we suffered some indecision as to unzip the tent to go out and water the cholla (those Boojums are really kinky against a starlit sky) a buggyist was curled about his fire in a nearby draw, waking up friz every hour to put more ocotillo on as it burns quickly. Going back the next day we found Ak over the ridge, by now well provisioned with beer and similar food, and he said the worst part was when the local bus came by and "if I'd had the fare to get on that turkey I'd a gone."

The funny thing, at least to me, was that I don't particularly like all the fuss and bother of camping, the endless stowing and unstowing, the business of zipping yourself in and out of the tent to go pipi as I am a nocturnal wanderer, the early bed, and yet I found myself becoming impatient as we moved back north where more people were. There is a powerful attraction to sitting there in absolute solitude and watching a cactus wren five feet away inspect you curiously or a tiny white-bellied mouse prospect energetically for crumbs near your foot. Cacti are a rather silent lot and offer no unnecessary conversation besides a slight muttering between themselves in the constant desert wind. In spite of the projected paved road down the peninsula, resulting in an even bigger crop of old beer cans and rusted-out automobiles, Baja California in most ways will still afford plenty of room for those of us who liked California looking as it did before the land pirates and big money boys got to it, who like nature to be real and not Disneyed. There will still be enough back roads where only something bullet-proof like the Land Rover will go, where you can be out of sight of jets and stereo decks and heedless oafs strewing their garbage around them. But come at least while everyone still waves as you pass by.

MANNEY IN MEXICO

ILLUSTRATION BY LEO BESTGEN

The perils of
motor homing south of the border

BY HENRY N. MANNEY III

FROM TIME TO time you have probably been belting along in your new Maserati, eager to get that smiling and silken bird alongside to that special little restaurant where you plan to get her (1) as full as possible of good food and Chateau Plonque (2) into the Mood (3) into Her Place or Yours. Once there, you plan to impersonate the Turks who received St Ursula's 10,000 virgins with open arms. Your body temperature is approximately the same as an NGK's center electrode at

97

Le Mans and the pit of your stomach feels like navy coffee on the boil. She keeps smiling and is switching about enough under her Pucci (she is the only thing under her Pucci) to wear the nap off the suede seats. Masterfully you boom through those winding country lanes, giving your best impression of P**l N*wm*n at Bonneville, and all of a sudden something white shows up in the lights. Lots of white. Acres and acres of white. It has tail lights and it's doing 26 mph. Sometimes even 24. For miles you follow that blivet through the lanes, occasionally dodging out to take a look, while you get wet under the arms, two of the plugs foul, broken twigs from the trees above clatter down on the Maser's aluminum, and the temperature needle creeps into the red. The nice girl now wears a mask rather like that of your ex-wife's. Finally you see a little hole and shoot through at 9000 rpm, glimpsing as you go by (1) on the right a family eating dinner (2) on the left a whole lot of towney-looking buildings and a State Copper sitting openmouthed in his car. Much much later, after it is all over, you start making plans to buy that James Bond Aston and start shooting holes in motor homes.

All I can say is, you have to drive one to find that you mustn't *tirez au pianiste* as he is doing his best. We rented one of these devices, a 20-foot Pace Arrow rectangular box, as the kids were temporarily out of school and we all wanted to go down into Baja California. Since there are very few hotels thereabouts and if there were we would be talking about $50 to $75 a night, taking our own house with us snail fashion was indicated. A couple of years ago a motor home would have been out of the question, but since then the Mexican government has paved the main road all the way down to Cabo San Lucas plus a couple of side "offs" such as the one to Los Angeles Bay on the gulf coast, about 300 miles south of the border. Renting a motor home at all isn't easy for Baja because if there is an accident, the mills of justice grind exceeding slow (not to mention capriciously), which may mean that the owner waits months to get his vehicle back. Purchase of Mexican insurance at the border helps a bit but still . . . anyway, I got offered a few unsuitable vehicles, mostly of ancient vintage and definitely long in the tooth, before an old friend with a VW agency let me have this device.

When I teetered out of the lot I wasn't so sure what sort of old friend he was as the motorhome's corners seemed as far away as the sharp end on a supertanker. Naturally enough the gas tanks were both empty and that cost me $30 straight off at the nearest Phillips 66, where the unwashed drongo didn't even wash the windscreen. If there had been anything but fumes, I could have made it to my cheapo station and saved about nine cents a gallon! The poo tank *was* full but as a consolation the twin butane tanks were topped up and there was air in the tires. In case all that causes confusion, without doing a road test one can say that we had a toilet-cum-shower with its holding tank and drain hose; a space heater, hot water heater, stove, and fridge all of which ran on the butane; a pressurized water system with its own tank; and the electrics which depended on the chassis' alternator/battery combination but could be hooked into 110 shore current at trailer parks if needed. Aforesaid chassis was Dodge truck, I think, with twin rear wheels and automatic transmission coupled to a monster V-8. Said V-8 had the dirtiest air cleaner I ever saw and could have used new plugs but otherwise ran like dependable American machinery is supposed to.

Inside, there was the driver's office, with a pair of bench seats (plus optional table) alongside, another bed that swung down from above the driver, and a dinette in the back which converted into a double bed. The benches alongside the driver formed an engaging puzzle in converting into a double (theoretical) but as neither of the Boys wanted to sleep with each other or God forbid with their sister, we took a pup tent plus an RAF survival suit and one Boy camped out. There were quite a few things that could have been a lot better (especially more working space around the stove) and just as many that were surprisingly good but this isn't a road test. Suffice it to say that before buying a motor home of any sort, it is wise to rent two or three different types; just like blind dating in fact.

Anyway, we got away late, partially because the vehicle wasn't delivered on time (loose battery lead) and we would have been delayed anyway because it takes time to stow everything aboard. Fortunately there are plenty of cabinets because the Mother always takes enough food and clothing to go across Siberia. Much baking and cooking went on and I think at last count we had seven loaves of bread for a five-day trip plus of course other food and wine. The camping stuff (tent, pads, Coleman lantern, etc) all went in the "cellar" while spare gas cans, eucalyptus firewood for coals, and any oddments were flung into the boot. By the time we were ready it was a bit too late to avoid the rush at the Mexican border so it was beddie byes. Just as well it was next morning because additional time gets eaten up stowing things in the fridge etc, etc and of course you don't make the average speed you would in a normal car. Freeways are no problem if the side overhang is kept in mind; this also contributing to a certain amount of mad zigging about when trucks pass due to the Venturi effect. More time was spent topping up in San Diego and then still more getting Mexican insurance and tourist cards at the border; none of these was avoidable but the last, but it would have meant a trip to the Mexican Consulate otherwise. The loss just has to be allowed for.

Getting down into Baja is pretty straightforward if you bypass most of Tijuana (see a good guidebook like Cross'), take the toll motorway, and slip into Ensenada by the quay road past the canneries. There you can park near the fish dock while the girls buy some yellowtail to grill later and visit the *supermercado* for canned juices like mango, guava or papaya which are much better there and not so watered down. If you forgot beer, Carta Blanca is better than American and some of the Santo Tomas red wines are as good as Californian. Try to keep the girls out of the souvie shops.

Exiting Ensenada requires as many lookouts as sailing out of a coral atoll; the locals don't have good judgment to put it mildly and an accident is bad bad news. This caveat applies to well past Maneadero, where you have to show the man your tourist card, and until you get out of populated areas. A lot of the road from there down is pretty good and winds among the mountains but there are a few towns. In one of them, the local ambulance is parked crosswise on the road and a nice little Indian lady in nurse's uniform hits you up for the local hospital. Actually there isn't too much traffic, the towns aren't much to look at, and come to that Baja isn't all that scenic until El Rosario which used to be the frontier with a vengeance as the telephone lines stopped there. It looks like a frontier town, too, but has lost a bit of its flavor as now everybody just thunders on through, barring people who remember what an almighty grind it was over the hill on dirt.

El Rosario used to be the last place you got gas out of a pump for nearly a thousand miles and they filled the pump with a bucket. Now there is a modern Pemex station 'round the corner and the prices are modern too; we filled up one ank at Colonet a ways before El Rosario and it came to $23 for ethyl! We thought we were being ripped off but it costs slightly over 3 pesos a liter for ethyl which makes just about a dollar a gallon. "Nova," the leaded regular, is around 2 pesos 50 a liter and is good for dry cleaning I suppose or perhaps 2cv Citroëns. However we hastily calculated our resources, turning out the kids' pocketbooks as well, and it was clear that we just wouldn't make it to Los Angeles Bay and back home at that rate, mashing vigorously on the throttle (resulting in six mpg approx) and buying "Extra" (ethyl) Pemex. So it was 40 mph or so, driving like one of the Economy Run cracks on the No. 1 butterfly, and Nova for the poor Dodge. It didn't like Nova.

The country after El Rosario is a succession of mountain ranges and valleys which meant slow speed up the hills and a Gadarene rush down the far side. The poor engine on Nova, after we had diluted the ethyl enough times, would just go gaaaaakkkkk and lose speed, necessitating a shift to second where it would pull all right but curiously, not dingle. On the way back when we calculated our mileage under the new regime at about 12 mpg, we developed a method of switching to the spare tank of American regular on hills and the engine would pick up and purr smoothly over in top gear. We also had to do the switching routine about five minutes before stopping for lunch as otherwise, on the key shutting off, the engine would commence this zany conga beat of hickychump puff hickychump puff and blow smoke rings out of the tailpipe indefinitely. I looked out once and here were the crew all doing the mambo to the hickychump puff cha cha cha; there was then a loud bang and the cockpit filled with this smell like an abo's armpit. Usually you couldn't shut it off, what with automatic transmission and all, even with Jim Crow's favorite method of leaving it in gear, so either it was the switch bit or let it idle. At a buck a gallon my memory got good. We also added American gas from our cans to the neat Nova and a workable mixture was about ten gallons Nova, three American, and two American ethyl with Bardahl 20:1 as we had one can with Bultaco premix in it. The smoke rings were better anyway.

Actually the reduction in speed was a good thing, both uphill and down. The road gets very narrow indeed after El Rosario and it is wise to stay on one's own side as Mexican trucks, not to mention American campers, take up a lot of room. The Mexicans don't really believe in road shoulders; you often find yourself travelling along a causeway with an unguarded drop of anything up to 15 feet on both sides and furthermore they put their little concrete stops right at the edge of the pavement. Also, at an even pace nobody gets thrown around too much and can look at the scenery besides moving around to icebox to toilet to dinette and back again. It is only fair to say that these motor homes have a roll center about as high as the Eiffel tower, that the chassis is apparently attached to the body by a small Sears Roebuck plastic toolbox hinge, and that you can't take your eye off the driving for an instant or the whole mass will make a determined lunge for one ditch or the other. Thus the planned Gadarene rush downhills became as sedate as the stately progress uphills and frankly I even enjoyed it more like that.

Progressing along in your own little house, you can look at all the pretty scenery and there is no hurry to get to a hotel or restaurant because you have those too. As we found out, an early start is the answer to covering an acceptable amount of ground; early starts are simple when early bed is the rule and that was easy enough because I wouldn't let anyone read

late (although the lights were quite good) as the Pace Arrow only had the one battery. It was pretty hard to start anyway with the automatic choke going out and who wants to be stuck out in the desert with a flat battery?

We camped only once in a trailer park and that because we wanted to pump out the poo tank. The rest of the time one just pulls off on a bit of the old dirt road that winds in and out, finds a reasonably flat place, and shuts everything off. Butane-operated devices operate on the pilot when not being used but tend to go out under way, either from being tilted or from draft. The neat way is to shut off the butane tap at the tank but that meant the icebox would quit working so every evening stop we scurried around outside opening trapdoors and lighting up the space and hot water heaters.

It is best to get stopped before sunset, both to find a nice spot sheltered from the wind (for the fire) and also because driving at night in Mexico is chancey. Scraggy black cows wander about the road and they tend to have sharp corners. Not only that, the local natives have been known to park their trucks on the road for a nap.

Los Angeles Bay is a cinch to get to now and looks exceedingly travel brochure, what with the surfless bay and big stark islands floating in it. Camping is no problem, if you stay off the airstrip that is, and you can even do a bit of sand road to get farther up the bay. Unfortunately the place is littered with tin cans and other rubbish; I spent several happy hours burying this junk while the family went shell collecting.

The nicest place on the trip, really, was just north of Rancho Santa Inez in the boojum forest, very science fiction with giant boulders, cacti, and boojums of course. A division of labor works best at times like this as one bod lights the butane, another builds a fire ring from rocks, another collects dried ocotillo and dead barrel cacti (they burn technicolor), another pitches the tent, another (people overlap, naturally) gets the Coleman out for light, and the Mother sets dinner on. This can be taken out or in as preferred and then it is time to sit by the fire and look at stars never seen in more civilized places, listen for coyotes, poke the coals, and just watch the boojums nodding to each other. Eventually you can go to bed . . . your own bed . . . in complete silence. And you can't hardly get that no more.

HENRY N. MANNEY III
1922-1988

TOO MANY OF us spend too much time thinking and talking about "the good old days." I'm as guilty of that as anyone, but occasionally something happens that makes that exercise all too viable. Henry Manney left us March 15, 1988, 12 days before his 66th birthday.

I didn't know Henry very well when he lived in California the first time. We became friends after he joined *Road & Track* as our overseas correspondent in early 1961. His first R&T report, published in the July 1961 issue, was the Targa Florio coverage, and it was wonderful—setting the tone for future Manney pieces to appear in, as he once put it, "the good grey pages of *Road & Track*."

Races, auto shows and new-car presentations in Europe were Henry's beat, but we used him to broaden the spectrum of R&T coverage with features on food (where to eat while touring Europe; he knew the best places) and travel (including the infamous Ile du Levant).

Henry was the best at what he did, and he worked with the best on the many excursions around the European automotive scene: Geoffrey Goddard for photography, Stan Mott and Russell Brockbank for art.

In spite of the seemingly relaxed style of Manney's writing, it didn't come all that easily to him. After the 1963 Targa Florio, Henry, his wife Annie and I had gone to Greece, partly for a vacation and partly because Henry was to cover the Acropolis Rally for *The Motor.* I watched him do the Targa report for *Road & Track* in our Athens hotel room.

Rolling a piece of paper into his Olivetti portable typewriter, he typed "47th Targa Florio—wherein Ferrari returns a 2-year-old favor to Porsche by handing over the race on the last lap . . . " Then he stopped to light his pipe, stare out the window (tempting, when the Acropolis is the major portion of your view), go over his race notes once again, adjust the tobacco in the pipe, then laboriously type the first paragraph using the first finger of each hand.

After each paragraph he would stop, consult his notes yet again, and go on. It seemed to take forever, but once he had finished the report, which would appear in the August 1963 issue, it was done.

No rewrite, no retyping, a few minor notes between lines or in margins with a fine-point pen, but his first draft was, basically, his finished story.

I learned a lot working with Henry Manney, particularly when I had the good fortune to accompany him to various races or shows. His attire at a race was almost always corduroy pants, tweed jacket, tie and hat, accessorized with cameras, a folding brolly and the ever-present notebook. Being used to scruffily dressed journalists, I asked why he chose to "dress up" when he was working at what could be a dirty bit of work. His reply was simple and straight to the point: "When you meet people, particularly for the first time, you are taken for what you appear to be. Dress like a bum and you're assumed to be a bum. Dress like a gentleman, and they'll think you are one."

His philosophy carried over to his personal contacts with car owners, drivers and mechanics. Henry never pushed his way into a situation, nor did he ask stupid or offensive questions. The interviewees were professionals, and he was one also. They respected him for his attitude and demeanor, and he, more often than not, got the information he wanted. After he had written a few race reports, they also knew that he could be trusted not to break a confidence and that his reports would be accurate and fair. He left them as a friend and was welcomed back the next time.

Henry was a dedicated car freak, but his interests were wide and his knowledge was vast. He knew a lot about music, particularly opera and ballet, which he studied in Los Angeles after his 3-plus-year stint in the military as a radar mechanic in WWII. In fact, he met his wife Anne Statz at a ballet studio. They toured, briefly, in a ballet company in the U.S. and Central and South America. His Army service must have been a shock to his family in view of his father being a Colonel in the Marine Corps and his grandfather a Navy Admiral.

He was also a baseball fan, his enthusiasm fanned considerably by his father-in-law, Arnold "Jigger" Statz, the best center fielder in the old Pacific Coast league and arguably one of the best fielders in baseball history. Henry and

his father-in-law could talk baseball as long as Henry could talk cars with the rest of us.

It was a double tragedy for Anne Manney when her father passed away the day after her husband died; Henry from the result of a cerebral hemorrhage that occurred six years and four months earlier, and her father from old age.

Henry is survived by his wife Anne; children Cecilia Schreyer, Patrick G. and Henry N. Manney IV; sister Frances Baer; and two grandchildren.

—Dean Batchelor

A fan and fans

IT'S MARCH 15. The Ides of March. Baseball is a couple of weeks into its exhibition season. The Toyota Grand Prix of Long Beach is coming up soon. And Henry N. Manney III has passed away. The Dodgers and F1 racing were two of Henry's great loves. I was born with Yankee pinstripes because my father spent a good portion of his life working at Yankee Stadium. As a result, I was a Dodger hater. So Henry and I used to have some real rock 'em, sock 'em arguments about the Bronx Bombers and da Brooklyn Bums. The real Yankees and Dodgers, pre CBS, George

PHOTO BY GEOFFREY GODDARD

Steinbrenner and Chavez Ravine.

I don't think any longtime Formula 1 racing fan would deny that it was Henry Manney who put Grand Prix racing on the map in the U.S. I grew up reading his accounts. And I came to know Henry quite well when I started working for R&T. By that time, Henry had relocated back to the States in nearby Corona Del Mar, only a stone's or baseball throw from our Newport Beach offices. But I had no appreciation of just how great an impact Henry had had on Formula 1 racing until Friday, April 26, 1976, the first day of practice for the first F1 race at Long Beach. Henry had been assigned to cover the race, the first GP he'd seen in nearly a decade. I was wandering through the pits when suddenly all activity came to a screeching halt. Was there an accident? A fire? I looked around. No, it wasn't a fire, but it was spreading like wildfire throughout the pits. "It's Henry. Henry Manney!" whooped his fans.

Henry, in his usual sartorial splendor of tweed jacket and tweed hat, was ambling through the pits. Cracking jokes. Shaking hands with all the mechanics. It was as if he'd never been away from the sport. I'll never forget that moment. I'll never forget Henry. Everyone at R&T is deeply saddened by his passing. Our heartfelt condolences go out to his dear wife Annie and the rest of his family.

—John Dinkel

Our friend

HAVING ARRIVED in what he called his "hundred-and-fifty-dollar Fiat" or on his ISDT Triumph 500 or BMW 750 Twin, he would walk into your office wearing his cardigan sweater, tweed cap and brown Wellington boots, one pant leg tucked in and the other out. He would strike a ballet pose, or some engaging parody of one, then throw himself down in the nearest chair, reach elegantly over his head and pluck the tweed hat from his head with two fingers, drop the hat onto his knee and say, "How is the famous Peter Egan today." (In Henry's world, anyone he addressed was "the famous," and anyone out of the room or otherwise offstage was referred to as "the dreaded," as in "Where is the dreaded Allan Girdler?")

Once your good health had been asked after and verified, he would often launch into a description of mechanical-restoration work in progress on his Velocette or his Manx Norton, illustrating the relative motion of levers, rockers, gears and hairpin springs with the kinds of hand movements most people use to make shadow pictures of geese and foxes on a wall. He loved oddball, funny Old English and Italian examples of archaic technology and couched his descriptions of them in non-technical jargon: "I'm trying to fix that diabolical clothespin tweeter the Brits always use to run the oil pump behind that trapdoor where they pile all the shims . . ."

Just prior to his illness, I think Henry's favorite vehicle may have been his motor home, which he bought at the peak of the second (or was it the third?) great American gas crisis, when motor-home dealers everywhere were wondering if they'd be able to give these behemoths away. "Now I don't have to wait in line at public restrooms when I go to a race," he announced proudly, "and I'll always have a place to sit in the shade!"

He brought the motor home to an Ontario motorcycle race I was competing in and insisted that my wife Barbara and I spend the hot, dusty hours between practice sessions in the air-conditioned luxury of the motor home, sipping cold drinks from his refrigerator. Henry later charmed his way past the cornerworkers (no credentials) and stood right beside the track with his camera, shooting the only really good pictures I have of my racing bike in action.

Charmed is the key word here. Whether at a race or our office, Henry Manney was ever the gentleman, joking, chatting, putting people at ease and leaving a trail of amusement and good humor. When you heard his voice in the hall, you smiled and said to yourself, *Oh good, Henry's here*, and genuinely looked forward to a good conversation, the way you look forward to a good meal or a cold beer when you're hungry or thirsty. He was a form of refuge from everything tedious and commonplace, just like his motor home.

Looking back at all of his fine writing and race reporting now, you realize he was an irreplaceable part of the grace and style he described, not just an observer. He added to the color and fun of great events simply by being part of the scene. As Allan Girdler said, after looking through an old copy of R&T recently, "Sometimes I'm not sure if Formula 1 racing in Europe during the Sixties was really that important, or if Henry just made it seem that way."

We'll probably never know, and that was Henry Manney's particular brand of magic. We've lost a rare man, a great writer and a good friend.*—Peter Egan*

PHOTO BY WM. A. MOTTA

PHOTO BY WM A. MOTTA

Henry N. Manney III, 1922–1988

Henry Manney has left us (R&T, June 1988). It was many years ago on the pages of *Road & Track* that I first met Henry. Later we came to know each other well and were close friends.

Thanks to Henry, my world was a richer and brighter place. I have missed our exchanges during his long years in the hospital. I'll miss him more now that he's gone. Rest in peace, Henry.

Robert J. Sinclair
President
Saab-Scania of America, Inc
Orange, Connecticut

Henry N. Manney III was the reason I subscribed to R&T 25 years ago. He was the dean of motorsports journalists—none were funnier, more erudite or more entertaining. Damn, Henry, we will miss you!

Yr fthfl svnt,
Dick Lees
Bellevue, Nebraska

As my mother, sister and only daughter will attest, "He ain't much of a writer," but a long overdue letter of thanks is due *Road & Track*.

I am brought to tears and deep sadness over what feels like a personal loss, the passing of Henry Manney III. This gentleman brought more smiles and laughs to me through the years than I can count. His passing leaves such a void.

Thanks, Henry, for giving me some of the best reading I've ever enjoyed during the past 20 years.

Nick Davidson
Waterburg, Vermont

As a constant reader since I first found R&T in 1948, I have seen staff and editors come and go. None have I enjoyed as much as Henry Manney III. As your tribute to him states, his style was interesting and believable. I appreciated his coverage of motorcycles in other magazines. One such story about an old English make reproduced in India stands out in my mind because of the picture of Henry in his tweeds and hat.

I have missed his writing these last six years and only hope his style and straightforwardness will rub off on some of our younger writers. Now, I guess I will have to go back and look for some back issues and reread some of his work. Thank you for the one you printed.

Merrill Rust
Corpus Christi, Texas

The excerpt from Henry N. Manney's coverage of the Targa Florio in the May issue brought back many memories of the wonderful Formula 1 coverage he provided in the Sixties, when I first subscribed to R&T and became hooked on this ultimate form of motorsports.

Wayne A. Zuehlke
Roseville, Minnesota

Henry N. Manney III will never be gone as long as some of his immortal phrases are passed on in our family. My daughter, as will her children, knows that many of our family code words are Manneyisms. "Crumpet collectors" and "old Indian names" will keep ever fresh the memory of one of the most amusing writers of his generation. Thank you for many hours of enjoyment.

Yr hmbl srvnt,
Douglas H. Skoyles
Calgary, Alberta
Canada

Henry Manney was our friend. He was also every car enthusiast's "fthfl svnt."

When I first read a Henry Manney race report at the tender age of 15, I didn't know what he was driving at half the time, but it was all very entertaining. Later I began to understand his wit and appreciate the wondrous fascination and joy that he brought to his craft.

Those of us who cherish his reports will remember:

"Practice was the usual shambles . . ."

"Race day dawned rather murky/gray/grizzly . . ."

"There was the usual panic on the grid . . ."

"lest he get squz out."

"returned to the fray."

"(Brabham) chin tucked well in and the tail well out . . ."

And his usual style gave us:

"iced lollies were selling like Christine's memoirs."

"All dose zilly liddle cars. Zoom zoom zoom."

"The great urge for a bit of company (perhaps there are ghosts on the backstretch?) . . ."

"the eerie skirling of bagpipes filled the air as a piper of the Scots Guards, especially imported at grrreat cost, mon,

Letters to the Editor

summoned up whatever Pictish spirits would be necessary to warn off the Sassenach peril."

To me, he was the best sports journalist of his time. Goodbye, Henry. May you forever be At Large.

James Kinder
Maryland Heights, Missouri

Reading Henry Manney's work gave me hours of pleasure over the years. He understood, as many automotive writers do not, that cars are supposed to be fun. Everything he wrote conveyed gaiety and a sense of enjoyment.

A Manney story was never routine. I remember one report from the Monaco Grand Prix in which he portrayed the sound of practice from his hotel room window by running the letter "r" up and down across the page. Critics who disparaged his writing style did not understand, as would anyone who has ever written professionally, how hard it was to do it well. I was not surprised to learn that he once pursued ballet, another art form that depends on making the difficult look easy.

In another article he told how he had somehow managed to get his hands on a Ferrari. He picked it up in Italy and headed north in the afternoon toward his home in northern Europe. He stormed an Italian pass, flinging the car higher and higher around the lacets, and arrived at the frontier post exhilarated and with the car smoking. The Italian border guards were delighted to welcome such a fine automobile.

"I am not made of stone," Henry said, and so he got out of the car and let the border guards sit in it and play with the controls, while they talked about Ferrari and cars. The object, to Henry, was the enjoyment, and the car was a means to the enjoyment.

As he said, he was not made of stone.

Michael Mahoney
San Francisco, California

Henry the III, Part II: from his friends

As a belated word on the passing of Henry Manney, he was one of the funniest men I have ever met. He also possessed this incredible ability to place his readers comfortably high up in the balconies of his mind to experience the joy and excitement he felt about everything from hot cars to nudist colonies to fine wine. Lucky us that he gave as much as he did.

Stan Mott
Little Harbor
British Virgin Islands

The passing of Henry Manney has saddened me greatly. Perhaps in some way, this letter will reach him.

I used to manage the now-defunct Saddleback Motorcycle Park in the foothills of the Santa Ana Mountains. Henry would come up to the park to ride the trials bike that I stored for him in the back of the parts room. It could be August and 103 degrees, but in would drive Henry in that dreaded Fiat or, later, in his clean, white Mercedes sedan. He would dismount with some ballet move I could never pronounce, and we would start in with the day's events, or lack thereof. Henry would drink a Pepsi, then when ready to ride, don a favorite "Porridge Pot" helmet, button his cardigan sweater and putt off up the main road.

Henry would bring me a Tupperware container of Annie's homemade chocolate mousse and dare me to eat the whole thing. I did. Each Christmas he would present me with a special ham from some farm in Virginia, or if he scored a good deal on a few bottles of Burgundy he especially liked, he'd bring a bottle and make me promise not to waste it in spaghetti sauce.

Henry did not like Motocross Racing, or the racers themselves for the most part. He called them "Drongos." He said a Drongo was a stupid French bird, but I never believed him. Henry first acquainted me with the term "Mouth Breather." I use it to this day.

I lost touch with Henry just after his cerebral attack, and I moved to Portland. Now, even after all this time I feel a great sense of loss. The literary loss to automotive journalism can never be replaced. His European reports of Formula 1 racing were classics. Henry took the stuffiness out of the European racing circuit for those of us here, lucky enough to have been educated by him.

I will miss seeing the dreaded "Henry N. Manney III" on your masthead.

Jeff James
Lake Oswego, Oregon

I loved and miss Henry, not just because he lent me money and let me drive his Ferrari GTO in Paris, or because he introduced me to the spiders living behind the toilet bowl in their home in Switzerland that coughed on cue when he sat down with his pipe or cigar; not even because he once sent me a marvelous set of color shots he had taken of a semi-nude Hindu dancer when he learned I had been contracted to produce a soft-core, nudie-cutie magazine. Though they are all damn good reasons, I miss him because he achieved something that to me is the rarest and most valuable thing a person can accomplish with his life—he is irreplaceable.

Joe Parkhurst
Costa Mesa, California
Joe Parkhurst is the co-founder of Cycle World *magazine.*

To all Henry's good friends, those who knew him, those who enjoyed his writing and those who wrote in tribute:

Our children join me in thanking you for your kind thoughts, prayers and many expressions of love and appreciation of him and his work. His was a unique talent nurtured by your continuing support and encouragement. Your friendship sustained us through the years of his illness. The Lord watches over us all.

Anne Manney
Corona del Mar, California